S0-APM-443

R0006946814

DISCARD

CHICAGO PUBLIC LIBRARY
HAROLD WASHINGTON LIBRARY CENTER

R0006946814

BUSINESS & INDUSTRY DIVISION

HG
255
.C26
1972
cop. 1

FORM 125 M

APPLIED SCIENCE &
TECHNOLOGY DEPARTMENT

The Chicago Public Library

Received _____ MAR 5 1976

WORLD AFFAIRS
National and International Viewpoints

WORLD AFFAIRS

National and International Viewpoints

The titles in this collection were selected
from the Council on Foreign Relations' publication:
The Foreign Affairs 50-Year Bibliography

Advisory Editor
RONALD STEEL

MONEY AND FOREIGN EXCHANGE AFTER 1914

By GUSTAV CASSEL

ARNO PRESS

A NEW YORK TIMES COMPANY
New York • 1972

BUSINESS & ECONOMICS DIVISION

MAR 5 1976

REF
HG
255
.C26
1972
cop. 1

Reprint Edition 1972 by Arno Press Inc.

Reprinted from a copy in The Wesleyan University
Library

World Affairs: National and International Viewpoints
ISBN for complete set: 0-405-04560-3
See last pages of this volume for titles.

Manufactured in the United States of America

∽∾∿∽∾∿∽∾∿∽∾∿∽∾∿∽∾∿

Library of Congress Cataloging in Publication Data

Cassel, Gustav, 1866-1945.
    Money and foreign exchange after 1914.

    (World affairs: national and international view-
points)
    Reprint of the 1922 ed.
    1. Currency question. 2. Foreign exchange.
I. Title. II. Series.
HG255.C26 1972   332.4'5   72-4266
ISBN 0-405-04563-8

BUSINESS & INDUSTRY DIVISION
MAR 5 1976

B & I
R

14.00

MONEY AND
FOREIGN EXCHANGE
AFTER 1914

MONEY AND FOREIGN EXCHANGE AFTER 1914

By GUSTAV CASSEL

AUTHOR OF "THE WORLD'S MONETARY PROBLEMS"

New York

THE MACMILLAN COMPANY

1922

All rights reserved

PRINTED IN GREAT BRITAIN BY
BILLING AND SONS, LTD., GUILDFORD AND ESHER

FOREWORD

In this book I have aimed at presenting a coherent account of the fortunes of the world's monetary system from the outbreak of the War up to the present time.

In my two Memoranda to the League of Nations I endeavoured to give an analysis of the world's monetary problem, as it presented itself at the time when the Brussels Conference was being arranged, and one year later. Those Memoranda, however, are written for a narrow circle of experts, and are therefore in a somewhat concentrated form. To suit a wider public a broader representation of the problem is desirable, and it is particularly desirable that greater attention be paid to the course of events that has led up to the situation in the face of which the task of restoring a sound monetary system has now to be taken up. For all future time the period through which we are now living will come to form one of the most important chapters in monetary history, and it will likewise offer the richest materials on which to draw for studying the question of the effects of a misguided monetary policy. A book of the character suggested thus undoubtedly has a task to fulfil. Only the task is of such dimensions that one's powers will never prove adequate to meet the demands made upon them.

I am much indebted to Mr. Leonard Bucknall Eyre, B.A. (Gonville and Caius College, Cambridge), for the very valuable assistance he has rendered me in preparing the English edition.

GUSTAV CASSEL.

DJURSHOLM,
March, 1922.

CONTENTS

PAGE

FOREWORD - - - - - - V

ABOLITION OF THE GOLD STANDARD - - 1
CREATION OF ARTIFICIAL PURCHASING POWER - 9
THE RISE IN PRICES - - - - 19
THE GROWTH OF THE VOLUME OF THE MEANS OF
PAYMENT - - - - - - 26
ARITHMETICAL EXPRESSIONS FOR INCREASE IN
CIRCULATION AND RISE IN PRICES - - 33
SCARCITY OF COMMODITIES AND ITS BEARING ON THE
RISE IN PRICES - - - - - 52
THE INFLUENCE OF INFLATION ON GOLD - - 63
THE EXCLUSION OF GOLD - - - - 79
THE DISCOUNT POLICY AND ITS EFFICIENCY AS A
REGULATOR OF THE MONETARY STANDARD - 101
THE EXCHANGE RATES - - - - 137
DEVIATIONS FROM PURCHASING POWER PARITIES - 147
POPULAR MISCONCEPTIONS - - - - 163
RELATIONS TO EARLIER THEORIES ON THE EXCHANGES 170
INFLATION AFTER THE WAR - - - 187
REFORM PROGRAMMES - - - - 203
THE ACTUAL OPERATION AND EFFECTS OF DEFLATION 230
THE RETARDED DIMINUTION OF THE CIRCULATION - 242
THE PROBLEM OF STABILISATION - - - 254

INDEX - - - - - - 283

MONEY AFTER 1914

ABOLITION OF THE GOLD STANDARD

THE first thing that happened in the financial sphere upon the outbreak of the World War was that the existing gold standard was abandoned—not only in the belligerent countries, but also in the majority of neutral states. Upon the entrance of the United States into the War, corresponding steps were taken in that country. A realisation of this fact is of fundamental importance for a proper understanding of all that occurred later. From the moment of the outbreak of war, the various currencies had in the main to be regarded as free paper currencies, and consequently as currencies which were not limited to any metal, and therefore were not in any relation to one another. Only an economic theory which from the very outset takes cognisance of a system of free currencies can be in a position to offer a true and intuitive picture of the essential points in the development which followed. Wherefore, it is of primary importance to realise that the value of the monetary unit in a pure paper currency can manifestly only be based upon the scarcity in the provision made by the country for means of payment, and that, therefore, the responsibility for the value of the currency, in cases where the gold standard has been abandoned, must exclusively lie with those in whose hands rests this provision of the means of payment.

1

When I say that the gold standard was abandoned, I refer to an actual fact. Its form one has everywhere sought as far as possible to avoid, and it may, therefore, be possible to assert, with a certain amount of plausibility, that the gold standard has not been abandoned—nay, even that it still obtains. But from an economic point of view that has no meaning. Economics have only to reckon with facts. When the essential conditions for a gold standard are removed, then the gold standard, as viewed from an economic standpoint, is abolished. The fact that a country has a gold standard implies that the currency of that country is bound up with the metal gold in a fixed ratio of value, so that the price of gold in the currency of the country is fixed—not absolutely, it is true, but so that it varies only within narrow limits. In so far as other forms of currency are valid within the country, such currency must clearly be redeemable in gold coin (or at any rate in a certain weight in gold). But this is not sufficient to maintain the fixed parity between the currency and gold. If the gold standard is to be effective, one must be able to obtain for a certain quantity of gold, lying either at home or abroad, a certain sum in the currency of the country, and, *vice versa*, one must be able to obtain for such a sum a certain quantity of freely disposable gold. The guarantees for this are, in the first place, the right of the possessor of the gold to free import and free coinage; and, in the second place, the right of the possessor of the country's gold coins to free export and free smelting. Besides, it is, of course, necessary that the coinage of the country be of full value. For this reason the Mint Laws generally lay particular stress upon the issuing of guarantees for the quality of the coins in circulation. But these guarantees are of no value whatever, unless the still more fundamental guarantees just mentioned are properly fulfilled.

Now, however, all these guarantees have been violated during the War, and in particular the right to receive for a certain amount in currency a certain amount of freely disposable gold was in general discontinued immediately upon the outbreak of the War. Whether this was caused by suspending the redemption of notes, or by the abolition of the right to dispose over gold, is not the point: actually the gold standard is equally abandoned in both cases. If one withdraws the right to export it and to smelt it down, then gold loses all its usefulness except as the country's coinage, and the redeemability of the currency in gold becomes then a mere pretence. In this connection the conditions for the redemption of notes in Denmark during the War period are particularly striking. In the National Bank's Report of the 31st July, 1919, occurs the following sentence: "From the month of March, 1916, the right to refuse the redemption of notes with gold has not been exercised, when there was no reason for believing that an illicit export of gold was contemplated, and by a Royal Decree dated the 30th July, 1919, it was laid down that redemption in gold coin may be refused when, in the bank's judgment, sufficient guarantee is not forthcoming that the gold will not be utilised in a manner contrary to the interests of the Danish monetary system." One can get over the difficulty still more neatly, as was done in England for a long time, not by introducing—even formally—an export prohibition law, but at least by actually preventing any kind of inconvenient export. Such a method makes no difference either way: from an economic point of view the gold standard has in any case ceased to exist.

The most immediate cause of the gold standard being suddenly dispensed with on the outbreak of war was the desire to preserve as far as possible untouched the gold reserves of the central banks. The extraordinary un-

certainty as to the future which governed the world during
the first days of the War would in all probability have led
to a sharply rising demand for gold as a means to the
maintenance of wealth, and as a means of payment,
especially to abroad. The central banks, therefore,
had to reckon with the possibility of being speedily
deprived of their gold, if they continued to redeem their
notes and other bonds in gold. The loss of gold cash
reserves—nay, even a considerable reduction of them—
would, it was supposed, seriously affect the general
confidence in the central banks' note issues, and thereby
in the future of the currency. Indeed, the central bank
was, as a general rule, legally bound to retain a certain
amount of gold in cover for its notes; a substantial drain
on the gold reserves would have involved the neglect of
that duty, and therefore had to be prevented.

Thus right from the beginning the maintenance of the
gold reserves stands out as the one essential factor, while
the protection of the currency itself was more or less
entirely disregarded. For a long time past the Bank Laws
had centralised their interest with regard to this protection
in regulations concerning gold reserves, while the public
had for generations been brought up to the idea of regarding gold reserves as all-essential. This detracting of the
attention to side issues now seriously became a deciding
factor in monetary policy. Gold reserves should represent
a guarantee for the redemption of notes, but at the very
first sign of a possibility of redemption being demanded
on a considerable scale, interest in the question of gold
reserves became such a predominant factor, that it
eventually proved a positive hindrance to any redemption of notes whatever. People respected the provisions
of the law as regards gold reserves, but the real object
of these provisions—to maintain the capacity for redeeming notes—was disregarded, and the most definite

regulations which the law laid down with regard to liability for the redemption of notes were set aside.

This idolising of gold reserves as an end in themselves has been continued ever since, and, in fact, is still being carried on to quite a large extent to this day. Main stress has been laid upon the fact that the central banks should outwardly appear to the best possible advantage. Striving after this end led to attempts to accumulate all the existing gold in the country in the vaults of the central bank. And so this gold was shown in the statistical reports, and even exhibited to admiring visitors—all this in an earnest endeavour to inspire the general public with the idea that the gold in the vaults in some mysterious way infused a value into the paper in circulation. The truth that the value of a currency must be determined by the quantity of the notes in circulation was, of course, particularly inconvenient at a period when their quantity happened to be steadily increasing. In Germany gold was collected on an organised plan like a sort of patriotic sacrificial feast, where, however, the aim showed itself to be hardly in fair proportion to the people's strong and noble desire to make the sacrifice. On the other side of the front this collection of gold was ridiculed, but the Allies themselves very soon followed along the same lines, with an appeal to their peoples to make every sacrifice for the strengthening of the currency. The curious thing was, however, that the currency refused to be strengthened on these lines, but relentlessly depreciated in value to the same extent that the masses of paper grew, without the slightest regard for the gold reserves.

With the abolition of the gold standard, then, a pure paper standard was adopted, the value of which was determined entirely by the scarcity of the currency recognised as means of payment in that standard. Where

there exists a gold standard, notes, except for the fact
that they are legal tender, are also at the same time bonds,
the value of which may be dependent upon the financial
standing of the issuer. But when the gold standard
disappears the notes are nothing more than a means of
payment, and their value, therefore, can only be determined by their scarcity. The altered character which
notes thus come to assume is a result of the disappearance
of the gold standard, a fact with which the public has
hardly yet managed to make itself acquainted. To the
utmost people have adhered to the idea that notes must
some time or other recover their former value, and people
have only with extreme reluctance appropriated the view
that the value of irredeemable paper can be depreciated
to an unlimited extent, provided their quantity is
sufficiently increased. People have stubbornly insisted
on regarding notes as acknowledgments of debt, and have
looked upon gold reserves as the last security for these
debts, and in so doing have also attributed to them a
significance which they no longer possess.

As the authorities concentrated their interest to such
a large extent upon the external aspect of their currency,
they would evidently not be at all ready to acknowledge
that the gold standard had been abolished. Indeed,
it would be interesting to know whether any official
acknowledgment of that fact has yet been made in any
country ! Consequently, in spite of the fact that the
gold standard was actually done away with, various
monetary laws had to remain in force, which in some cases
proved at a later date a serious obstacle to a wise monetary
policy. This obstacle has especially made itself felt
where countries have been bound together by monetary
unions. Nominally these latter were left undisturbed,
even after any real ground for their retention had ceased
to exist, and all reasonable prospect of a future restoration

of such a union has disappeared. Sweden and Switzerland, in particular, have suffered very considerable inconvenience from this inherent contradiction in their monetary situation.

With the abolition of the gold standard began the lengthy struggle in which Governments and central banks engaged, during and after the War, in order to prevent the public from realising what was happening, and from being able to criticise the manner in which the administration was protecting the currency of the country. Responsibility for the disastrous course which events took was on no account to be allowed to fall upon the administration. The position was as far as possible to be painted in glowing colours, and the highly disastrous consequences, which were naturally not slow to arise, were for as long as possible to be laid at the door of others. This aim permeates the whole of the world's monetary policy, not only during the War period, but all too clearly afterwards as well. It is against such a position, maintained with all the resources which those in power have had at their disposal, that science has had to carry on its campaign for a view of the matter more in accordance with the real state of affairs.

Circumstances have led to such a point of view gradually gaining ground, in spite of all opposition. The reduction in the value of the monetary units went too far to allow of the official fictions being kept up for any length of time, and much of the earlier official teaching has, in the light of later developments, proved to be of such a character that probably not even its most ardent supporter would now be willing to champion it. But a perfectly clear understanding of the monetary problem, brought about by the World War, can never be attained until officialdom's interpretation of affairs has been disproved point by point, and full light thrown on all the delusions with which the authorities attempted as long as possible to obsess the public mind. The first step in thus solving the monetary problem is for the public to learn to realise that the gold standard was in reality abolished by the act of taking those measures which were adopted upon the outbreak of war.

CREATION OF ARTIFICIAL PURCHASING POWER

FOR a belligerent state to conduct war from the very first moment with the utmost possible energy is always regarded as a matter of the highest principle. Money must be found at any price. To procure out of taxes means for carrying on war is, as a rule, at any rate to begin with, out of the question. One must feel thankful if the proceeds of taxation prove sufficient for ordinary State expenditure. Generally speaking, direct taxes have to a large extent to be written off, or their payment postponed, while the returns from indirect taxation, and particularly from customs, diminish, owing to the impossibility of getting commodities into the country, or of carrying on the home production of taxed commodities on a normal scale. Nor, in fact, can the issuing of a real State loan be calculated upon at the very outset. It requires extensive preparations, and even if these should have been made in advance, still the appalling economic disruption brought about by mobilisation must in some way be overcome, before one can expect success for any considerable State loan. The old theory that an accumulated amount of funds in gold could form a basis for financing the first period of a war has been definitely demolished by the experience of the World War.

Purchasing power, however, must be placed at the disposal of the Government, and in a modern community this can always be done at once, and to an unlimited extent, by increasing the amount of bank currency—

i.e., notes or balances on cheque accounts. The State issues treasury bills, and discounts them either at the central bank or at other banks, and thus creates balances against which it can either issue orders for payment, or receive banknotes directly. The problem is thereby solved. The solution is too simple for anyone not to avail themselves of it; nor, indeed, were any of the belligerent states able to avoid the use of this method of financing war. The forms may vary according to the different ways of effecting payment in each country. But the main factor remains the same. Whatever happens, there is always the creation of an artificial purchasing power for meeting the immediate requirements of war.

When it has become possible later on to take up special loans, the floating debt has by that time usually increased to such an amount that the loan is mainly required for reducing the floating debt. Treasury bills previously taken up by the public are exchanged for State bonds; notes which have been accumulating in extravagant quantities in the pockets of the private individual are paid in, and the bank balances of the private individual are reduced. The creation of an artificial purchasing power is thus for a time avoided. The longer the War lasted, however, the shorter that time became. Very soon again must one proceed to the production of new bank currency to meet the country's daily requirements.

Moreover, even the borrowing process itself has usually been based to a very large extent on assistance from the banks. Private subscribers to State loans, urged on by patriotism, or simply by exterior pressure, subscribed over and above what they could afford out of their available savings. Under the most favourable circumstances subscriptions were paid by means of funds which had to be saved up during one or more of the succeeding years. In the meantime the banks had to step into the breach, and whatever the State managed to obtain at the moment was then only an artificially created purchasing power. To such a method of employing bank credit subscribers were encouraged by the fact that the later State bonds were made discountable at the central banks at a particularly low discount rate. But the consequence of this was that the banks were flooded with State paper on a scale which rendered impossible any rational restriction of the credit requirements of the public. This circumstance, the import of which will be further explained later on, has been an outstanding one everywhere, but may, perhaps, be best borne out by a study of the war finance of the United States.

In this way, then, the creation of an artificial purchasing power became a continuous process, though, maybe, one continuing with ever shorter and shorter interruptions. The range of this financial method can scarcely be directly determined, but must be judged by its effects. These will be more closely studied in the succeeding paragraphs.

The actual creation of an artificial purchasing power in itself involves a dilution of the currency. It is exactly this process that is indicated by the term *inflation*. The whole study of the development of money after 1914 is very largely the study of this inflation, its meaning and its effects. The definition just given suffices for outlining the essential character of inflation, but in order to be able to gauge inflation on an arithmetical basis, it will be found necessary to give below a more exact definition of the term.

The process of creating an artificial purchasing power spread very rapidly from the belligerent states to the neutral countries. The most immediate cause was, in the case of the neutrals as well, the needs of State finance. The maintenance of neutrality during the earlier period of the War demanded very considerable outlays, while

later on there appeared the claims of social politics, which
laid an exceptionally heavy burden on State finances.
The example of the belligerent nations and their financial
methods proved infectious, and there was a feeling in the
air that money was always to be obtained, so long as
there existed the will to create it. It was this way of
thinking which, more than anything else, rendered hope-
less any opposition to the ever-increasing extravagance
in national administration.

The second principal cause of the creation of an
artificial purchasing power in neutral countries was the
belligerent nations' demands for credit. One would
imagine that it would have been in the option of the
neutral states to limit this granting of credit according
to means and opportunity. The fact that in reality this
was not the case, but rather that the credits they granted
to the belligerents far exceeded the amounts their
available funds should have allowed, was mainly due to
the interest neutral states had in keeping up their exports.
It was a matter of life or death for the belligerents to
be able to buy, but their ability to pay was limited. The
neutrals, therefore, had to give credit, if they wished at
all to keep up their exports; while, on the other hand, the
scope for marketing their goods was practically unlimited,
provided credit could be granted on a large enough scale.
One can distinguish three different stages in this credit-
giving. During the earlier period private exporters sold
on credit, often in the currency of the belligerent state.
In this absolutely unorganised credit-giving, all the
advantages lay on the side of the belligerents, the neutral
private exporters not being in a position to demand a
suitable security to cover their credits; and they ran the
most serious risk when, without special guarantees, they
sold in a currency which might at any time sink to any
level. In the next stage the banks in the neutral countries

endeavoured to organise the granting of credits to the belligerents, and succeeded in obtaining important advantages—*e.g.*, in the form of establishing a guaranteed rate of exchange, or of selling in the currency of their own country; or, again, of the right to purchase from the belligerent state certain quantities of particularly necessary articles. As soon, however, as agreements of this sort were made with one of the belligerent parties, the other side at once demanded similar credits, and in order to maintain neutrality it was necessary to meet their demands. In this way the giving of credit to the belligerents went on extending further and further. Whenever the belligerent Powers discovered that the neutrals had urgent need of a quantity of articles which the belligerents were in a position to deliver, or over the supply of which they possessed control, they promptly availed themselves of their position of power to wring credits out of the neutrals. In this third stage the granting of credit became unavoidable for the neutrals, and owing to force of circumstances had to be organised on State lines. It was then in the interest of the neutral state to reduce to a minimum the amount of credits granted, and to obtain therefor as much compensation as possible in the form of a supply of necessary commodities. For the purpose of dealing with these credits there was formed in Sweden, under State management, a special company, Svenska Kronkreditaktiebolaget (the Swedish Crown Credit Company).

During the whole time goods were naturally sold by the private exporters to the belligerents against bills either in their own currency or in that of the foreign country. The neutral country's banks discounted these bills, and thus became, in so far as they accumulated them in their portfolios, granters of credit to abroad. Through the purchase of such bills, or through the direct purchase

of foreign exchange in one form or another, Sveriges
Riksbank (the Bank of Sweden) accumulated during
the War very considerable amounts of foreign exchange,
a proceeding which, later on, when the sharp fall in the
exchange values took place, naturally caused the bank
heavy losses.

To this form of credit, which was directly concerned
with the financing of exports to foreign countries, was
now added a credit-giving of a quite abnormal character.
The heavy fall in the rate of foreign exchanges led private
individuals in neutral countries to buy up such exchanges
in the hope that their rates would rise. The belligerent
states, and amongst them particularly Germany, availed
themselves of this to sell out their currency wholesale
to the neutral countries. At every fresh fall in the rate
there appeared a fresh flood of speculators, who started
with the idea that now, at last, the lowest point must have
been reached, and that a rise must inevitably follow.
Now, on looking back, it may seem curious that people
could be so credulous. We must, however, bear in mind
that, according to the theory which was officially
enunciated in every country, the depreciation of the
currency of a country on the world's market was only a
temporary disturbance resulting from the disorganisation
of international trade. This official opinion was, as a
matter of fact, shared, even until quite late in the War,
not only by a vast number of private business men,
but also by many leading and intelligent bankers. "As
soon as ever there is any talk of peace," people said, "the
exchanges of the belligerent countries will rush up to their
former quotations." Later on, of course, the realisation
that this was an error of judgment came to most men,
but by then certain exchanges had sunk so low that
people in ever-widening circles reckoned upon a substantial improvement being in any case inevitable. So

there gradually came one catastrophe after another, which ought to have taught people that a currency can be reduced to any value whatsoever, and may even become practically valueless. But not a single one of these experiences prevented people from buying depreciated exchanges on speculation. As a matter of fact, this form of credit is still being given to-day on an enormous scale, in the shape of the speculation in German marks which is rife over the whole world.

Through all this giving of credit, purchasing power on the neutral market has been placed at the disposal of the belligerents, without a corresponding increase in the total mass of commodities available on the neutral market. The same, however, is also the case if the purchasing power on the neutral market is placed at the disposal of foreign countries through the purchase of securities from abroad. If it is a question of purchasing the bonds of the foreign state, this obviously constitutes a form of credit-giving. So is it also in a case where other securities are purchased from a foreign source. But the effect is exactly the same, even if the import of securities consists in redeeming the country's own bonds. In the last-mentioned form purchasing power has been placed on a very large scale on the part of the neutral countries at the disposal of the belligerents. The rates at which these bonds could be redeemed were, on the whole, so profitable that one cannot be surprised at these operations being carried out on such a large scale.

The purchasing power in the neutral country's currency, which was thus in one way or another placed at the disposal of the belligerents, was to a great extent artificially created. There existed no real saving on which could be supported all this giving of credit to abroad or this buying up of securities. In so far as saving was actually carried on in neutral countries, probably this

saving was in most cases entirely consumed by those
countries' own capital requirements, which, owing to the
demands of both State finance and industry, were
abnormally increased. It is a question whether these
requirements had not already in themselves exceeded
the amount of the current savings, so that by their means
a certain degree of inflation had already developed. In
the majority of neutral countries, this has probably been
the case, at any rate during certain periods. It is quite
evident that at those times no effective reserves were
available for abroad. Only through the continual
creation of fresh means of payment has it been possible
for neutral countries to provide the belligerents with all
the purchasing power that was actually placed at their
disposal.

Under normal circumstances it is, indeed, possible for
a wealthy country to grant annually large loans to abroad
—*i.e.*, to provide foreign countries with purchasing power
in that country's own market. Whether this is possible
or not depends on the nation in question setting aside
yearly savings to a corresponding amount—*i.e.*, reducing
its consumption to such an extent that a certain quantity
of the real commodities which the nation would have
been able to buy with its income remains over, and may
be set up against the purchasing power which the credits
have placed in the hands of foreign countries. During
the War the neutrals, generally speaking, had no such
savings available, and the purchasing power which they
provided abroad could not, therefore, be obtained in any
other way than by continually creating fresh supplies
of means of payment. With this purchasing power in
their hands, the belligerent states were enabled to appropriate a considerable portion of the real commodities
which represented the regular income of the neutral
nations, and which the latter all too clearly needed for

themselves, either for their own daily consumption or
else for the formation of real capital—*i.e.*, for building
purposes and for expansion of industry.

In spite of the very serious considerations which this
creating of purchasing power for account of the belligerents involved for the entire economy of the neutral
state, this procedure was nevertheless supported by very
strong interests. The artificial stimulus to export which
it induced did, indeed, bring in very considerable profits
to the export industries, and made it possible for them
to employ an increasing number of workers at increasingly higher wages, incidentally overcoming thereby the
difficulty of unemployment which threatened them during
the first years of the War. Every criticism of the excessive
credits which were being granted to foreign countries
was met by the argument that it would never do to stop
the country's export, to ruin the export industries, and
to reduce the workers to starvation. Without doubt all
these arguments contained gross exaggerations. Export
could certainly have been kept going to the extent of its
being paid for in commodities to be delivered to the
neutrals from abroad. It is even quite certain that, at
any rate in the first years of the War, the belligerent
nations would have allowed the neutrals considerably
larger quantities of goods, had it not been so easy to
acquire purchasing power by other means. Every credit
given to the belligerents, over and above what was
absolutely unavoidable, unnecessarily stimulated exports
from the neutral country. The productive forces of the
country were thereby directed to the export industries
to a disproportionate degree—that is to say, were with-
drawn from those industries which worked for the
immediate supplying of the nation's needs. By that
means the regular supplies of the nation fell off. In
Sweden it is particularly remarkable how building enter-

prise was made to give way to industrial expansion for export purposes to such an extent that every kind of house production—except in connection with this expansion—was almost completely stopped. In like manner all the timber which could possibly be raised was utilised on such a vast scale for export purposes—as fuel for the manufacture of pig-iron, pulp, pit-props, etc.—that the people in Sweden had to freeze.

On account of the circumstances just described, inflation developed into a process which extended throughout the whole world, although its influence was felt in various countries in very different degrees. Its economic purport and its consequences, however, are principally the same everywhere.

THE RISE IN PRICES

UNDER normal conditions all fresh purchasing power arises through commodities being placed on the market at a value corresponding to the amount of fresh purchasing power. The total purchasing power during any given period, therefore, is equivalent to the total quantity of commodities available for purchase. An increase in the purchasing power can only take place through a corresponding increase in the actual production of commodities. If now there is created in a community an artificial purchasing power in the form of bank currency, this false purchasing power will inevitably compete with the genuine. The consequence of this competition must be a rise in prices. The rise in prices must actually reach such a height that the available real commodities are brought up to a total value corresponding to the total purchasing power. Not until then is any equilibrium reached. This rise in prices involves for all possessors of purchasing power a restriction in the quantity of commodities they are able to purchase, and it is just this restriction which sets free a certain quantity of commodities for the extra created purchasing power to buy. The rise in prices is thus a method of depriving the members of the community of a portion of the real income which should have been at their disposal for the money income to which they are entitled. Just so much real income may then be placed at the disposal of the owners of the artificially created purchasing power, whether they are the country's own Government or foreign borrowers.

Inflation thus leads always and inevitably to a rise in prices, and it is just by means of this rise in prices that the ultimate object of inflation—namely, to place real commodities at the disposal of one who can offer nothing in exchange—can be realised. Upon a continuous process of inflation there generally follows a rise in wages and other incomes. But this rise comes for the most part only gradually, so that wide classes of people are compelled to restrict their expenditure. If one could raise all incomes equally, and on the same scale as the rise in prices, then no restriction in satisfying requirements would be made, and consequently there would be no real commodities freed for balancing the artificially created purchasing power. It is therefore part of the object of inflation to force up the price of commodities, while at the same time this rise must be sharper than the simultaneous rise in wages and other incomes.

Naturally there are always some kinds of income which derive direct advantage from inflation, and which are raised far more rapidly than the price of commodities. Persons in this favourable position have their real purchasing power increased, but this only means that the restriction in the real purchasing power of the rest of the people, which is incomparably larger, becomes still more intensified.

War finance manifestly requires that a very considerable amount of real commodities, in kind and in services, are immediately available for the management of the war. Since production cannot be increased at this pace, but rather has a tendency to go down, this is only possible when the needs of the civil population are restricted to the utmost. Such a limitation of consumption is also attained by means of taxes and loans, but by a slower and by no means so effective a method as by a general rise in prices. It is only by causing an immediate and sufficiently sharp rise in prices that a belligerent Government can set free an adequate amount of real commodities for its requirements. It is on account of this fact that effective warfare under really serious conditions is practically impossible without inflation. All belligerent states during the War were obliged to employ this method, and it seems quite certain that in spite of all the tragic experiences the world has reaped in the serious consequences of applying this method, yet in every war to come the very same method will be adopted, as soon as ever it becomes a question of to be or not to be. Though economic science may utter ever so many warnings in condemnation of inflation, it will nevertheless not be possible to prevent it. The only effective prescription for the prevention of such a disaster for the community is, obviously, Cease making war !

In view of the fact that the revolutions which have taken place in latter years have brought about a far more violent inflation than even the War, a warning against inflation should likewise invariably include the warning, Cease making revolutions ! The only certain result of a revolution in any case appears to be an exceptionally sharp depreciation of money, with accompanying misery for the great mass of the population, and unearned profits for a small minority.

When one comes to realise that a rise in prices is only one side of the financial system which we characterise by the name of inflation, one must find it somewhat curious that all countries, simultaneously with their pursuit of a more or less pronounced policy of inflation, have endeavoured to fight against a rise in prices. Lack of clear insight into the real purport of the financial policy adopted appears in this case peculiarly characteristic. But this lack of insight has not been altogether involuntary. It has been so obviously dictated by a

reluctance to look unpleasant facts in the face, and a desire
to avoid responsibility for the inevitable consequences
of an unsound financial policy, that criticism cannot
altogether disregard that side of the psychological basis
on which the economic policy of the past few years has
been founded. It was a question of preventing the public
at all costs from realising the true connection between the
rise in prices and the inflationist methods of finance.
Responsibility for the rise in prices was under no possible
conditions to be laid at the door of the State authorities
or of the central banks, and therefore all other imaginable
means of explaining it away had to be employed. The
ruling authorities have thereby distinctly, and very
materially, contributed towards debarring the people
from economic enlightenment, and have confined public
opinion to false ideas, which have naturally since proved
a serious hindrance to the return to a sounder economic
policy.

Above all, the popular desire to thrust liability for
every fresh rise in prices upon the shoulders of middlemen
and speculators has been taken advantage of in the
official explanation of the causes of the high cost of living.
Even in enlightened circles, people have with visible
satisfaction indulged in the use of those insulting expressions which in common language have won popularity,
as indicating those whom they wish to make scapegoats
for the rise in prices. Laying stress on this point in no
way involves any moral absolution of the so-called
jobbers and profiteers from all that they may have on
their conscience. But in order to have a clear idea of
what actually took place, it is of the very first importance
to establish the fact that the true cause of a general rise
in prices can never be found in profiteering. It is the
process of inflation which with irresistible power forces
up the price level, and when prices rise, it will always

happen that large and, one might well say, unearned profits fall to certain groups of persons. These groups comprise above all others those who are in possession of the permanent means of production or have stocks of goods. But the groups are not closed to outsiders: anyone can attain to such a position through timely purchases, and then the unearned profits will fall to his share. This is called "profiteering," and the public easily imagine that the profit thus reaped "is put on to the price of the article," and that, therefore, profiteering is a directly contributory factor in raising prices. In particular cases, of course, this may be true, but generally speaking the popular idea represents a complete inversion of the combined causes.

Officially inspired pronouncements and the popular notion as to the causes of a rise in prices have combined to bring about attempts at preventing a rise in prices. Such attempts have been carried out on a large scale in all countries, while at the same time the process of inflation has been unblushingly continued. In these democratic times of ours, the road to power has been via the highest possible appreciation of the economic wisdom of public meetings. For the elementary political idea, it has always been the natural thing to try and prevent all troubles and nuisances in the life of the community by forbidding them to occur. So also here. A rise in prices was an evil thing, and consequently should be simply prohibited by legislation. Thus "maximum price" legislation came into being. In vain did scientists point out the unreasonableness of this arbitrary attack on the most vital factor governing the economic life of the community, the natural formation of prices. In vain did they foretell the series of grave consequences which such attacks were bound to involve. The modern community must, ever to its shame and hurt, go through that stern system of education in the first principles of social economics and finance which so many peoples have had to undergo during periods of inflation ever since the days of ancient Egypt, and that without having learned one single jot from all the wealth of experience gathered during these thousands of years.

Naturally the rise in prices could not be prevented by such means. It went on relentlessly. The price actually paid for things differed more and more from what the law allowed; illegal dealings gradually became, at any rate in countries with the worst inflation, the ever more and more predominant part of trade, and legislation has had again and again to raise its maximum prices to a level still barely adequate to meet the actual situation.

In doing this people generally tried as long as possible to retain particular prices at a lower level. The consequence of this was a violent disturbance in the mutual correlation of prices to one another, and, further, a dislocation of the whole mechanism which the natural formation of prices represents for the regulation of the entire economic life of a country. The community became inadequately provided with those commodities whose prices were kept too low, while consumption was freed from that restriction which a price determined upon rational principles will normally exercise. Further study of these social-economic consequences of attempting to prevent a rise in prices does not fall within the scope of the present work. Here the attention of the reader will only be drawn to the efforts at " alleviating the pressure of high prices " which all Governments have pursued, while at the same time forcing up all prices through continued inflation. Obviously such efforts were not capable of preventing a rise in prices, nor indeed of freeing the mass of consumers from that restriction of consumption which was the financial purport of inflation. Relief could

only be obtained in the case of particular commodities, or
of certain groups of the population. But relief again
involved the dislocation of the mechanism of normal
price-formation. These efforts at relieving distress took
a number of different forms: direct financial support to
certain groups of citizens; grants for lowering prices,
in order to facilitate the selling of an article below cost
price; losses being covered by Government funds; the
retention in State-owned concerns of tariffs below working
expenses, etc. The financing of these measures proved,
in the majority of cases, a direct cause of fresh inflation
and of fresh rises in prices, which again evoked fresh
demands for relief of distress. The total result of the
State's interference thus constituted a complete disorganisation of the normal process of price-formation and
a further aggravation of the inflationist policy.

Through the general rise in prices which the creation
of artificial purchasing power induces, inflation constitutes
a depreciation of money. All prices come to be calculated
in terms of a lower unit, they tend to grow higher, just
like figures denoting lengths and areas when expressed
in terms of a smaller unit of measure. To begin with,
when the rise in prices is still very unsettled and keeps
within fairly reasonable bounds, it is difficult for the
public to view the matter in this light; and attempts on
the part of economic science to point out the true import
of this rise in prices were met, during the first years of
the War, by strong feelings of distrust, and in general by
an openly hostile attitude. This attitude found further
strong support in the interest entertained by the Government authorities and the central banks in preventing
the public from realising that an actual depreciation was
taking place. Not until after a long struggle, and after
depreciation had gone very far, did this opposition begin
gradually to give way.

THE GROWTH OF THE VOLUME OF THE
MEANS OF PAYMENT

THE creation of artificial purchasing power immediately takes the form of a creation of bank currency, whether as notes or cheque balances. In previous discussions about the effects of inflation one has generally looked upon this increase in the quantity of currency as the real cause of the rise in prices, and one has declared that the rise in prices must be proportional to this increase in the quantity of currency. This idea is known by the name of *the quantity theory of money*. On the part of theorists this theory has been proclaimed self-evident, but it has always met with objections, without the opponents themselves being able to produce a tenable explanation of their own. The foremost objection, and the one which lies nearest to hand, is that the currency which is put into the hands of the public need not remain in the possession of the public, but may at any time return to the banks. Ever since the period of inflation in England during the time of the Napoleonic Wars, the banks have declared that they cannot force upon the public more currency than trade requires, and that the banks are therefore in no way responsible for an increase in the quantity of the currency. This point of view was also keenly supported by the central banks during the years of inflation we are now considering: they did not issue more currency than trade demanded. The increased demand was explained away by all possible circumstances—and amongst others by the rise in prices.

26

To clear up all this disorder is the first duty to be performed, if we want to get a true idea of the process of inflation which has been going on ever since the outbreak of the War. It is, no doubt, quite true that the public, generally speaking, does not hold more currency than it has need of. The Quantity Theory is, therefore, untenable as it has generally been formulated hitherto. One must, however, not presume from that that the artificial creation of fresh purchasing power has no effect. It is proved above that a rise in prices must occur when extra purchasing power is put in the hands of a Government, or, in fact, of whomsoever it may be who directly takes advantage of this purchasing power. The heightened competition for the non-increased supply of commodities which the newly created purchasing power evokes cannot help having this effect. To what height the rise in prices will go cannot be determined theoretically, but for the purpose of accounting for the chain of causes here at work, it is quite sufficient to establish the fact that a rise in prices must take place in consequence of the creation of artificial purchasing power. This rise in prices in its turn manifestly brings about an increased need for currency. Obviously, one must expect that the quantity of currency required by trade grows in proportion to the rise in prices. Any contrary hypothesis must necessarily imply that the people's habits of payment had in one respect or another become altered, or that the amount of commodities available to be put on the market had increased or decreased. Such changes would, of course, have the effect of altering the need of currency, even without any rise in prices taking place, and must, therefore, be regarded as independent factors in the problem. In a first discussion of the effects of inflation the possibility of such factors having any bearing on the subject must be set aside. Attention, how-

ever, must be paid to them at a later stage in the
discussion.

At this point, then, we can proceed from the assumption
that the increase in the quantity of currency retained by
the trading community is proportional to the rise in
prices. It is not at all sure that the whole of the amount
of fresh currency, which at a certain moment has been
placed at the disposal of a belligerent Government,
remains in the hands of the public. The Government will
be using this currency in various ways, and thus the currency comes into the possession of private persons or business firms. But these latter pay in to their accounts
with the banks the currency they do not consider they
require. More currency than had been usual before,
however, will always be kept by the trading community,
because a general rise in prices has taken place. The
argument may then be summed up as follows: The primary
cause is the artificial creation of fresh purchasing power;
this produces a rise in prices, and the rise in prices in turn
renders necessary a proportional increase in the quantity
of currency.

If, now, this process continues, and fresh artificial
purchasing power is being continually created, one has
to reckon with a steadily increasing rise in prices and an
equally steadily growing increase in the quantity of bank
currency. Between this quantity of currency and the
general price level a proportionality will establish itself.
If one expresses both the quantities by index numbers,
both referred to 100 as the basis, then these index numbers
ought to tally. If one represents these index numbers
by curves, then the curve denoting the rise in prices should
coincide with the curve indicating the increase in the
quantity of currency. It would be incorrect to describe
any one of these variations as a cause and another
as an effect. The primary cause which produces the

entire disturbance is the creation of artificial purchasing power.

In this new form the Quantity Theory is unassailable, and gives us the right starting-point for an analysis of the complicated ramifications of the monetary systems and of the formation of prices, which we have set ourselves the task of studying here. Reality will, of course, always show divergencies from the results derived from this Quantity Theory. But even in this case a sound theory of the fundamental phenomenon itself is useful, by making it clear that here exist divergences which must have special causes, and by directly inducing an investigation into those causes.

If a uniform rise took place in all prices, then, as pointed out above, a proportional increase in the need for means of payment would be quite natural. Now, the rise in prices is in practice never uniform. Different groups of prices usually show a different percentage of rise. If we select only one of these groups, we cannot expect the rise in prices thus calculated to correspond exactly to the increase in the quantity of currency. Such a proportionality can only be expected if due attention be paid to all prices, and, consequently, to the index numbers both for wholesale prices, retail prices, and cost of living, as well as for wages. With the incomplete knowledge we possess of the changes in these different groups of prices during the period of inflation, considerable difficulty and uncertainty generally attaches to determining the true position of the general level of prices. This fact must always be borne in mind when we want to compare the rise in prices with an increase in the quantity of currency.

Generally speaking, we may assume that the need for means of payment has grown practically in the same proportion for the various kinds in practice. The currency in circulation (notes and coin) should in the main

have increased in about the same ratio as the balances
at the banks which can be disposed of by cheque. The
ways of payment practised by the different nations appear
for the most part to be fairly constant; a nation that is
accustomed to effecting payments in coin or notes prefers
to continue to do so, and can only very gradually adapt
itself to the practice of paying by cheque. The relative
need for circulating currency, which, owing to the various
methods of payment in practice, is very different in the
case of different nations, is also probably quite constant.
The French, for instance, have a far greater need for
circulating currency per inhabitant than the majority of
other nations. This fact holds good even after inflation
has taken place, and must be duly noted if we wish
to make comparisons between the circulation per head
of the population in France and in other countries.
Nevertheless, the period of inflation has, without doubt,
been accompanied by certain alterations in the methods
of payment, especially in the ratio between circulating
currency and balances on cheque accounts. The necessity for an immediately available reserve may also affect
the demand for means of payment without any direct
alteration in the methods of payment. This seems
actually to have taken place on a considerable scale in
some countries with regard to balances on cheque accounts.

In times of violent economic disturbances it is natural
for the public to keep larger sight balances at the banks
than usual, without, perhaps, for that reason, utilising
in the same degree these balances for payments. In other
cases, particularly when moratoria are in force or are
apprehended, the public may find it necessary to keep a
reserve in the form of notes. To verify these changes
statistically, and to give an idea of their extent, is generally
very difficult. Perhaps specialised research may gradually
come to throw more light on this point.

Authorities have taken advantage of this insecurity to distract public attention from the alarming increase in the note circulation. They have endeavoured by every means imaginable to explain away this increase. Amongst other things, they have pointed out that payments during the War necessarily had to be effected in cash on a larger scale than usual. When the use of bills declined, this fact could be exploited in explanation of the increased need for cash payments. The reasoning is not very convincing: payment by bill actually involves only a postponement of a payment which in any case must be effected sooner or later. Upon examining the whole evidence with regard to the increase in the circulating medium, we find no reason whatever for taking refuge in the official explanation which was so stereotyped during the War, that the practice of paying in cash increased the need for circulating media. In certain cases the explanations given for the increase in the note circulation have had more justification; it has then been a question of factors whose influence one ought to have been able to estimate quantitatively, and, therefore, also to eliminate, so that a proper grasp of the effective increase in the circulation might have been obtained. No particularly keen interest in having the question thus cleared up, however, seems to have been evinced either by central banks or by State authorities.

The desire to prevent the public from realising what was actually taking place induced certain central banks at times to keep the reports on the note circulation secret. This was for years the case with the Bank of Austria, and even the Bank of France suspended its reports from the outbreak of war up to the 28th January, 1915. On the whole, however, this direct withholding of information proved dangerous. Efforts were then directed towards letting the general increase in means of payment appear as little as possible in the note circulation. It was this desire which inspired the advice to " economise in notes " and to make use of cheque payments instead, which played so important a part during the War in the central banks' monetary policy. The central banks expended much energy on enabling the public to go over to cheque payments, and showed thereby a readiness to meet the public demand for accommodation which, in itself, was thoroughly commendable. In the annual reports of the French and German central banks it may be seen how the bank managements lay stress on these efforts. The craze for economising in notes spread also to smaller states, and to this day, in the case of Switzerland for example, this may be observed by every person who receives a letter, the post-mark consisting of exhortations printed in French and German to the effect that "payments by cheque save notes and coin."

Apparently these attempts to encourage payments by cheque had, on the whole, comparatively little success. To the extent to which they proved effective and therefore, relatively speaking, brought about a diminution in the need for notes, we must of course take them into account when estimating the increase in the circulating medium of the country in question. The increase in total circulation in the case of such a country, when calculated directly, gives a false idea of the increased supply of the means of payment. The calculated figure must be adjusted with regard to the larger increase in balances on cheque accounts or in their utilisation. If such an adjustment is made, the "note economy" policy will probably, from our present point of view, offer but little satisfaction to its originators.

ARITHMETICAL EXPRESSIONS FOR INCREASE IN CIRCULATION AND RISE IN PRICES

FOR all investigations into the extent and effects of inflation it is of the highest importance to have as accurate information as possible on the increase in circulation and on the rise in prices. The difficulties in the way of obtaining such information, however, are very considerable; sources of error are numerous, and are not so easy to eliminate. We shall first discuss them here in regard to the *increase in circulation*.

The most obvious source of error in an estimate of the increase in circulation which only takes account of the notes is the existence before the War of a considerable circulation of coins, which has since disappeared. Gold coins were, indeed, in circulation in considerable quantities both in Germany, France, and England, as well as in the United States. In the smaller and poorer states the gold circulation, on the whole, played a comparatively .unimportant part, while in the Scandinavian countries there existed, practically speaking, no gold circulation at all. Nowadays the gold circulation has almost entirely disappeared. The gold had accumulated in the vaults of the central banks. In order to gauge the real increase in circulation, one must add to the quantity of notes which existed before the War the amount of gold then in circulation. But, generally speaking, this amount is not known with any certainty, and the uncertainty seems to be relatively greatest in those countries where the circulation of gold was common. An exact estimate of the increase in circulation in such countries is therefore impossible. One has to be satisfied with approximate calculations based on estimates of the gold circulation before the War. Such calculations have been made in the case of England, but do not seem very reliable. As the figure indicating the relative increase in circulation comes out obviously too high, the estimate of the gold circulation before the War must have in all probability been too low.

Clearly the increase in circulation may be established with the greatest certainty in those countries where no gold circulated before the War. For that reason it has been possible in the case of Sweden, ever since the outbreak of war, to determine with fairly true accuracy the increase in circulation. However, regard must also be had to the silver circulation. Its extent before the War is probably on the whole better known than that of gold circulation, for the silver coinage used to be so debased that melting it down or exporting it did not pay. In countries with high inflation silver has since disappeared from circulation. If, then, one reckons the silver circulation before the War in the total circulation, one must now also include the notes of corresponding value or the coins of baser metal which have displaced the silver coinage. But one can equally well leave out of the reckoning both this note circulation and the silver circulation, and yet obtain fairly accurate figures for the total increase in circulation.

In the case of Sweden the estimate of the present silver circulation presents considerable uncertainty, as a number of Danish and Norwegian silver coins found their way into the Swedish circulation. It would be of some interest to try, by means of systematically examined amounts of cash, to find out the relative percentage of these foreign coins in the Swedish silver circulation. One could then form some idea of the total silver circulation in the country.

Probably the increase in the silver circulation is, relatively speaking, somewhat less than the increase in the note circulation. In regard to this the index figures for the note circulation must possibly be reduced by some small percentage, in order to give a true indication of the variations in the total circulation. But what adjustment should be made here cannot be exactly stated. Like difficulties exist with reference to the calculation of the increase in the circulation in Switzerland. For that country, too, being a member of a monetary union, has had a silver coin circulation, which has not been definitely closed to the outside world.

Another of the chief difficulties in determining the growth of the circulation is offered by the usual yearly variation in the note circulation. If one is to follow with any accuracy the development of the circulation month by month, and to determine whether it is rising or falling, one must pay attention to the annual variation in the note circulation which is normal for the country. This annual variation is, in the case of some countries, irregular, while again, in other countries, it is so regular that one can speak of a normal annual variation. In order to arrive at this one must proceed from a series of years which, from an economic point of view, have been fairly normal, determine the annual variation for each year, and on that basis reckon the average variation. With particular accuracy this method could be employed in the case of Russia for the period immediately preceding the War and by working on such a basis I have managed to determine, with a comparatively high degree of certainty, the relative increase in circulation in Russia during the first years of the War right up to the time when, with the revolution, the Russian monetary system completely collapsed.

Even in the case of Sweden the annual variation in

the note circulation is sufficiently regular to allow of a normal variation being determined. I have calculated the average of the Riksbank's note circulation for every month throughout the years 1910–1913, having for that purpose reference to both the weekly and monthly reports. I also worked out the annual average figures for the said years. Then I divided the monthly averages by the respective annual averages, and thus obtained the percentage figures which indicate the variation in the note circulation for each month of the year. By calculating the average for the four years of these percentages for each separate month, I obtained the following series, representing the normal variation of the Riksbank's circulation:

January	..	92·5	May	..	96·5	September	104·8
February	..	93·0	June	..	101·1	October ..	106·0
March	..	99·8	July	..	98·6	November	104·5
April ..	..	98·7	August	..	98·2	December	106·3

If one examines the development of the Riksbank's note circulation for a series of normal years, one will find a fairly regular rise year by year—a rise which naturally expresses the general economic development. It is impossible to neglect the influence of this rise on the figures expressing the seasonal variations of the note circulation. In the series of figures just quoted is included an annual rise of 4 per cent. (The annual average for 1909 is, in fact, 179·3 million kronor, and for 1913 209·9 million kronor, which represents a rise, calculated by logarithms, of 4 per cent. per annum for the four years.) When making up my circulation index, however, I realised that I ought not to reckon upon any real economic progress beyond what corresponds to the growth of the population, which I assumed to represent ¾ per cent. per annum. I have therefore taken an annual increase of ¾ per cent. as a basis for determining the

normal variation of the note circulation during the year.
The seasonal variation given above must further be
reduced to a seasonal variation with an annual rise of
¾ per cent. By means, then, of an increase adapted for
this purpose for the first six months of the year, and a
corresponding fall for the latter half of the year, we get
the following normal variation:

January	..	94·0	May	.. 97·0	September	104·0
February	..	94·3	June	.. 101·4	October ..	105·0
March	..	100·9	July	.. 98·3	November	103·1
April	..	99·5	August	.. 97·7	December	104·6

If we now start from the yearly average for 1913—
i.e., 209·9 million kronor—we can thus, by assuming an
annual rise of ¾ per cent., calculate the normal circulation,
first for 1913, and then for each month during the whole
period of the War. Having by this means discovered, for
example, that the normal circulation for December, 1916,
is 224·6, we can prove, with the knowledge that the
actual mean circulation for the same month was 393·8
million kronor, that the relative circulation for that
month was 175·3 (expressed in per cent. of 100 as normal).
By this means I have calculated an index number for
the circulation for every month from the commencement
of the War. This index series has the whole time been,
and still is, a good basis for judging the real variation in
the note circulation. Without such an index series one
cannot determine with any certainty whether, for example,
an actual rise in the note circulation from one month to
the next means a continued inflation or not. If the
absolute increase is less than that which should correspond
to the normal increase for the month, then really a
relative retrogression in the country's supply of currency
has taken place. The quarterly means of my index
numbers together with diagrams are given on pp. 58–59.

The yearly averages for the index of circulation are as follows:

1915 ..	.. 132·2	1918 ..	.. 297·9
1916 ..	.. 154·9	1919 ..	.. 323·7
1917 ..	.. 207·3	1920 ..	.. 320·7

In the case of other countries, which before the War possessed a metallic circulation, it would, generally speaking, be hardly worth while trying to make such detailed calculations, since the lack of knowledge as to the metallic circulation before the War involves too much uncertainty in estimating the increase in total circulation.

A third cause of uncertainty in determining the true increase in circulation which took place during the War period is the hoarding of notes. Upon the outbreak of war it seems that hoarding became a general practice in the countries of Europe. Apprehension and the complete uncertainty as to what was going to happen made people try to get into their hands as much cash as possible, and this they stowed away in their pocket-books, writing-desks, and safes. This nervousness on the part of the public was natural enough at a time when central banks suspended payment, and the private banks applied more or less far-reaching moratoria which rendered it uncertain to what extent, if at all, balances could be disposed of. More normal conditions in this respect having been restored, the public everywhere stopped this hoarding. The notes then either returned to the banks or went into circulation. Where inflation was violent, cessation from hoarding could not be traced in any direct decline in the circulation. But in the majority of neutral countries the note circulation already began a few months afterwards to show a certain decline from the high level to which the hoarding of the first period had brought it.

The official efforts to hide the significance of the

increase in the note circulation often found expression in an endeavour to attach to hoarding a far greater importance than it really possessed, and to keep up the idea that hoarding was going on long after it had become quite apparent to everybody that this was no longer the case. A repetition of the hoarding mania on quite a large scale appears to have occurred in Germany in connection with the revolution, and it is believed that considerable amounts of notes remained for a long time in private possession, particularly in that of the peasant population. By now even these notes have probably begun to appear again, one of the reasons being that the peasant population has been drawn into the general speculating in shares which has assumed such enormous dimensions in Germany in consequence of the stupendous inflation characterising the last year or two. It is often said that considerable quantities of notes were hoarded by the French population. This idea is certainly exaggerated. The French have always made a practice of keeping large amounts of cash at home. In proportion as inflation progressed and the value of the notes was reduced, naturally the nominal amount of these cash reserves was increased. Such an increase, however, involves no actual hoarding, and therefore does not represent an independent factor in accounting for the increase in circulation. Nevertheless it has been possible to observe how, on the various occasions when the French Government took up permanent war loans, the country was, one might say, overfed with notes. A certain amount of notes were, in fact, used for paying for war loans, and the note circulation decreased for a short time by some small percentage.

In order to ascertain the true increase in the circulation, one must, of course, subtract the hoarding from the published figures showing the circulation. But one has

to accept statements regarding hoarding with reserve,
and it is certain that after the first few months of the War
hoarding occurred only in exceptional cases to such an
extent as to influence the figures of circulation. Where
events turn out as they have done in Eastern Europe,
resulting in notes being reckoned by the cartload, the
line of demarcation between hoarding and circulation
disappears, but there again practically no sure means for
calculating either the increase in circulation or the rise
in prices can be found.

In the calculation of the increase in circulation we
have sometimes to take into consideration a change in
the geographical sphere within which the currency circu-
lates. Any widening of this sphere is naturally accompanied by an increased demand for notes, and a corresponding increase in the circulation does not then imply
inflation. This fact has been made use of to place the
figures showing the circulation in as favourable a light
as possible, and to impress upon the public the idea that
no inflation existed, but that the circulation was merely
supplied with the currency it required. This was
particularly the case in Germany during the War, when
the victorious German armies had occupied wide territories both east and west. One could indeed then
apparently assert with some reason that the increased
sphere of circulation fully justified an increase in the
circulation. I criticised this standpoint at the time: in
the occupied areas the former circulation was probably
in most cases retained and increased or else a new one
organised—as, for example, in Belgium. It is true that
at the beginning mark notes were deposited as security
for the Belgian note circulation, but these mark notes
were later transferred to Germany, and were substituted
by balances in the German banks. In the occupied
French territories a municipal note issue was organised

on quite a large scale. Naturally the German armies brought with them very large quantities of mark notes: but these amounts ought not to be regarded in their entirety as fresh additions to the need for circulation; for if all these men who were now taking part in the War on foreign soil had been at home instead, they too would have had considerable need for currency. Certainly the demand for notes was to some extent increased through the occupation of enemy territory, but at no period did this factor account for more than a small fraction of the actual increase in notes. The principal cause of the growth of the German note circulation has the whole time been inflation. This is obvious now to all the world, when, the German armies having been driven back, the issuing of notes none the less goes on at a steadily increasing pace. In order to be able now to gauge accurately the development of the German circulation we must take into consideration the diminution in the extent of the German state which has taken place as a result of peace. Alsace-Lorraine is a case in point, for there the mark circulation has been substituted by a franc circulation; but the French Government, which undertook the task of substitution, found themselves burdened with the whole stock of German notes previously in circulation in those provinces, and it is not known whether they have since succeeded in getting this amount exchanged. In computing the increase in the note circulation of France the alterations in the sphere of circulation during the War and after have to be taken into consideration. In the case of Denmark, too, the peace has resulted in a small increase in the sphere of circulation, which must be taken into account.

Finally, we must also take into account, when calculating the increase in circulation within a given country, a circumstance which, particularly in latter years, has

begun to have an important bearing—namely, that notes
to a large extent are taken out of the country and remain
abroad.   In this are involved two separate phenomena
which are partly of a contrary nature.   In the one case
it is a country with an inferior currency attracting to
itself better and more reliable currencies from other
countries; in the second case it is countries with comparatively sound currencies buying inferior currencies,
speculating upon their rising in value.

The export of sound currencies certainly goes on to
a not inconsiderable extent.   It is said that Dutch notes
circulate on a large scale in the north-west of Germany,
and are even used as a means of preserving property.
Swiss notes are believed in like manner to be widely
distributed in neighbouring countries possessing unsound
currencies.   It is not improbable that English notes are
lying abroad in considerable quantities.   It may be that
to some extent the retardation in the contraction of
circulation, which was a widely discussed phenomenon in
most countries during 1921, and one which we shall take
into consideration later on, can be accounted for in this
way.   Similarly it is possible that a number of Swedish
notes are being used in Norway and Denmark, as well as
in some other countries whose currencies have proved
less sound than the Swedish.   There is hardly any
question, however, of any very large sums being involved.

The export of bad currency has assumed far larger
proportions, especially in latter years.   In this sphere
it is Germany which holds the first place.   The German
estimates of the amount of mark notes lying abroad have
perhaps at times been too high, and must be accepted
with some reserve.   But it is certainly true that at the
present time there are many milliards of marks in German
notes lying abroad, and further that this note export is
still continuing.   Amongst these milliards are included

the mark notes which the French and Belgian Governments have redeemed in the regions evacuated by Germany: for the rest the foreign mark note holdings are due to the export of notes from Germany which has been carried on on the largest possible scale. The reason for this export has been partly the demand of private business men as well as of municipal authorities for foreign currency, especially for the purchase of provisions and raw material, partly a general desire to substitute balances in a falling currency for a surer investment, or, again, attempts to avoid by this method the heavy German taxation. Quite an overwhelming proportion of this export, however, has been required for providing the German Empire with the sums of foreign exchange it found necessary, particularly for meeting reparation claims.

The sale of mark currency to abroad has naturally to a large extent taken the form of selling balances with German banks as well as bonds and treasury bills. But it is an undoubted fact that notes, too, have been sold in vast amounts. This amazing export has apparently gone to practically every country in the world, probably mostly via Holland. In Amsterdam I saw one day in the spring of 1920 thousand-mark notes being offered in bulk to tightly packed crowds out in the open air on the Square facing the Bourse, and the selling of mark currency in that way has, it seems, long been customary. According to an estimate from the end of 1921 the total sales of mark currency to abroad has reached 60 milliards of paper marks. In the economic sense the export of mark currency to abroad constitutes a form of borrowing. When all other possibilities of obtaining foreign loans fail, a needy state has no other recourse but to sell its currency to speculative investors who are willing to take it over in the expectation of an early rise in its value.

As such loans bear no interest, and as they involve a considerable measure of insecurity, the probable margin of profit must be fairly large. Heavy selling therefore forces down the exchange rate quite sharply, and naturally the more so as less and less confidence is felt abroad in the economic future of the selling country. Where this confidence begins to fail the sales of the currency in question are rendered more and more difficult to effect, and maybe even come to cease altogether—which indeed seems to have been the case with certain Eastern European currencies. That the sale of mark currency has been able to continue for so long and goes on even to this day on such an enormous scale is clearly due to the fact that, in spite of everything, the world is maintaining as long as possible unwavering confidence in German energy and German ability to succeed in overcoming all difficulties and in restoring sound currency conditions. At the beginning, in fact, it was always imagined that the mark must return to its former gold parity. Since then, hopes have gradually grown fainter and fainter, but at each particular stage people have imagined that the then current quotation marked the bottom rate, that a further fall was impossible, and that a considerable rise with its accompanying colossal profits must inevitably come. Owing to this false but worldwide notion the German mark has always found buyers. The early buyers, it is true, have suffered untold losses, but new buyers have come steadily forward, and the sale of mark currency has been able to continue. On certain occasions also a rise in the value of the mark has taken place, whereupon the latest buyers actually made considerable profits, and this circumstance has naturally induced fresh speculations when the value of the mark again commenced to fall. The losses which have been incurred on these speculations must be enormous, and for those

countries which have been the keenest participators in
this speculation they must have amounted to such sums
as considerably to affect those countries' entire economic
position. These losses should at any rate have one good
effect—namely, that of testifying to the whole world this
truth, that there is no limit to the depth to which a
paper currency can fall, so long as the quantity of the
means of payment in that currency is arbitrarily allowed
to increase. During the first years of the War people
were everywhere obsessed with the idea that a currency
had some sort of mysterious innate power of keeping
itself at its original value, independent of all arbitrary
increase of the means of payment. Much would be
gained if this idea could now be definitely overcome.

The fact that currency is exported abroad on a large
scale is one of the most extraordinary experiences in
the sphere of economics which the World War has brought
in its train, and it is therefore a matter of particularly
wide interest that the extent and the effects of this export
should be determined as accurately as possible. This,
of course, can only be done by official means, and it
would be eminently desirable for all countries to lend
their co-operation in having this matter gone into as
fully as it deserves. In many ways, of course, it does
not admit of exact estimates being made, but there must
undoubtedly be a quantity of material to hand capable
of helping to elucidate the subject, but which has not
yet been brought into the light of day.

We have also now to pay some attention to the possibility of mathematically determining the extent of the
rise in prices and the difficulties to be encountered in
that process. As is well known, people had already
attempted before the War, by means of index numbers,
to throw light upon the movements of the general price

level. The methods employed for this purpose are so
familiar and have been so thoroughly discussed elsewhere
that it is hardly necessary here to give an account of
them. But attention must be drawn to the fact that the
chances of inaccuracy attaching to the calculation of
indexes increase with every rise in prices. Every index
calculation implies to some extent weighing the importance of the various commodities whose prices are
being included in the calculation. This weighing is no
exact process, but is based rather on judgment; and it
must always be so, even if we attempt to have recourse
to figures representing production and consumption or
other such material for weighing the importance of the
various commodities. Now this unreliability in the
weighing process has no very great influence on a price
index, so long as the variations in prices are confined
within reasonable limits. But with the violent rises in
prices that have recently been taking place in every
country, the unreliability of index figures becomes
essentially greater. One gets some idea of the degree
of uncertainty in this respect by studying the different
index figures calculated in any given country for the
same category of prices, as, for example, the prices of
wholesale merchandise. The uncertainty in any case is
not so great as to prevent the price index giving a good
idea of the development of inflation in a country. If in
this connection we wish to make comparisons between
different countries, it is quite likely that the uncertainty
in the calculation of the index numbers gives rise to a
somewhat greater measure of uncertainty, and we must
therefore regard with some caution the inferences we
draw from such comparisons.

Index numbers representing rises in prices are com-
posed for various special purposes. One must differentiate between wholesale prices, retail prices, cost of

living, and wages. An index for wholesale prices may be based on statistics of general prices or else on statistics of the prices of import and export goods. Those index numbers which concern import and export goods are limited to a small class of commodities, and are therefore subject to variations, which make them unserviceable for any other purpose than that for which they are primarily intended.

In all calculations of index numbers very great difficulty has resulted from the State's interference in the natural formation of prices. A price index is, in fact, intended to be an indication of the prices actually paid. As, however, the State's regulation of prices is hardly ever fully respected, and as illegitimate trade—particularly at certain periods—was practised everywhere on a very large scale, a price index which, in dealing with commodities subject to controlled prices, only has regard to legal prices is very apt to be misleading. If no illegitimate trade existed, then such a price index would certainly offer a true indication of the prices actually paid. But it might then always be objected that the price level thus indicated was artificially too low and did not correspond to the real economic situation within the country. This objection is of immense interest, both from a theoretical and a practical point of view, but it is directed less against the index calculation than against the actual fact that the entire system of prices is disorganised through State interference. However, maximum prices obtain on the whole only in the case of a few commodities. Any reduction in the prices of these below the level required by the economic situation has this effect, that the public gets a greater free purchasing power than it would otherwise possess, and this purchasing power, when brought to bear upon other commodities, only forces up *their* prices. It is therefore always a vexed

question how far the policy of State-controlled prices
leads to a reduction in the general level of prices.
Certainly, the fall in the general level of prices which
the maximum prices may possibly have brought about
is considerably lower than people have been inclined to
imagine.

Very serious difficulties stand in the way of an attempt
to establish an index number where the question of
wages is concerned. For this purpose statistics are
generally very incomplete and not very reliable. When
making use of figures to indicate the standard of wages,
it is important to differentiate between those figures
which refer to working hours and those which refer to
working days or working weeks. These index numbers
generally differ very considerably, when calculated for
the past few years, for the reason that the daily working
period has been shortened by the introduction of the
eight-hour day. When wages rose with the advance of
inflation the result was that the index number for the
weekly income went up more slowly than the index
number for hourly income. Moreover, these index
numbers are of importance for two different problems. If
it is a question of determining the rise in the cost of
production in connection with the depreciation of money,
then, of course, it is the index number for the hourly
income that is the deciding factor. If, on the other
hand, we want to find out how the income of labour has
altered in relation to the cost of living, and on that basis
to form an idea of the development in the standard of
living on the part of the workers, then we must use an
index number based on the daily, or still better the weekly,
income. Moreover, in a case like this we should of
course have to take into consideration the question of
how far labour has been employed on full time, so that
the fact that industries may have been working for, say,

only a few days a week must be duly noted. A wage index which is to form a basis for the calculation of the total demand for currency, must obviously be based on statistics giving the workers' real incomes per week or per month, or possibly per year.

For all calculations of price index numbers it is of importance that they be made quickly, so as to allow of the figures being published, if possible, immediately after the end of the month they concern; and further that they are worked out uniformly for all countries, so that they may at once be employed for international comparisons. In the matter of being up-to-date the calculation of indexes in the case of many countries still leaves much to be desired. The value of those index numbers which are actually placed at the disposal of the public a few days after the end of the month is considerably diminished by the fact that the corresponding figures for other countries are delayed, often several months. It must be borne in mind that index numbers are not only intended for the research workers of the future who will one day rake up all the economic errors and delusions of our time. First and foremost should index numbers serve to assist scientists and experts in at once getting to know what is happening to-day and in being able to fathom the true meaning of it. Carefully worked-out statistics of the form of index numbers should be of particular value in serving as a guide in bank policy for purposes of judging what the situation demands, and it makes all the difference whether this guide is available a month or two before or after. The same naturally holds good, though not quite to the same extent, as regards the indication needed by Government authorities in looking after financial matters or in judging the situation in other countries. It is also important that index numbers be calculated as far as possible for all countries alike. In this connection surprisingly much has been neglected. Before the War regular calculations of price indexes were made only in England, and to some extent in a few other countries. Even the appalling upheaval in the sphere of prices brought about by the World War and the general inflation failed to induce the authorities to take any steps to establish public index numbers for prices and wages. It really appears to have been the economists' sharp criticism of inflation and its effects which first evoked by degrees a methodical calculation of index numbers of that sort. As a matter of fact, in several countries they do not exist even yet, and where they have been established it has for the most part been brought about by private initiative. This does not indicate that either the Government authorities or the central banks have had any particularly keen interest in throwing light upon the full import of the process of inflation.

The official calculations of index prices which have actually been made seem for the most part to have been the result of the desirability of having a standard for that increase in wages which the progressive inflation made necessary. This was at any rate the case in Sweden.

It entails considerable inconvenience and a good deal of uncertainty if index numbers are not calculated on a uniform basis. It is of some importance how one chooses the period before the War which is to serve as a starting-point for estimating the rise in prices, and whose price level is consequently to be indicated by 100. Not even in this simple detail have people managed to arrive at any uniformity in the calculation of indexes in the different countries. However, people seem to agree more and more in choosing the year 1913 for their starting-point, but this is still far from being uniformly carried out. As uniform as possible a system of calculating price indexes in different countries, with the publication of these index numbers in a uniformly compiled table as soon as possible after the close of each month, is very desirable. Such a programme seems to be peculiarly suitable for that international co-operation to which the interest of the world has to such a high degree been drawn since the War. The International Institute of Statistics at The Hague* has recently made a beginning in such statistics, but these statistics still suffer very much from the absence of a lot of countries, and from lack of uniformity in the index numbers, as well as from their publication being in a good many cases unreasonably delayed, so that the table fails to present a coherent picture of the actual situation with regard to the world's currencies. If steps could be taken to remedy these defects, if the compilation and publication of such a table could be effected with sufficient rapidity, if, finally, this table could be at once distributed telegraphically throughout the world, then this would contribute much towards solving the extremely important problems which are closely connected with the continual fluctuations in the values of the various currencies.

* Institut International de Statistique. Bulletin Mensuel de l'Office permanent.

SCARCITY OF COMMODITIES AND ITS BEARING
ON THE RISE IN PRICES

ONE of the principal methods of explaining away the rise
in prices, and of escaping the reproach of having caused
depreciation of money during the War, was to draw
attention to the prevailing scarcity of commodities.
When there is a lack of commodities, prices must rise—
that is so natural and simple a phenomenon that only
a spirit of ill-will, combined with an incurable tendency to
theoretical speculations, could induce people to believe
that the rise in prices was a sign of depreciation in the
value of the currency ! The official argument had here
a point in common with the views of the general public,
which are, of course, governed by personal impressions
of everyday variations of individual prices. On the
evidence of such experience no other conclusion is
possible than that the price of a particular commodity
must rise if there is a scarcity of that commodity. This
elementary observation is now generalised, and is applied
without hesitation to the case where a scarcity of all
commodities has come about. In so doing one forgets
that prices are essentially relative; they are an expression
of the valuation of different commodities in relation to
one another. A rise in one price may, indeed, be compensated for by sundry falls in other directions, so that
the price level in its entirety remains unaffected. If the
community as a whole is worse off for commodities than
before, but relatively about equally well supplied with
the one kind of commodity as the other, then there is no

reason why the relative valuation of the various commodities should alter, and the prices in that case might
well be imagined not to have altered, in spite of the poorer
supply of commodities. If any sudden changes have
taken place in the community's relative supply of various
commodities, then a relative change in prices must be the
consequence, but there would be no reason for a rise
in the average level of prices. If such a rise does occur,
it can only be accounted for by a reason of a monetary
nature—*i.e.*, the reason must lie on the side of the
currency.

A diminution in the supply of commodities should
properly call for a corresponding reduction in the community's supply of currency. If this is done, then the
price level must remain unaltered. If, on the other
hand, it is not done, but the community's supply of
currency remains unaltered, in spite of a scarcity of
commodities having arisen, it is obvious that a general
rise in prices must follow. This rise in prices must be
proportional to the plentifulness of the supply of currency
—*i.e.*, it must be determined by the relation between the
actual quantity of currency and that which would have
conformed to the new reduced supply of commodities.
Let us imagine that it would be possible to express the
supply of commodities statistically by an index number,
and let us further imagine that this index number has
sunk from 100 to 80—*i.e.*, that the community's supply
of commodities has been reduced by 20 per cent.—then,
according to this reasoning, the supply of currency would
also have gone down from 100 to 80. If it has not done
so, but has remained at 100, then it is too plentiful in the
proportion 100 : 80, and the consequence must be a rise in
prices in the same proportion—*i.e.*, the general price
level must be raised from 100 to 125.

During the War there was unquestionably a scarcity of

commodities, and this, too, has undoubtedly proved a
contributing factor in the rise in prices. But this has
manifestly been a factor of quite secondary importance.
For a reduction in the community's supply of commodities by an average of 20 per cent. all along the line
is a very serious matter, and inevitably gives rise to great
privation amongst wide classes of the population. But
even such scarcity cannot, as we have already seen, serve
as a basis of explanation for a rise in prices of more than
25 per cent. Now, as the index figures showing the
general price level in the majority of countries soon came
to exceed 200, and afterwards, even in the most favourably
situated European states, went beyond 300, and in other
countries rose even much higher, it is quite clear that
there cannot be any question of a possibility of accounting
for the rise in prices on the ground of scarcity of commodities. In spite of all the economic arguments brought
forward on this subject, the official pronouncements for
a long time stubbornly adhered to their explanation
that the scarcity of commodities was the real cause of
the rise in prices. After the War ended, however, the
supply of commodities in the Western European States
began once more to be normal, and at certain times it
has even been exceptionally plentiful. According to the
official theory prices should then have gone back to their
former level. But they showed no inclination whatever
to do this. On the contrary, after a slight reduction
during 1919, prices showed a further rise in the course
of the first half of 1920. A price index for wholesale trade,
showing 360 as an average for the second quarter of 1920,
such as existed in Sweden after the country was practically
filled to overflowing with goods, must cause some embar-
rassment to a theory which wanted to make the scarcity
of commodities the true ground of explanation for the
rise in prices. The experience we are now undergoing

offers final judgment in the long struggle between the teaching of science and the numerous opinions which have refused to acknowledge a rational analysis of the questions at issue. From this judgment there can be no appeal.

Furthermore, it is now quite evident that the much-used argument that the rise in prices is due to the keen demand for goods, which naturally made itself felt during the War, is a false one. A demand for goods, if it is to have an economic significance, must be backed up by ability to pay. There is, of course, always an unlimited demand incapable of paying for itself, and therefore without influence on prices. Now, when people say that during the War the demand reached an unprecedented pitch, and that prices therefore had to go up, this can only mean that there arose a demand which was backed up by full ability to pay, and that this forced up prices. This is just how it turned out. But this ability to pay has been artificially created by a steadily increasing production of additional currency. In fact, the driving force in the rise in prices has been just what we mean by inflation. Whenever this suggestion has been made, the usual answer from the central banks has been that they could not suppress the demand. When the scarcity of commodities became aggravated, the public clung as long as possible to their claims upon life, and bought, in spite of the fact that prices rose. It was commonly imagined that the public were by no means limited in this buying up of goods by the amount of their current incomes, but that they could draw on their balances at the banks for as much as they wanted, and could thus procure the purchasing power they needed in order to supply themselves with goods at however high a price. This reasoning is quite false, and it may not be out of place to say a few words in explanation of where the error really lies. The public's deposits at the banks are, as a rule, loaned out to industry and trade. If the public withdraws any part of its deposited funds in order to gain extra purchasing power, then a corresponding amount of funds must be withheld from industry and trade. In consequence of this the purchasing power of enterprises, and ultimately also that of the workers, is diminished, and therefore no increase takes place in the total purchasing power which the community has at its disposal. This is only the case if the banks create fresh bank currency in order to be able to pay back the deposited funds which the public demands to withdraw, and therefore do not make the reduction in their granting of credit to industry which this consumption of the savings should rightly have required. But thereby we find ourselves involved in a regular process of inflation, with a rise in prices as the inevitable consequence.

During the War inflation went on side by side with a growing scarcity of commodities. The rise in prices then was a result of both these price-raising tendencies which thus made themselves felt. If we suppose that the community's supply of currency was increased to double the normal amount, while the supply of commodities went down from 100 to 80, then from the first cause a rise in prices from 100 to 200 must result, and from the second cause a rise in prices from 100 to 125. The total rise in prices must, then, have been from 100 to 250. This sketch illustrates how the increase in the normal purchasing power in conjunction with the growing scarcity of commodities tends towards a heightening of the general price level. The connection of ideas, indeed, is, one would suppose, not so technical but that any and everybody should be able to grasp it, and the fact that so much obscurity ruled on this point testifies in no favourable manner to the results of mathematical education in our schools.

Now, generally speaking, there exists hardly any possibility of gauging the scarcity of commodities statistically. Whereas, if we had a fully reliable gauge of the general rise in prices, and similarly a fully reliable gauge of the increased supply of currency, then we should be able to estimate from them the extent of the scarcity of commodities. If—to keep to the example given above—we know that the level of prices has risen to 250, but that the community can be content with a supply of currency at 200, this means that a scarcity of commodities has been brought about which has reduced the supply of commodities in the proportion 250 to 200—*i.e.*, from 100 to 80. Under the conditions as stated, therefore, the diminution in the supply of commodities represents 20 per cent.

At present, of course, neither our knowledge of rises in prices nor of the supply of currency is so exact that we can expect any very accurate results from such a calculation. The reliability of the calculation would be further reduced if, in the course of events, a variation took place in the community's customary ways of effecting payment, such as, for example, would lead to an increased demand for currency where the price level was still unaltered. Even if, however, there exist no immediate reasons for supposing that this has come to pass, a calculation of the kind here given should in any case be made, in order to gain some ideas of what has probably taken place, and especially to enable us to see whether there is any necessity for supposing a variation in the methods of payment to have taken place.

In the following table I have placed side by side the figures for the rise in prices and those for the increase in circulation, which are available, as far as regards Sweden, right from the outbreak of the War up to the end of 1920. In order to gain a more comprehensive idea I have

worked it out in quarterly averages. The table further
shows the quarterly average figures for the index of the
Swedish Trade Journal representing wholesale prices,
and also the Social Board's unweighed index for food

Year and Quarter.		1 Trade Journal's Price Index.	2 Social Board's untested Price Index.	3 Relative Note Circulation.	3 in % of Arithmetical Average of 1 and 2.
1914	3	113	103	121	113·1
	4	120	108	128	112·3
1915	1	135	114	133	106·8
	2	143	121	130	98·5
	3	147	129	131	94·9
	4	155	138	136	92·8
1916	1	164	143	144	93·8
	2	175	148	151	93·5
	3	191	162	156	88·4
	4	209	175	168	87·5
1917	1	225	190	185	89·2
	2	229	197	201	94·4
	3	249	208	210	91·9
	4	272	235	233	91·9
1918	1	305	268	260	90·8
	2	331	350	285	89·6
	3	351	330	307	90·2
	4	370	372	339	91·4
1919	1	360	364	340	93·9
	2	331	352	328	96·0
	3	320	343	313	94·4
	4	311	332	314	97·7
1920	1	338	316	316	96·6
	2	360	316	320	94·7
	3	363	331	326	93·9
	4	325	323	322	99·4

prices, as well as that of my own monthly figures showing
the relative note circulation. These series of figures
are illustrated by the diagram (Fig. 1). The general
agreement between the rise in prices and the increase
in circulation is clearly indicated, and it is particularly

striking that the agreement is, practically speaking,
absolute for the final quarter of 1920.

However, one glance at the diagram shows also that
during the years of war the rise in prices was somewhat
greater than the increase in circulation. This, in fact,
should, theoretically speaking, be the case, since the
country's supply of commodities during these years
was undoubtedly scarcer than usual. Seeing that the

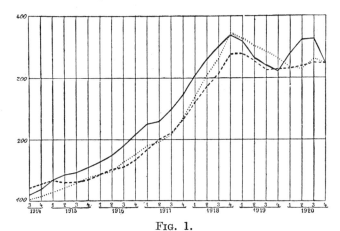

FIG. 1.

——— Wholesale price index of the *Swedish Trade Journal*.
.... The Social Board's index for retail prices of food, fuel,
           and light.
--------- Relative note circulation.

circulation came into general use in both the wholesale
and the retail trade, the demand for notes must clearly be
referred to the rise in prices in both the one and the other
of these branches of trade. We can thus quite well
start from the average of the rise in prices taken from
both index numbers. If we now divide the index of
circulation by this average, we get a figure which shows
how large the circulation would have been if the price
level throughout the whole period had been constant.

This circulation, which is shown in the last column of the table, clearly offers a gauge of the quantity of the commodities which were available for the market at each given period.

The diagram (Fig. 2) presents this reduced circulation figure. It shows that from the second quarter of 1915 inclusive it lies below the standard average (which is indicated in the diagram by 100). The fall of the curve

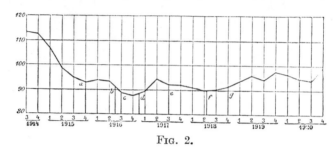

FIG. 2.

(a) Important extension of export prohibition in Sweden for bacon, butter, etc.
(b) England and France cease to apply the rules of the London Declaration regarding transport by sea.
(c) English total prohibition of export to Sweden.
(d) Important Swedish State regulations for trade in grain, bread, and manufactured goods.
(e) The United States establish practically total export prohibition.
(f) The so-called " Great Trade Agreement."
(g) The Armistice.

below the standard average gives an idea of the scarcity of commodities which prevailed in the country during the succeeding years. No exact measure of the scarcity of commodities, of course, can be obtained by this method, as the material from which the figures are supplied can never be absolutely relied upon. Besides which, alterations in the methods of effecting payment may have been made, though the diagram gives no cause whatever for presuming any such thing, since the movements of the curve very naturally explain themselves without recourse being had to any explanation of that sort.

The vertical lines drawn on the diagram, indicated by the letters *a–g*, are intended to recall certain events which were of particular importance for Sweden's supply of commodities, and the effects of which may be traced in the movements of the curve.

It is understood that the curve represents the scarcity of commodities actually handled on the market. During certain periods there probably existed a larger quantity of commodities, although speculation withdrew a certain portion of them from the market. During these periods the curve must lie lower than it should do by reason of the total supply of commodities. That has apparently been the case, in some degree, from the third quarter of 1916 inclusive up to the first quarter of 1917 inclusive, as also in the middle of 1920.

During the first months of the War there were hoarded in Sweden, as is well known, considerable quantities of notes. As a result of this the total note circulation far exceeded that actually in current use. This particular rise in circulation can clearly be read off on the curve; the curve even gives an approximate idea of its extent and its duration. Already, by the second quarter of 1915, hoarding had apparently ceased.

By the end of 1920 the supply of commodities, according to the diagram, is once more normal—that is to say, the note circulation merely corresponds to the prevailing price level.

If no scarcity in commodities exists, as at the end of 1920, then the rise in prices is to be accounted for as a result of the more plentiful supply of currency—in other words, as a result of inflation. The general level of prices, on this hypothesis, is a measure of the extent of inflation. If a scarcity in commodities sets in, then, as we have already seen, the rise in prices is thereby intensified. But even this further rise in prices may be regarded as a result of a too plentiful supply of currency, and consequently of inflation. Thus, the meaning of inflation must be extended, but this extension of the significance of the term is justified both on the grounds of the intrinsic character of the matter, and also particularly because then the rise in prices, as expressed by the general price level, becomes under all circumstances the measure of inflation. It is an advantage thus to have the measure of inflation given, even before we have succeeded in completely determining its causes, and even if it should never be possible accurately to find out what bearing the scarcity in commodities has on the rise in prices. It is therefore natural to conceive the idea of inflation in a limited as well as in a wider sense. In both cases the essential point of inflation is a too plentiful supply of currency. In the former case we estimate this excess only from the standard which prevailed before; in the latter case we also take into consideration the excess in the supply of currency which arises through the former standard being retained even after the supply of commodities has diminished.

THE INFLUENCE OF INFLATION ON GOLD

THERE is an old saying that bad coinage drives the good out of circulation. In accordance with this saying the gold coinage since the outbreak of the War has everywhere been driven out of circulation by the depreciated notes. This movement, however, has assumed peculiar forms, which it is somewhat important to study. If the movement of gold had been left entirely free, the result would naturally have been that all gold would have disappeared from the belligerent countries of Europe and have found its way to such countries as still maintained a gold standard, and whose coinage retained the highest purchasing power. On the whole, this actually has been the result, although by various indirect means and with important limitations.

In countries where a gold coinage circulated the export of gold coins on the outbreak of war was either formally prohibited or at any rate practically prevented. Steps were likewise taken to prevent gold being melted down, and some countries even went so far as to prohibit the paying of an agio for gold coins. As by this means gold was of no practical use, it became comparatively easy for the central banks to carry out their policy of accumulating gold, of which I spoke in a previous chapter. In this way practically all gold coinage in the countries of Western civilisation has disappeared from the circulation and has found its way to the central banks. The private banks also have been induced to part with their gold more or less completely. Even as late as in the Spring

of 1920, the English private banks had to hand over the
rest of their gold reserves to the Bank of England, having
during the War supplied both the Bank of England
and the Government with considerable sums in gold.
The Chairman of the London Joint City and Midland Bank
announced at the Annual Meeting in January, 1921, that
his bank had had to give up its remaining gold reserves
of 8 million pounds and had been refunded in Bank of
England notes; this happened in view of an agreement
between the Government and the banks: " We were sorry
to lose it," remarked Mr. McKenna, " but we recognised
the necessity which led the Government to demand it
of us."

However, gold did not remain in the belligerent countries' central banks, but was used by them in a greater
or lesser degree in payment for war necessities from abroad
or to support loan operations on foreign markets.   The
latter method of employing gold proved to be the most
effective when it was a question of procuring as large
amounts as possible in foreign exchange. The foreign
market could, in fact, be presumed to have a greater
capacity for absorbing a loan if the lending country's
central bank was able to show a high percentage of gold
cover for its notes.   France's gold exports to England and
England's and France's gold exports to the United States
are a good example of a method of financing in accordance
with this point of view. In one form or another, therefore, during the War period, gold went from the belligerents
to the neutrals, as well as to the United States and Japan,
and in consequence the gold reserves of these countries
have been continually increasing.

In order to indicate in figures the international movements of gold since the outbreak of the War, it will be convenient to express the amounts in one and the same
currency, and in view of the United States' present

position as sole maintainer of a gold standard, it will suit our purpose to use the dollar.   Early in the first years of the War the Austro-Hungarian Bank had to surrender the main portion of its gold reserves to the German Reichsbank, and in this way the former bank lost 206 million dollars.   On the other hand, the gold reserves of the German Reichsbank increased very substantially during the first period of the War.   From the end of 1913 to the end of 1914 the rise was equivalent to 120 million dollars, and by the end of 1916 an additional 100 million dollars had found its way there.   It was the bullion of the Austrian Bank and the German domestic circulation which represented the principal sources of this supply of gold.   At the same time, however, a considerable amount of gold exportation was going on from the German Reichsbank, either in direct payment for provisions and other necessary commodities, or in support of the falling mark rate.   After the Peace of Brest-Litovsk 50 million dollars' worth of Russian gold was transferred to the German Reichsbank, and the latter's stock of gold at the time of the armistice reached the figure of 607 million dollars.   The greater portion of this gold, however, has since been sunk in various payments which Germany has had to effect, especially for the immense import of food which became necessary after the raising of the blockade, so that by the beginning of 1921 the bank's remaining gold reserves consisted of only 260 million dollars, which was somewhat less than the stock it held at the end of 1913 (279 million dollars).   Taken as a whole, then, the movement may be described as such that the whole of the German domestic circulation, plus the rest of the gold which accumulated within the country during the War, as well as the entire contribution of Austrian gold, has been exported.   In France a corresponding movement has taken place.   The French Bank's stock of bullion, owing to the withdrawal of gold from circulation, was first brought up to 968 million dollars by the end of 1915, as against 679 million dollars at the end of 1913. After 1915, however, France was obliged to export gold in considerable quantities, so that the stock of gold went below 700 million dollars. In the Bank Report of the 30th September, 1920, the gold reserve within the country is stated to have been 3,531 million francs; but after that comes an item, "Gold abroad," which is given at 1,948 million francs. The latter figure has been maintained ever since, while in the former figure a slight increase has taken place. The item "Gold abroad" represents the French Bank's direct gold export, but the question must be left open how much gold may otherwise have been exported from France. Of particularly vital importance has been the Russian export of gold. Before the War, the Russian State Bank had the largest gold reserve of any country—namely, 787 million dollars (at the end of 1913). This gold reserve had by the end of 1915 an amount of 831 million dollars. This increase had probably almost completely absorbed the Russian gold circulation. At the same time, however, the exportation of gold was carried on, principally to Great Britain, and it is said that from October, 1914, to the spring of 1917 this export covered about 330 million dollars. During the Roumanian War the gold reserve of the Roumanian Central Bank was transferred to Russia, to be kept in security during the German invasion, but it is believed that this gold was afterwards appropriated by the Bolsheviks. It is said that, besides this amount, the Bolshevik Government has had in its possession between 400 and 500 million dollars' worth of the gold which formerly belonged to the Russian Imperial Bank. Latterly, however, this gold too has probably been very largely exported, finding its way principally to America.

It is apparent, therefore, that, in spite of all the efforts of the Governments to prevent it, the inflation existing in the belligerent countries of Europe finally forced the gold abroad. Nevertheless in some of these countries the central banks have managed to retain considerable

GOLD RESERVES: 1913 AND 1921.

(In millions of dollars.)

Belligerent States on the Continent.	1913.	1921.	Increase + Decrease −
France ..	678·9	688·3	
Italy ..	288·1	236·5	
Belgium	59·1	51·4	
Germany	278·7	260·0	
Austria-Hungary	251·4	0·0	
Total	1556·2	1236·2	− 320·0
England	175·2	763·3	+ 593·1
Neutral States (including Japan).			
Sweden	27·4	75·5	
Norway	12·8	39·5	
Denmark	19·7	61·0	
Netherlands ..	60·9	245·6	
Spain	92·5	479·2	
Switzerland ..	32·8	104·9	
Argentine	225·0	450·1	
Japan	65·0	558·8	
Total	536·1	2014·6	+ 1478·5
United States	691·5	2529·6	+ 1838·1
Sum total	2954·0	6543·7	+ 3589·7

reserves, which are more or less completely excluded from the world market; this is especially the case in England and France, but also in countries with a still more depreciated currency, such as Italy and Germany. At the same time gold production has been going on, and has supplied to the world very considerable quantities of gold, which have been mainly at the disposal of the other countries for increasing their public gold reserves.

Ever since the beginning of the War, a stream of gold has in this way been flowing to neutral countries, as well as to the United States and Japan. The table (p. 67) gives an indication of the movements of gold since the outbreak of the War, in so far as these movements find their expression in variations in the gold reserves.

This table does not give a complete survey of the movements of gold. The gold reserves of the Russian and Roumanian central banks have for the most part, as stated above, been exported, and this gold is now to some extent included in the gold reserves officially reported as being in other countries, particularly in America. Nor, indeed, have the colonies of the British Empire been accounted for in the table. Of still greater importance, however, is the fact that the table only takes account of public gold reserves, and therefore disregards the very considerable movement of gold to and from the East, which is not included in that category. An estimate of these latter gold movements is given below.

The world's gold production has turned out as follows (the figures representing millions of dollars):

1913	..	.. 459·9	1917	..	.. 423·6
1914	..	.. 439·1	1918	..	.. 380·0
1915	..	.. 470·5	1919	..	.. 365·2
1916	..	.. 454·2	1920	..	.. 338·0

An English statistician, Mr. Hitchin, has made the following calculation regarding the use to which this newly produced gold has been put (the figures in millions of pounds; the minus sign represents export):

	1915.	1916.	1917.	1918.	1919.	1920.
Industry (Europe and America) ..	17	18	16	16	20	
India (the year up to following March included).. ..	1·4	5·1	19·6	−3·3	27·7	3·9
China	−1·7	2·6	2·6	0·4	13·5	
Egypt	−0·8	−0·2	−0·1	−0·0	−0·0	
Available for monetary purposes ..	80·5	68·0	48·2	65·9	14·0	
Total	96·4	93·5	86·3	79·0	75·2	70·0

For 1913, when the total production amounted to 94·5
million pounds, the amount consumed in the arts was
27·3 million pounds. For 1915, on the other hand, it was
only 17 million pounds, though production then reached
its maximum. During all the War period the industrial
consumption of gold remained at a relatively low level.
During 1915, too, the requirements of India were small,
while China and Egypt show an export which is more
than sufficient to cover India's requirements. The
quantity of new gold available for monetary purposes—
that is to say, for the public gold reserves—reached a
maximum in 1915. The amount has since then shown
a sharp decline, as is seen from the table, and for 1919 is
very low, owing principally to an exceptional demand from
the East, secondly to reduced gold production, and finally
also to a somewhat increased industrial consumption.
The total quantity of new gold which, according to these
obviously very approximate estimates, should during the
years 1915–1919 have gone to the world's public gold
reserves, amounts to 276·6 million pounds, or 1,345 million
dollars. If we add to this a figure of 325 million dollars,
which represented the corresponding gold supply for
1914, we get a total figure of 1,670 million dollars, which
should thus represent the increase in the gold reserves

in question after 1913, in so far as this increase arises from
new gold.

The result, therefore, of the gold movements after 1914
is that the central banks of the belligerent states on the
Continent lost 320·0 million dollars, while England's
public gold reserves gained 593·1 million dollars, those
of the neutral states and Japan together 1478·5 million
dollars, and the United States 1838·1 million dollars.
In its entirety this means an increase in the public gold
reserves, in so far as they are included above, amounting
to 3589·7 million dollars. If out of this amount 1,670
million dollars may be considered to have been covered
by the gold production during the same period, then at
any rate about 1,900 million dollars must have been drawn
from the gold which was formerly in circulation in the
countries of Western civilisation.

It follows from these figures that, after the outbreak
of the War, the amount of gold offered on the world market
was on an altogether extraordinary scale, at the same time
as the monetary demand for this gold was limited to
whatever sums the central banks and exchequers of the
neutral countries, the United States and Japan might be
prepared to accept for increasing their gold reserves.
This situation has involved a complete disorganisation
of the market for gold, and the result has been a very
sharp fall in its value.   The best gauge for the depreciation of gold during this period will probably be found in
the rise in the general level of prices in the United States.
According to the Bureau of Labor, the index figure
for wholesale prices reached a maximum of 272 for May,
1920, as compared with 100 for 1913.   Of course, the rise
in prices cannot be judged on wholesale prices only,
but we have no index numbers for retail prices and wages
that are of equal reliability.   Nor does the highest index
number for a single month give any very reliable indica-

tion of the level to which the purchasing power of gold has sunk. Even if, therefore, we do not rely merely upon the highest point reached by the curve of wholesale prices, but base our calculations on a maximum general price level of only 250, then gold will in any case have gone down to 40 per cent. of its former value in relation to commodities. It is quite true that, owing to the complete disorganisation of the gold market, this figure can in no way claim to be an exact one, but all the same it is without doubt essentially correct. The fact is that, after the outbreak of war, the value of gold was subject to a more violent revolution than history has ever at any time previously witnessed, and this depreciation of gold is on the whole one of the most remarkable phenomena in the entire revolution of the world's monetary system that has taken place after 1914.

With the superfluity of gold which resulted from the cessation of the gold circulation, and from the fact of certain countries having parted with a very large portion of their central gold reserves, it was practically inevitable that some fall in the value of gold should follow. But the extent of this depreciation was largely dependent upon the reception which the central banks of the gold countries gave to the gold which poured in. Had the influx of gold been comparatively moderate, and had the central banks concerned admitted this gold into their gold reserves without increasing their note circulation on that account, or else without creating any additional currency, then certainly the value of gold might have been kept up. An increased monetary demand for gold would then have arisen, and would have represented an independent factor in that market where the value of gold was determined. But, as it happened, the influx of gold was very strong, and at the same time it was accepted in this way only to a relatively small extent by the central banks

of the gold countries. In fact, the central banks everywhere built upon their augmented gold reserves an ever-
increasing quantity of means of payment, and this newly
created purchasing power could not help forcing up the
price level of commodities in the various currencies which
were affected thereby. This was equivalent to a reduction in the purchasing power of gold. By a continual
inflation of their currencies, therefore, the central banks
of the gold-receiving countries offered a kind of resist-
ance to the extraordinary influx of gold; they impaired
the market for gold and brought down its value.

In some cases, it is true, the central banks have kept
the increase of their circulation proportionately lower
than the supply of gold would have warranted had the
former percentage of gold cover been taken as normal.
This means that the gold cover reckoned on a percentage
basis increased. Particularly has this been the case
in Holland, Switzerland, and Spain. But even in such
cases the country's supply of means of payment has
increased in absolute figures, and the artificially expanded
purchasing power has brought about a rise in prices.
Thereby pressure has been exercised upon the value of
gold.

The explanation of the inflation which was thus going
on in the neutral countries side by side with the import
of gold lies in certain economic interests which for both
parties was closely bound up with the transfer of gold.
From the point of view of the belligerent states the
export of gold was merely a link in the chain of their
financial policy, which aimed at obtaining as much purchasing power as possible in other countries without
having to send them commodities. The export of gold,
as pointed out above, could best be utilised for this
purpose if credits could be established on that basis in the
countries receiving the gold. These credits might perhaps

amount to several times the total quantity of the gold exported, but this meant the creation of fresh purchasing power, and thus inflation in the receiving country was an inevitable consequence. Naturally these continual rises in prices proved to be a source of great inconvenience to the gold-exporting countries. But it is probable that they scarcely realised this at the time, and even if they had done so, they would have paid but little attention to it, since their principal interest in any case lay in procuring for themselves as large a supply of commodities as possible.

Again, in the gold-receiving countries the central banks have, with a view to interior economy, had an interest in making their recently acquired gold stocks interest-bearing, which could only be done by creating more currency on the strength thereof. There can scarcely be any doubt but that this motive constituted a contributing factor in the spirit of concession displayed by the central banks in the countries in question, not only towards belligerent states, but also towards their own Governments or the internal business demand for credit.

Further, the idea was very generally entertained, and even still prevails in wide circles, that no inflation can be considered to have taken place so long as the percentage of gold cover has not been lowered. Here we again have the old superstitious belief that gold cover is the true basis of the value of a currency. Had people realised that a currency's purchasing power can never be determined by any other factor than the scarcity of the means of payment valid in that standard, then they would have understood that every increase in the quantity of means of payment which came into active use must mean a reduction in the value of the currency and consequently involve inflation.

In some of the gold-receiving countries the creation of new purchasing power in connection with the influx of gold was driven to such lengths that the value of the currency dropped lower than that of gold. It was then no longer worth while exporting gold to these countries. With every such expansion of inflation the market for gold became narrower. Finally, the United States became practically the only country which could take gold. The value of gold during the whole of this process was, of course, determined by the purchasing power of the currencies of those countries which still had a sufficiently sound money to make it worth while sending them gold. Theoretically speaking, the value of gold in all those countries which were able to import gold should have been identical. If gold could have been sent to a country where it would have had higher purchasing power, it would certainly have gone there rather than to the country possessing the next best currency, and this movement would have gone on until the best currency had, through an excessive influx of gold, been forced down on a level with the next best currency. In that way gold would have possessed exactly the same purchasing power in all the various countries to which it was sent. If any country had depreciated its currency to a greater degree than these best currencies, then it would not have been able to get any more gold. In reality conditions did not prove quite so simple during the War. Freedom of trade was far too restricted to allow of such a complete adjustment of the purchasing power of gold in the various countries taking place. The belligerent states had first and foremost to see to it that they procured commodities from those countries where commodities were to be had, and for that reason they sent their gold even to countries where gold possessed a smaller purchasing power than in others.

It was not until the War ended and some freedom of trade was restored that it became realised that a number of those countries which had previously managed to import gold had actually carried the inflation of their currencies to such lengths that these currencies were far below gold in value. This was so in the case of all the neutral states of Europe, as well as of England. The currency of the United States then stood at a level by itself, gold could go only to the United States, and the value of gold was determined by that of the dollar. As, however, inflation of the dollar currency was going on all the time, it was inevitable that the value of gold was proportionately depreciated. Inflation actually continued, with slight interruptions, right up to the spring of 1920, and consequently the depreciation of gold likewise continued up to that time.

It should, however, be observed that even the United States did not find it possible to maintain an effective gold currency during the War. Gold export was prohibited from September, 1917, and this prohibition was not annulled until June, 1919. During that period, then, the dollar could depreciate in relation to gold. At times gold has probably also possessed greater purchasing power in the Far East than in the United States. That such was the case is evident from the considerable export of gold to the East which began as soon as the American embargo was removed in June, 1919, and which, in conjunction with the large exportation of gold to South America for over a year, caused the gold trade of the United States to show a net balance of exports. During the period of restriction gold still found its way to some extent from Europe to the United States, though at the same time also from the United States to other countries, particularly to the Far East and the Argentine. From September, 1920, however, the United States have

every month had a net balance of imports of gold over
exports, which at times has been exceptionally large.
Thus, no sooner had the world's trade become free than
gold streamed in large quantities into that country where
it possessed the highest purchasing power.

How different the purchasing power of the currencies
of the gold-importing countries actually was may best
be seen from the following table, which illustrates the
yearly average index of wholesale prices in some of the
gold-importing countries:

	Sweden (Swedish Trade Journal).	England (" Economist ").	U.S.A. (Bureau of Labor).	Holland (Central Bureau v.d. Stat).	Japan (Bank of Japan).
1915 ..	145	123	100	149	97
1916 ..	185	161	123	234	117
1917 ..	244	204	175	298	148
1918 ..	339	225	196	398	196
1919 ..	330	235	212	303	240
1920 ..	347	283	244	285	260

The fact that Holland and Sweden, with their comparatively very strong inflation during the War, were
able to import considerable quantities of gold is an
outcome of the above-mentioned abnormal conditions in
the world market. But the final figures show that all
the European currencies under review here actually fell
in value to points essentially lower than the dollar.
These countries, therefore, can only retain their gold by
locking it up. The free gold goes to the United States.
In the case of England, the actual fall in the currency
below the gold parity is shown in the now regularly
published London quotations for gold. They are given
in shillings per ounce troy of fine gold, the old parity
being 84·96s. (=84s. 11·5d.). For June, 1921, the mean

quotation was 108s. 10d.—*i.e.*, about 27 per cent. above parity. For December, 1921, however, the mean quotation had fallen to 99s. 4d.

An increase in note circulation and deposits in the gold-importing countries has shown itself to act as a check on the influx of gold. Were it not for such an increase a country possessing a gold standard would have had to import still more gold, and this gold could doubtless to some extent have forced up the price level. By creating additional currency and thus voluntarily forcing up the price level, the country can prevent the influx of gold, and, if the process of inflation is carried to sufficient lengths, even completely shut it out. We may say, then, that the new bank currency in the group of countries we are now discussing competes with gold and reduces the world's capacity for absorbing gold. As this is manifestly so in the case of those belligerent countries which by means of inflation were the first to expel gold, we are justified in regarding the competition between the fresh bank currency and gold as the general cause of the fall in the value of gold.

That a process of inflation can in this way become a reason for a fall in the value of gold is a fact which only the experience of the War brought to light. It has, of course, long been realised that a country which fails to redeem its notes with gold is reduced to a paper standard having a lower value than gold. When valued in that currency the gold gets an " agio " and disappears from the country. Then people have been quite content with stating that the currency in question has lost in value. It has apparently never occurred to anybody that this change may also have had some influence on the value of the gold. When, however, as now, a revolution of this sort takes place simultaneously in the majority of the most important countries of the world, one cannot

get away from the fact that the total increase in the
quantity of currency in the world must also cause a
reduction in the value of gold. In consequence of the
competition of artificially created currency the monetary
utility of gold has been relatively reduced. If all countries
had simultaneously adopted a paper currency depreciated
in an equal degree, and had to a similar extent reduced
their demand for gold in cover thereof, then the pressure
on the value of gold would have been enormous, and we
might perhaps even have witnessed the paradox of the
gold falling as low as the paper currencies, with the
result that their gold parity would have been maintained.

THE EXCLUSION OF GOLD

THE gold-receiving countries have by still more direct means tried to protect themselves from the undesirable influx of gold—viz., by simply excluding the gold from their respective monetary systems. For this purpose free coinage has been suspended in certain countries, and where the central banks had been under an obligation to buy gold at a fixed price they have become exempt from this obligation. This *gold-exclusion policy* is one of the most remarkable phenomena in the history of money after 1914. For thousands of years gold had been the chief of all the means of payment, and it was now to be degraded and regarded as inferior to a purely paper currency. Sweden, by taking the lead in this gold-exclusion policy, has attracted the attention of the whole world to her monetary conditions, and a somewhat detailed account of the measures adopted in this respect in Sweden may not be out of place in the present work.

The gold-exclusion policy was formally carried out in Sweden by the passing on the 8th February, 1916, of a special law, and by various royal edicts. By means of this legislation Sweden had freed her currency from its connection with gold, and the value of the Swedish krona was thus enabled to rise above the gold parity.

In adopting this extraordinary measure the Riksbank gave no other motive than a consideration of its own economic interests, and it is curious to see now how petty were the points of view from which even these interests were considered. The Riksbank's gold reserve, which at the

end of 1914 amounted to 108·5 million kronor, and even
by the end of November, 1915, did not exceed 113·3
million kronor, had by the end of the latter year increased
to 124·6 million kronor. Thus from the beginning of
1916 the bank found itself in a position to resume the
redemption of notes with gold. On the further events
the bank's Year Book for 1916 makes the following
statement:

"The gold reserve continued to increase from 124·6
million kronor at the turn of the year to 142·3 million
by the 31st January, and to 160·3 million by the
5th February, 1916. In view of this rapid rise in the
gold reserve the Board sent on the 4th February a
communication to the Government in the following
terms:

"'According to para. 10 of the law governing the
Swedish State Bank, the Riksbank has to redeem bullion
delivered to the Mint for the bank's account at a price
of 2,480 kronor per kilogramme fine gold, less ¼ per cent.
for cost of minting.

"'This ordinance was made and is intended to be put
in force under normal conditions when the bank is
in a position to sell without difficulty and without appreciable loss any gold not required for the bank's own
purpose. The present rates on the exchange market,
however, make it impossible for the bank to dispose of
such gold as is not required for the bank's own needs
without very considerable loss.

"'Furthermore, as the gold reserve of the Riksbank
at present reaches an amount which is regarded as fully
adequate to meet all possible requirements, the Board
consider that the liability to buy gold which devolves
upon the Riksbank according to para. 10 of the State
Bank Law should be suspended; wherefore the Board
respectfully submit that the Government be pleased to

propose to Parliament that the clause in question be duly amended to that end.'

" As a consequence hereof opportunity must be afforded for suspending the universal right as given in accordance with para. 9 of the Mint Law to receive against gold delivered at the Mint twenty- or ten-kronor pieces."

Thus we find that the Riksbank has treated this matter as if it concerned only the bank's private convenience. Nothing in the above communication gives us to understand that the Board had any conception of the fact that the unrestricted admission of gold into the circulation of a country is an entirely characteristic feature of a gold standard. The suspension of the free influx of gold was in reality equivalent to a suspension of the Swedish gold standard in one very essential point— namely, that of the limit placed by law upon the rise in value of the currency above the value of gold. In principle such a measure implies that the Swedish currency had been converted into a free standard limited as to any downward tendency by the value of gold (notes always being redeemed by gold), but free to assume any higher value.

Personally, I was of the opinion that such a radical change in the character of the Swedish currency ought not be made merely out of consideration for the Riksbank's private interests, which, with the significance they may have for the finances of the Swedish State, must nevertheless be regarded as of quite secondary importance in a matter of such fundamental consequence to the whole economic life of the country. If any alteration were made, it would have to be based on motives of national economy, which alone would justify a change in the monetary system. But the situation was such that it was of vital interest for Sweden to protect her currency from being further involved in the fall in

the value of gold. The only way to avoid this was to
exclude the Swedish currency from any further influx
of gold from abroad.

When, therefore, in the end of January, 1916, the
Riksbank asked for my opinion in this matter, I submitted
that the motive for an exclusion of gold ought to be based
on its being necessary " for preventing a further considerable rise in the general price level within the country
and other harmful consequences arising out of an unnecessary increase in the means of payment." This point of
view ought, in my opinion, to have been argued as follows :

" The general rise in prices caused by the War asserts
itself not only in countries with a paper currency at present
unredeemable, but also, though of course in a lesser degree,
in countries with an effective gold standard, and must
to that extent be regarded as implying a depreciation of
gold itself. Since the Riksbank has now resumed the
redemption of its notes with gold, and the value of Swedish
currency is thus determined by the value of gold, the
abnormally low internal value of the monetary unit
is altogether to be regarded as an indication of the depreciation of gold itself. So long as gold can be freely imported into Sweden, it is impossible for the general price
level at home to be kept appreciably lower than in other
countries possessing an effective gold currency, and every
additional decrease in the value of gold must then cause
a corresponding depreciation in the Swedish krona, and
consequently a proportional increase in the general price
level. . . .

" As the Riksbank is bound to buy all the gold which
is offered to the bank, foreign countries have the option
of effecting their payments to Sweden to any extent they
like by consignments of gold instead of commodities.
Under present conditions, however, it is particularly
desirable that liabilities of foreign countries should be

paid as far as possible in the form of commodities of which we are in need. This Swedish interest could of course be more easily satisfied if further gold payments could be avoided. It is also clear that, while gold payments have a direct tendency to increase the volume of the means of payment, and thereby the general price level, payment in kind has the opposite effect of increasing the quantity of commodities (the total amount of the means of payment remaining unchanged) and thus of tending to reduce the price level at home.

"This influx of gold, with which the neutral countries have for the present to reckon, is apt to cause an unsound increase in the quantity of the means of payment, which in its turn tends to promote a speculative expansion of industry that may lead to overspeculation and will then probably end in an economic crisis. Although we have in the main escaped these consequences in Sweden, they are nevertheless of so serious and so threatening a nature that we have every reason to protect ourselves against them."

By the 8th February a bill had already been passed giving the Riksbank the powers for which it asked. The right of free mintage, however, was not suspended until the 28th April, after the necessary agreement had been come to with Denmark and Norway regarding the suspension of the regulation made by the monetary union.

With the passing of this legislation the tie was loosened which had hitherto prevented the Swedish currency from rising above its gold parity. This gold exclusion was a measure of such importance that the very highest interest will always be attached to it by future writers on monetary history. True, it has happened before that a metallic currency has been closed to the metal on which it was founded. But then the question has been one of silver,

and the intention has been to raise the value of the currency above a depreciating silver, in order, if possible,
to keep the currency in a constant relation to gold, and
possibly even to establish an actual gold standard.   The
action of the Netherlands in 1873 and also the much-
spoken-of closing of the Indian mints to free silver in June,
1893, offer examples of this.   But closing a gold currency
from the free entrance of gold was something hitherto
unheard of, and is, in fact, a measure which lies on an
altogether different plane from the exclusion of silver.
For now there is no longer any thought of basing the
currency on a metal of a higher or a more constant value.
The exclusion of gold implies, in principle, the transition
to a free standard which will be regulated irrespective
of any metal and exclusively with a view to the country's
interest in having a standard of value as stable as possible.
The development of money had long tended to make the
gold standard universal, and before the outbreak of the
War this result had, practically speaking, been attained.
That even this gold standard should come to be regarded
as inferior, that a paper currency should come to receive
a higher value than gold, this is what makes the Swedish
proceedings of February, 1916, extremely remarkable.

It is never a matter of indifference as to what is put
forward publicly as the motive of an important action.
It is often the motive which gives to the action its particular character.   The reason on which action is based
gives the most reliable support for pursuing a consistent
course of action in the ever-changing conditions of
life.   The exclusion of gold from Sweden was an action
of such importance that it must have been dictated by
powerful motives.   But the motive which was here officially put forward was, as may be gathered from the
foregoing, a very poor one indeed.   Consideration of
the private economic interests of the Riksbank ought

really to have been deemed a far too weak motive for the measure in view. Nor would it be long before it was proved that the lack of definite motives and of deliberate purpose rendered impossible the rational fulfilment of the Swedish policy of gold exclusion, and that the very pettiness of the motive made it essentially more difficult to obtain the active co-operation of the Scandinavian neighbours in a united Scandinavian monetary policy.

No complete exclusion of gold supplies from abroad had been effected by the above-mentioned legislation. Indeed, by virtue of the still valid Scandinavian monetary union, both Norwegian and Danish gold coin were fully legal tender in Sweden, and the Scandinavian neighbours could thus have Swedish purchasing power at their disposal by sending their gold coin to Sweden. In accordance with the agreement made with Norway and Denmark as to the suspension of the right of free coinage, these countries had also put a ban on the importation of gold from abroad. It was thus not possible for foreign countries to nullify the Swedish gold-exclusion policy by shipping gold to Norway or Denmark and, after having it minted there, introducing the gold into Sweden. This did not, of course, preclude the possibility of these countries themselves—i.e., their central banks—having gold minted and the gold coins sent over to Sweden. It was, however, taken for granted in Sweden that this course would not be adopted, but that Sweden's desire to cut herself off from the supply of foreign gold would be duly respected.

This hope, however, was not fulfilled. From the autumn of 1916 inclusive Norwegian and Danish gold coin to a considerable amount began to be imported into Sweden. The Riksbank's holdings of Scandinavian gold coin increased during 1916 by 17·8 million kronor, and during 1917 by 36·5 million kronor—that is, for both years together by 54·3 million kronor. This increase did not

begin until September, 1916. By the end of 1915 the
bank's stock of Scandinavian gold coin amounted to
55·4 million kronor, and thereafter remained practically
constant up to and including August, by the end of which
month it was 54·9 million kronor. What made the Danish
and Norwegian central banks send gold to Sweden was
the fact that their currencies sank in value in comparison to Swedish currency, falling definitely below par
from August, 1916, inclusive. The average rates of
exchange per month for Christiania and Copenhagen are
as follows:

		Christiania.	Copenhagen.
1916	July	100·00	100·00
	August	99·95	99·02
	September	99·15	97·47
	October	98·26	96·60
	November	97·98	95·88
	December	96·10	94·19
1917	January	95·15	93·28
	February	95·05	93·47
	March	98·52	96·45
	April	98·07	95·57
	May	98·04	95·83
	June	97·60	96·18
	July	94·93	93·96
	August	92·01	91·71
	September	91·32	91·06
	October	86·19	86·13
	November	86·95	86·43
	December	95·90	93·11

It appears from this table that shipping gold to Sweden
from Denmark and Norway did not pay until August–
September, 1916, and it is therefore quite natural that,
as may be gathered from the above-quoted figures, the
import of Scandinavian gold coin to Sveriges Riksbank
did not begin until September, 1916. By the end of
September the Riksbank's holdings of Scandinavian

gold coin had amounted to about 60·4 million kronor, and the rise continued right up to the end of 1917, when the total reached 109·7 million kronor.

Under pressure of this undesirable import of Scandinavian gold coin the Riksbank sent a letter to the Government on the 10th February, 1917, petitioning for the opening of negotiations with the Norwegian and Danish Governments with a view to preventing this import. The letter includes the following passage:

" According to the Scandinavian monetary convention of the 27th May, 1873, Article IX., Danish and Norwegian gold money coined in accordance with the rules of the convention is legal tender in Sweden. This opens a way for an unlimited invasion of gold into Sweden. The Riksbank, which at present is not a buyer of gold either in bars or in the form of foreign gold coins, has on several occasions latterly been offered to buy foreign gold coin. Although this has been obtainable at prices considerably below parity, these offers have been declined. There is, however, nothing to prevent this same gold which the Riksbank refused to buy being bought for Danish or Norwegian account and, after having been reminted into gold coin in Denmark or Norway, imported into Sweden. If this is done, the consequence will be that the Riksbank is compelled to take over at par in the form of Norwegian or Danish gold coin the very same gold which the bank had previously declined to buy at a price considerably below par. The cost of the minting is of no importance in this connection, as it represents only a fractional part of the disagio at which the Riksbank could have bought the gold prior to its being reminted. It is obvious that the disposition to pay Norwegian and Danish debts to Sweden in Scandinavian gold coin grows in the same degree as the depreciation in the Danish and Norwegian currencies as compared with the Swedish currency increases. At present the depreciation amounts to about 7 per cent. for Danish and 5 per cent. for Norwegian currency.

" According to an agreement privately come to between them the three central banks have undertaken not to recommend any licenses for export of gold from any one of their own countries to either of the other two Scandinavian countries without having first consulted the central bank of the country to which the gold is proposed to be sent. Although the Riksbank, in a pronouncement issued in consequence of this agreement, has definitely declared itself unwilling to receive gold, nevertheless gold in the form of Danish or Norwegian gold coins has been sent to the bank. By this means Denmark and Norway have managed to procure Swedish kronor at par, whereas, had this recourse not been open, they would have had to pay the agio on Swedish kronor prevailing at the time in Christiania or Copenhagen. In other words, the Riksbank has had to stand the loss in exchange which the parties concerned in Norway and Denmark would themselves have had to bear if there had been no clause in the monetary convention making Danish and Norwegian gold coin legal tender in Sweden.

" In order that the object of the above amendments of the law may not be defeated through Danish and Norwegian gold coin being sent to Sweden, it is the opinion of the Board that steps should be taken to come to an arrangement for revoking the clause in Article IX. of the monetary convention to the effect that gold coin minted in conformity with the convention shall be legal tender in the three kingdoms, irrespective of which kingdom has minted it. If this clause is revoked, it follows that the regulation in Article XIII., at present suspended, concerning the right to obtain gold coin for bullion delivered to the mint, will also have to be struck out of the convention.

" No doubt to arrive at such an agreement, which will require the co-operation of the Parliaments concerned, will, even under the most favourable circumstances, take some time. All trouble in this connection, however, would be avoided if the three Governments unanimously declared themselves willing strictly to maintain, as far as Scandinavian gold coin was concerned, the prohibition in force against the export of gold, as long as negotiations were going on for an agreement on the amendments in the monetary convention."

In consequence of the Riksbank's proposal, representatives of the three Scandinavian Governments met in conference in Stockholm on the 17th April, 1917. Besides the heads of the three central banks, one additional representative of each of the countries also attended the conference. The only result was an agreement to submit to the respective Governments that the existing prohibition against the export of gold should be stringently observed.

Some time elapsed before this agreement was carried out, and the importation of Scandinavian gold coin continued to influence the note circulation of the Riksbank " right up to the autumn of 1917 " (Report on Measures taken for Regulating the Value of Money, dated the 30th July, 1918, p. 12).

It is evident from the foregoing that in 1916 Sweden was for a period of seven months actually closed against the free importation of gold. After that comes a period, lasting about one year, when, in spite of legislation against gold, Sweden is exposed to an influx of Scandinavian gold coin. From the autumn of 1917, however, the gold-exclusion policy was effective, and Swedish money thus became a free paper standard, the value of which could not be drawn down by the continued fall in the value of gold.

A closer study of the development of the Swedish currency during these different phases may be of interest. In spite of the gold-exclusion policy, the Riksbank continued to buy gold on its own initiative, probably mostly at prices below the former gold parity. Below are quoted, in millions of kronor, the total quantity of gold held by the Riksbank at the end of the years stated:

1913	..	.. 102·1	1918 ..	.. 285·6
1914	..	.. 108·5	1919 ..	.. 281·2
1915	..	.. 124·6	1920 ..	.. 281·8
1916	..	.. 183·5	1921 ..	.. 274·7
1917	..	.. 244·5		

At the time when the gold-exclusion policy was adopted the gold reserves of the Riksbank amounted to 160·3 million kronor (5th February, 1916). From that time, up to the end of 1917, the gold reserves were increased by 84·2 million kronor. As the import of Scandinavian gold coin during the years 1916 and 1917 amounted to only 54·5 million kronor, it follows that, from the date when gold was first excluded to the end of 1917, the gold reserves increased by 30 million kronor (in round numbers) on account of gold supplies from other quarters. Since this could be so in spite of the considerable import of Scandinavian gold coin at the same time, it can hardly be contended that the import of Scandinavian gold caused an increase in the gold stock over and above that which would otherwise have taken place. Existing facts give the decided impression that the gold import from Denmark and Norway was not in itself so inconvenient for the Riksbank as the fact that through this import the bank was forced to accept gold at par which it could itself buy considerably below par. It has since always been contended by the Riksbank that it could not be held responsible for the inflation of the Swedish currency which went on until the autumn of 1917, as it was not until then that the bank really controlled its gold imports. It may clearly be gathered from the figures quoted above how much heed is to be paid to this defence as regards the period from the adoption of the gold-exclusion policy to the autumn of 1917.

Moreover, that a forced import of gold did not, as has sometimes been contended, decide the monetary policy of the Riksbank is obvious on account of the fact that, in the period from the adoption of the gold-exclusion policy to the end of 1916, during which time this policy was effective, the bank increased its holdings in foreign assets from 177·6 million kronor (5th February) to 236·4 million kronor (31st August), or by no less than 58·7 million kronor. From the point of view of maintaining the value of the Swedish currency, there could be no sense in closing itself against the import of gold, while at the same time saddling itself on a large scale with foreign assets. It is true that, as far as interior economy is concerned, it might seem more advantageous to the Riksbank to base its note issue on interest-bearing foreign assets, instead of on gold holdings unproductive of interest. But even this consideration of private advantage would prove to be a fatal mistake, as afterwards the Riksbank suffered enormous losses on its foreign assets owing to the fall of exchanges.

In order to illustrate how comparatively negligible has been the influence which the influx of gold forced upon the country has had on the inflation of the Swedish currency, it may be expedient to quote some figures showing the increase in the Swedish note circulation since the outbreak of the War. For the last quarter of 1916 my index number for the relative increase in the circulation was 136. The circulation had consequently already increased by 36 per cent. before any undesirable gold import whatever had been forced upon the Riksbank

through the international fall in the value of gold. The
influx of gold which provoked the gold-exclusion policy
brought up the index number for the circulation from
136 for the last quarter of 1915 to 144·3 for February,
1916. Although the Riksbank was now relieved from
the inconvenience of forced gold supplies, the circulation
index nevertheless rose to 157·8 for August, 1916. For
the third quarter of 1917 the average index number is 210,
but it would manifestly be wrong to ascribe this important
increase in the circulation to the forced import of
Scandinavian gold coin, considering that the bank at
the same time itself bought gold on a large scale (7·5
million kronor) from other quarters, and that the note
increase during the period in question was several times
larger than the amount of the Scandinavian gold imports.
In absolute figures the note circulation of the Riksbank
amounted to 345·5 million kronor on the last day of
August, 1916. On the corresponding day of 1917 the
circulation was 467·1 million kronor. The rise for that
year thus amounted to 121·6 million kronor. The
holdings in Scandinavian gold coin increased during the
same period from 54·9 million kronor to 86·2 million
kronor—*i.e.*, by 31·2 million kronor. This increase does
not come to much more than a quarter of the increase in
the note circulation during the same period, and anyone
who seeks to account for the unreasonable increase in the
note circulation during this time by the forced importation of gold from Denmark and Norway will thus find
himself in an obviously untenable position.

After the pressure of the Scandinavian gold imports
had, even in the opinion of the Riksbank, ceased to
influence the note circulation, a rise in the latter took
place on even a greater scale than before. From 210·0
for the third quarter, 1917, the index number rose to a
maximum of 350·0 for December, 1918. Thereafter it

dropped to a minimum of 307·1 for September, 1919, rising again, in August, 1920, to a fresh maximum of 330·1. It is obvious from these figures that other factors, culminating in an internal Swedish inflation, had been in operation since the outbreak of the War, and are in reality to be held responsible for the enormous increase in the note circulation. A forced gold import may possibly be considered a contributory factor for the period November, 1915, to the 8th February, 1916, but the figures do not suggest that there is any truth in the assumption that the note increase would have been discontinued for just this period if no forced gold import had taken place. Apart from this period, the increase in the Riksbank's gold reserve has not been forced upon it from outside, for practically the whole time the bank had to buy gold in order to maintain the prescribed amount of gold cover for its increasing circulation.

Further, a study of the rise in prices suggests that the forced import of gold has in no way exercised any very considerable influence. According to *Svensk Handelstidning* (*Swedish Trade Journal*), the index number for wholesale prices was 155 for the last quarter of 1915, from which we may infer that these prices must have risen by something like 50 per cent. before they were influenced by the import of gold. For the first quarter of 1916 the index number is 164, which is a by no means very remarkable increase. For the third quarter the index number is 191; it has thus undergone a considerable rise in spite of the gold-exclusion policy practised during this period. From this time onward until the third quarter of 1917, during which period, according to the Riksbank, a forced import of Scandinavian gold coin was a deciding factor in the inflation in Sweden, the index number rose to 249, a somewhat modest increase

as compared with the rise to 351, which occurred during
the following year up to the third quarter of 1918. A
similar result is arrived at by studying the rise in the
unweighed price index for food, as calculated by the
Social Board. It would never occur to an uninitiated
person examining the diagram on p. 59, which illustrates
the increase in prices and note circulation, that, from the
latter half of 1915 to the first quarter of 1916, any factor
having a particular tendency to cause a rise had made
its influence felt and then disappeared.

It cannot be denied that the Swedish policy of gold
exclusion proved a serious miscalculation. As events
afterwards proved, it would have been far better if Sweden
had continued to allow gold free access as under normal
conditions, and had thus allowed the purchasing power
of its currency to be regulated by that of gold. The
Riksbank would in that case have acquired a large stock
of gold, and it is possible that the bank's domestic loans,
as well as its other interest-bearing assets, might have
been reduced to a minimum, and even that the notes in
circulation would have been entirely covered by gold.
The loss of interest thus incurred would certainly have
proved to be very insignificant as compared with the
enormous amounts the Riksbank afterwards had to
write off on its foreign assets. After the end of the War
Sweden would then have had an effective gold currency,
and the former parity between the Swedish krona and
the dollar might at any rate approximately have been
maintained. Now, Sweden did actually for a short time
succeed in keeping her currency at a higher value than
what corresponded to the gold parity. Little was gained
by this, however, as in any case inflation of the Swedish
currency continued, and was pushed so far that its
purchasing power against commodities finally went far
below that of gold. After the end of the War it gradually

dawned on the country that the Swedish money was actually a depreciated paper currency.

When, therefore, people began to claim the redemption of notes with gold, the Riksbank was again compelled to ask for exemption from this liability. This request was granted on the 17th March, 1920, and from that time onward the Swedish currency showed itself openly as a depreciated paper currency. This ignominious outcome of a policy which had once set itself the task of keeping the value of the Swedish money above that of gold is solely to be ascribed to the continued internal depreciation. Had the impossibility of resisting the factors which forced on this inflation been fully realised, there would, of course, have been no sense in introducing a gold-exclusion policy. Swedish economists have sometimes been criticised abroad for having supported a measure so unsuccessful as the Swedish gold-exclusion policy proved to be. The fault, however, does not lie with them, but with the Riksbank, which from the beginning had no definite monetary policy in view when adopting the gold-exclusion measure, and in continuing that measure proved incapable of such an administration of the money as would have maintained Swedish currency at any rate approximately in parity with gold. In justice it must be recognised that the belligerent countries' steadily growing demands for credit from Sweden, together with the enormously increased public expenditure within the country, made it infinitely more difficult to oppose a continued inflation than could reasonably have been anticipated when the gold-exclusion policy was first adopted.

The Swedish gold-exclusion policy has no doubt had an important influence on the gold policy of the other neutral countries of Europe. Denmark and Norway followed the example of Sweden and closed themselves to

the free influx of gold. The central banks in these
countries, however, continued to buy gold on a large
scale, although, during the first years, they were probably
in a position to acquire this gold considerably below par.
Denmark and Norway never displayed any particular
interest in the policy that dictated the exclusion of gold;
the advantage to the central banks of being able to buy
gold below cost price, and their reluctance to have forced
upon them an unnecessarily large gold reserve bearing
no interest, probably proved deciding factors in the
policy they adopted. Denmark and Norway have succeeded even less than Sweden in maintaining the internal
purchasing power of their currencies. From 1916 inclusive, inflation became more violent in these countries
than in Sweden, and when a free gold market was established in the world, it became clear that the Danish and
Norwegian currencies were far more depreciated in relation to their gold parity than the Swedish currency.

In Holland, where the gold standard was officially
adhered to and gold was said to be accepted at par, the
central bank nevertheless apparently had it in its power
to decide how much gold it wanted to buy, and availed
itself of this power to refuse any gold imports deemed
to be undesirable. The result of this restrictive policy
was that the large increase in the gold stocks of the
Netherlands Bank, which had been going on ever since
the outbreak of the War, was interrupted in the middle
of 1916, to be resumed, however, on a somewhat reduced
scale in the middle of 1917.

During a period characterised by heavy falls in the
value of gold, a gold-exclusion policy would have been
quite reasonably justified on the part of the neutral
countries of Europe, if it had been founded on a conscious
desire to prevent their own currencies from being involved
in this depreciation. The only possible way of pre-

venting the purchasing power of a currency from sinking in the same proportion as that of gold was, of course, to preclude the possibility of all connection between that currency and gold. This need not in any way have implied a definite abandonment of the gold standard. It might, indeed, have been assumed that the fall in the value of gold would be only temporary, and it was to be expected that a rise in the value of gold would occur as soon as world conditions became more normal. Under this assumption, which, in fact, has since proved to be correct, it might have been a reasonable policy to try to prevent the currency from following the gold in its decline right down to a minimum. A country's interest in the stability of the purchasing power of its own currency demanded that efforts should be made to keep this purchasing power on the level to which the purchasing power of gold could be expected to return at some future time. This would have served to avoid a fluctuation in the value of the currency which would only have added to the difficulties of the problem.

A rational aim of this sort, however, has hardly anywhere been set up by the central banks in their gold-exclusion policy, and in no case have any of them been able to keep to such an aim. This was due simply to the fact that none of these neutral countries succeeded in stopping the process of inflation. The increasingly insistent demands for credit on the part of the belligerent countries, together with the abnormally high State expenditure and a banking policy which maintained far too low rates of interest, necessitated the creation of artificial purchasing power to an ever increased degree. This caused the neutrals' currencies to depreciate irrespective of the import of gold, and would have done so even if the country had been ever so completely closed to the free import of gold. In actual fact, the depreciation

7

of the currency went so far that its value dropped even below that of gold, in spite of the continual fall in the value of gold. This depreciation of the neutral currencies did not become fully manifest until after the end of the War, and after the world's gold market had recovered so much freedom that an approximately uniform value of gold could be said to exist. But that a very violent inflation went on in the neutral countries even after they had begun to close themselves to the entrance of gold from abroad is perfectly evident from the continual increase in the note circulation, as well as from the rise of the price level in these countries. In none of the neutral countries, therefore, has the fall in the value of gold, particularly after 1916, been any essential cause of the depreciation of the currency, which rather has been the result of a process of inflation going on independently in each country.

This will be most clearly seen if we consider the alterations in the exchange rates. Already at the outbreak of the War the gold standard began to be abandoned, and the neutral currencies were reduced to free paper standards in which gold and such currencies as the pound and the dollar were quoted above par. In Stockholm the mean quotation for the pound sterling (£1 at par= kr. 18·16) in August, 1914, was 18·36. It continued to rise steadily up to March, 1915, when it reached a maximum of 19·43, after which it declined, not going definitely below par until September. The dollar rate (1 dollar at par=kr. 3·73) showed for August, 1914, an average of 3·78, and later reached a maximum of 4·05 for March, 1915. Then came a fall, which eventually brought the dollar below par in November, 1915. In Christiania and Copenhagen the conditions were similar. By the end of 1915 the Swiss currency dropped far below its parity with that of Sweden, and the gold agio was consequently still higher there. Of all the neutral currencies that of the Netherlands was best kept up on a parity with gold; but in Stockholm it was also quoted above par (kr. 150 for 100 guilders) up to February, 1916, inclusive. For certain months the mean quotation even exceeded 160, and for January, 1916, was still as high as 159·99. From the outbreak of the War up to about the end of 1915, therefore, there can be no question of the fall in the value of gold having forced down the internal values of the neutral currencies, except in the case of the Dutch currency. The very considerable rise in prices that took place during this period, in the other neutral countries here mentioned, was due to a separate inflation going on in each particular country. The scarcity in commodities is, as we have seen, to a certain extent a contributory factor, but, comparatively speaking, it was not very pronounced at the period in question.

From the autumn of 1915, when, on account of the conditions of the exchange market, it began to pay to send gold to the neutral countries, the gold import actually had a tendency to force up the price level in those countries. But they very soon found means to avoid the forced import of gold, firstly, by a more or less strictly carried out policy of gold exclusion, and then through an inflation which brought the respective currencies far below their parity with gold, and later on caused the dollar exchange, which during the War and the period that immediately followed had not been a fair indication of the true value of the dollar, to rise considerably above its parity with the neutral currencies of Europe.

A reduction in the value of gold must evidently cause a corresponding reduction in the value of an effective gold standard. If the depreciation of gold is expressed in a general rise in the prices of commodities on the world's market, it is useless for a country with an effective gold standard to try to restrict the rise in prices within its own frontiers. During the War this simple truth was eagerly exploited by the central banks when on their defence against the accusation that they had themselves forced up the price level within the country by inflating the currency. Oddly enough, the central banks sometimes received support in this from economists of narrow views who were unable to rise to a wider survey of current events. With the experience we have now gained, the connection between the depreciation of gold on the one hand and that of the various currencies on the other is quite patent, and there can no longer be any doubt as to how far the direct process of inflation is to be held responsible for the internal depreciation of the currencies. In the main, this depreciation, even in the case of the neutral currencies, must be considered the result of an inflation developing independently in each country. The immediate responsibility for this inflation lies always with the respective central banks. But certainly there have been conditions, even in the neutral countries, which have encroached upon the central banks' independence, and which may in a certain degree be said to have forced on inflation. This pressure, however, has been very relative and would certainly have to some extent been evaded if the central banks had used their influence wisely. As they have not done so, but on the contrary have keenly supported the official announcements which endeavoured to prevent the public from gaining a true idea of what was going on, they cannot truthfully be freed from all responsibility for inflation.

THE DISCOUNT POLICY AND ITS EFFICIENCY AS A REGULATOR OF THE MONETARY STANDARD

THE question of the central banks' responsibility for inflation brings us to the question of the influence exerted by the central banks on the value of the currency, and to the question as to how far they have it in their power to maintain stability in the general price level. The principal instrument in the hands of the central banks to maintain a fixed value of the currency is their rate of discount. It has been recognised for a century past that a proper discount policy, possibly supplemented by certain other measures for limiting credits, is not only an effective means of regulating the value of the monetary unit, but actually *the* means by which this regulation is in practice carried out. Now the central banks, having during the War completely lost control of the monetary system, proved themselves only too anxious to exonerate themselves from all responsibility, and with that object in view gave out that, while the old theory was of course sound enough in normal times, the bank rate no longer had any influence either on the increase in the note circulation or on the rise in prices. Even now, after the War, when there is a tendency to revert to a settled monetary system, the demand for a rational discount policy is perpetually being met with such objections as that it is impossible to regulate the value of a monetary unit by " artificial means."

Under such circumstances it is manifestly of fundamental importance first of all to make clear *exactly what is meant by discount policy, and its "modus operandi" under normal conditions.*

In a progressive community the steadily growing demands for capital must be met by a continued saving. Fresh savings are placed daily at the disposal of those having fresh capital requirements. In this the banks only act as intermediaries. They can increase their loans only in proportion to the amount of fresh savings that are available. Lending on the part of the banks, however, is done in bank currency, to the creation of which there are no absolutely definite limits. The criterion for a really sound bank policy, then, is that the quantity of bank currency does not increase, except, of course, in so far as the general economic expansion in the country makes increased demands for means of payment. But, as is well known, these demands vary with the seasons and with industrial conditions. At certain times of the year and under prosperous conditions the turnover on goods, and the volume of payments on the whole, show a particular rise, even if the price level is supposed to remain unaltered. The supply of currency should be adjusted to this varying demand. The banks, however, must constantly see to it that the quantity of bank currency is never unduly increased—*i.e.*, that bank currency is not arbitrarily created merely to meet capital requirements which cannot be met with available savings. As a guide for this kind of bank policy it would, of course, be very useful, even under normal circumstances, to have an index of circulation which, independent of seasonal fluctuations, indicates the relative variation of the circulation. In employing such an index due account would, of course, have to be taken of alterations in the methods of payment, which, at any rate where long periods are concerned, may require a different supply of currency.

A complete daily adjustment between demands for capital and fresh savings is scarcely possible. It is therefore of advantage if the issue of bank currency is given a certain elasticity, so that demands for capital may be met without unnecessary disturbance. This elasticity, however, must not be taken advantage of to meet, during prolonged periods, demands for capital on a higher scale than the amount of savings effected within the same period permits.

If the banks allow more credit than they are on these grounds economically justified in giving, then the active purchasing power in the country is raised without a corresponding increase of purchasable commodities. The inevitable result, therefore, is a rise in prices. This conclusion brings us to a new rule for a true bank policy. The supply of credit must be so regulated that no rise in prices, and, naturally, no fall in prices either, takes place. In order to keep demands for credit within the limits of available means, the banks must apply interest rates fixed with that object in view, but in their continual scrutinising of the demands for credit must also be able to effect the necessary restrictions. The main factor determining interest rates throughout the entire banking system in a country is the central bank's discount rate, and in addition the central bank naturally possesses a very great influence owing to the general advice it is able to give to the private banks as to their credit policy.

Demands for credit vary in their intensity. A bank policy bent on maintaining a fixed value for the monetary unit, therefore, must be continually adjusting its discount rate so that it may thereby actually succeed in limiting the demand for capital in proportion to the supply of available savings. The interest rates of the banks have in this respect exactly the same function as any other price. The social-economic function of prices is just this: to procure on all points an adequate restriction of the demand; and the correctness of the system of prices must, therefore, be judged from the point of view of how far this object is attained. So is it also particularly with regard to the discount rate. It is sometimes said that the banks must adapt their rates to the actual interest on capital. If we take this to be some sort of average rate of profit, then the statement is theoretically false. If, on the other hand, it is meant that the bank interest is to correspond to the proceeds of the last capital investments which show a profit, then the rule is practically inapplicable. Whatever rate of interest the banks maintain, the last capital investments which may be counted upon will be found to bear interest on a level with the bank rate, and in that fact the banks can have no guide whatever for their interest policy. The only rational and at the same time practically useful rule to go by, therefore, is that *demands for capital must, by means of the rates of interest of the banks, be limited to the amounts of funds supplied by current saving, so that no artificial purchasing power, with its accompanying rise in prices, will be created.*

Under normal circumstances the value of the monetary unit in a country possessing a gold standard is kept in a certain parity with gold by aid of the discount rate of the central bank, or, more generally, by its limitation of credit. That gold is made the measure of a fixed value of money is indeed the characteristic of a gold standard. Thus a gold standard is nothing more than a paper standard which, by aid of a proper bank policy, is kept at a certain fixed ratio to gold. Through a proper limitation of credits the currency's parity with gold can be broadly maintained. The exact parity can then be assured by strictly upholding the redeemability of the currency in gold coin. For this purpose the banks, and particularly the central banks, must keep a certain amount of gold in reserve. But no gold reserve in the world can guarantee the redeemability of a currency if a general parity with gold is not maintained through a proper discount policy.*

The value of a gold standard, therefore, is determined by the scarcity of the country's supply of means of payment. In this respect a gold standard in no way differs from other forms of money. A stock of bullion in the vaults of the central bank possesses no mysterious power to infuse a value into the currency. On the whole, value is no inherent quality in the stuff, but is an economic phenomenon determined by the scarcity of supply in proportion to demand. The value of money is no exception from this rule. It is therefore an absolutely false idea to regard the percentage of gold cover in the banks in any way as a factor essentially determining the value of the currency. Nor, indeed, is the value of a currency, as it is often declared to be, determined by the State's credit, financial standing, economic resources, etc., but only by the scarcity of the supply of means of payment. Unsound State finances may, of course, indirectly influence the value of the currency since, as we know by experience, it tends to the creation of an excess of bank currency to support the State. If it were possible to prevent this, the State might become bankrupt, while the currency of the country nevertheless possessed its standard value.

The liability to redeem notes compels the central bank to adopt a right discount policy, and thus has its importance for the maintenance of the value of the monetary unit. But it is not a means to that end. A fixed value

* This argument is reasoned out more closely in the theory of money contained in my "Theoretische Sozialökonomie," Leipzig, 1921. (English edition in preparation.)

can only be kept up by properly limiting the granting
of credit and principally, therefore, by a suitable discount
rate. As a discount policy is actually capable of regulating the value of the monetary unit in the case of a gold
standard, so as to maintain its level with gold, it is an
inevitable conclusion that a right discount policy must
also be capable of regulating the value of a free paper
standard. It must, of course, be assumed in both cases
that the State, by its demands for credit, does not force
a creation of bank currency nor itself create fresh paper
money to cover its own expenditure. If, however, this
condition is fulfilled, the central bank undoubtedly has
a determining influence over the intrinsic purchasing
power of a paper currency. If anyone disputes this, he
must undertake the impossible by answering the question :
What else determines the value of paper currency ? If
there were no determining factor, then a paper currency
could never possess even a comparatively stable value.
It seems to be quite commonly held that even in the
case of a paper currency the notes represent a promise
to pay in gold, and that this promise is the true basis
on which the value of the currency is founded. It might
be excusable if such a view were entertained at periods
when a paper currency, depreciated by only a slight
percentage, gave grounds for that view. But one who,
in face of the complete disorganisation of currencies
caused by the War, still adheres to the idea that mark
notes, for example, represent a promise to pay in gold,
thereby displays such poor ability to familiarise himself
with the realities of economic life that his judgment on
the question of the present difficulties of monetary
policy can scarcely claim to possess much value. We
must get accustomed to regard a paper currency as
a purely abstract numerical unit, whose value is exclusively determined by the scarcity of the means

of payment which in that currency have actual paying power.

The truth that the value of a monetary unit in the case of a paper standard is determined by the central bank's control of credit is of fundamental importance in forming a right judgment not only on what has taken place in the monetary sphere since the outbreak of the War, but also as to what must now be done to re-establish a sound monetary system. A general and unreserved acknowledgment of the responsibility of the central banks is the first condition of our ever attaining to a monetary policy characterised by strength of purpose.

Parallel with that discount policy which we have touched upon here the central banks also carry out under normal conditions what is generally called a foreign discount policy. Its main function is to protect the gold reserves from any excessive claims from abroad, and in pursuing this purpose the central banks are guided by the rates of exchange on other countries with a gold standard. When foreign demands for gold have temporarily increased, the desire to safeguard its gold reserves may induce the central bank to raise the discount rate, and it may thereby go beyond what would have been necessary if the maintenance of stable money at home only had had to be taken into account. The foreign discount policy may occasionally, therefore, disturb the domestic discount policy. But on the whole the foreign discount policy of a country has the effect of maintaining its currency on a general parity with all other gold standards, and thereby also with the metal gold. This is the degree of steadiness in value—somewhat relative indeed—which one can at all pretend to maintain in a gold standard. Under such circumstances it is natural enough that the central banks should have directed their attention chiefly to the foreign discount policy which, in fact, claims their daily interest. The management get accustomed to look upon their function from its purely technical side, and as experience shows, provided conditions remain normal, succeed in carrying on that function quite well without ever going deeply into the real significance of discount policy. But when confronted with such disorganisation as was brought about by the War, such a management is necessarily somewhat at a loss. The actual conditions of foreign discount policy have, of course, been profoundly affected by the War, even if there is considerable exaggeration in the common assertion that the discount rates no longer have any bearing whatever upon the regulation of international payments. When the managements of the central banks now talk of the discount rate having lost its usual effectiveness, it is probable that they are chiefly thinking of this upsetting of the conditions underlying their foreign discount policy. This is the psychological explanation of the misjudging of the situation so frequent on the part of the central banks after the outbreak of the War. If we look deeper we must acknowledge that what was really affected was simply the exterior technical machinery of the discount policy, while the essential part of its function, that of maintaining the currency at a stable level of purchasing power at home, still remained, the means to that end being in the main the same as before.

The doctrine of the ineffectiveness of the discount rate, so readily accepted in certain quarters, is, as a matter of fact, by no means so generally recognised as its advocates would have us believe. In England, which is the Mother Country of rational discount policy, people have a far clearer view of these things, and there too the effectiveness of the discount rate has been very strongly supported by men in a leading position. For all efforts at restoring sound monetary conditions in the world, such recognition of the effectiveness of the discount policy is, as I have said, a primary condition.

It is true that an alteration in the conditions of the discount policy has taken place, in so far as, since the outbreak of war, we have to regard as normal quite other discount rates than those to which we were formerly accustomed. But even on that point it has taken the mentality of the authorities a long time to adapt itself to the new real conditions with which nowadays we have to reckon. The War has, of course, caused an extraordinary scarcity of capital, and it was quite irrational to suppose that interest rates could be allowed to remain on a level which but slightly exceeded what would generally be considered as normal in times of ordinary prosperity. The rates of interest which the various central banks of the world have applied since 1914 have presented an absolutely false picture of the true situation of the capital market. Apparently people have for the most part assumed that, by some mysterious law of nature, 5 per cent. should represent the standard beyond which interest rates ought not to be allowed to rise— even during a World War! On the 1st August, 1914, the German Reichsbank went up to 6 per cent., and continued at that rate till the 23rd December of the same year, when a 5 per cent. rate was introduced, being afterwards retained throughout the entire war, and remaining so to this day. It is true that the Bank of England went up to 10 per cent. on the 1st August, 1914, but it lowered the rate to 6 per cent. on the 6th August, and to 5 per cent. on the 8th August, 1914. At this level the discount rate remained right up till the 13th June, 1916, on which date it was raised to 6 per cent. As early as the 18th January, 1917, however, the bank returned to 5½ per cent., and on the 5th April of the same year to 5 per cent., which obviously far too low rate was retained for over two and a half years, embracing the most critical period of the War as well as the dangerous speculation period which marked the early days of peace. From the 6th November, 1919, an interest rate of 6 per cent. was again applied, after which the bank went up to 7 per cent. on the 15th April, 1920. This high rate was maintained right up to the 28th April, 1921, when the bank rate was reduced to $6\frac{1}{2}$ per cent., and after that it was lowered to 6 per cent. on the 23rd June, and to $5\frac{1}{2}$ per cent. on the 21st July, 1921. The Bank of France went up to 6 per cent. on the 2nd August, 1914, but lowered this rate as early as the 21st August to 5 per cent., at which figure the bank rate remained during the whole war right up to the 8th April, 1920, when the discount was raised to 6 per cent. On the 28th July, 1921, the bank again went down to $5\frac{1}{2}$ per cent.

Even the neutral states during the War adopted a much too low discount rate. The Bank of the Netherlands after the outbreak of war went up to 6 per cent., but shortly returned to 5 per cent., and from the 1st July, 1915, it has applied without interruption a discount rate of $4\frac{1}{2}$ per cent. After the outbreak of the War the Swedish Riksbank applied the following interest rates: From the 3rd August, 1914, $6\frac{1}{2}$ per cent.; from the 28th August 6 per cent.; from the 7th January, 1915, $5\frac{1}{2}$ per cent.; from the 1st May, 1916, 5 per cent.; from the 10th November, 1916, $5\frac{1}{2}$ per cent.; from the 28th September, 1917, 6 per cent.; from the 12th December 7 per cent.; from the 1st February, 1918, $6\frac{1}{2}$ per cent.; from the 2nd March 7 per cent.; from the 25th April, 1919, $6\frac{1}{2}$ per cent.; from the 13th June 6 per cent.; from the 19th March, 1920, 7 per cent.; from the 17th September, 1920, $7\frac{1}{2}$ per cent.; from the 27th April, 1921, 7 per cent.; from the 6th May $6\frac{1}{2}$ per cent.; from the 6th July 6 per cent.; and from the 19th October $5\frac{1}{2}$ per cent.

Apart from the first days of the War, then, we see that the discount rates during the War were on the whole maintained at a particularly low level, having regard to the circumstances, and, as pointed out above, they scarcely exceeded what would be a normal rate during any time of prosperity. It is not until towards the end of the War, and especially after the armistice—when we find people beginning to realise that inflation is a continuous process and one which even threatens to increase ever more and more—that any serious attempt at combating inflation by means of higher interest rates can be observed, and even then only in certain countries.

The cause of the central banks' weak discount policy naturally lies first and foremost in the extremely vague notions as to the true import of the monetary phenomena entertained by bank managements. In fact, as we shall see in a moment, the managements have shown themselves very eager to demonstrate by actual documents the vagueness of their ideas. But the managements also considered themselves obliged, and were indeed sometimes actually compelled, to keep the discount rate low in order to prepare the way for State loans. In particular, it would seem that the desire to facilitate the public's subscribing to State loans has induced the banks to keep interest rates down. The influence which such points of view have exercised over bank policy has manifestly been a very serious factor in the general process of inflation.

The rise in interest rates, as compared with those usual before the War, appears to have been considerable in England and France, while that in other countries, and especially in Sweden, has for the most part been smaller.

Further, when speaking of the discount rates in different countries, one must always remember that they are not directly comparable with one another. The discount rate of the central bank has actually a different position in different countries on the scale of the various interest rates. A lower discount rate need not at all necessarily imply that the interest rates are to the same extent lower than in other countries applying a higher discount rate. A proper estimate of the general standard of interest rates and of the severity of the credit restrictions which it brings about presupposes a thorough study of all the interest rates applied in each country, and of their height in relation to the interest rates customary in peace-time. In each particular country inflation depends to some extent on the relation in which the interest rates have stood to the corresponding interest rates before the War. A comparison of the discount rates of two countries gives no very sure indication as to the extent of inflation in those two countries. As it is sometimes pointed out that a low discount rate in this or that country has not been accompanied by a particularly violent inflation, and as the inference is drawn from that that inflation does not depend on discount policy, it must be borne in mind that such an objection can have no meaning, unless due consideration is taken of all interest rates, as well as of the varying degree of the scarcity of capital in the different countries during the War.

During the period of inflation it is probable also that the relation between the discount rate and other interest rates has to a very large extent been disturbed. The discount rate, and, in general, interest rates for short loans, may have remained on a comparatively low level, while the interest rates for long term loans have risen considerably higher. Thus the margin between the rates for long and short term loans has become wider. This variation has corresponded to an actual variation in the capital market. The continual increase in inflation, which immediately expresses itself in a creation of fresh currency, has permanently kept the money market well supplied, so that low rates for short loans have become natural. Holland, and to a certain extent Switzerland also, would seem to offer interesting fields of study in this connection.

During the War a special theory was developed to explain the easiness of the money market, and in this theory central banks have often shown themselves particularly interested, for they found in it a support for their efforts to represent the comparatively low official discount rate as simply and solely an indication of the objective conditions of the capital market. This theory holds that productive enterprises sold out their stocks during the War and received money therefor, which they found it most convenient to keep at the banks or else to lend out at short term. The surplus of "floating capital" thus created has forced down the rates for short term loans and made it impossible for the central banks to maintain a higher discount rate.

In the form in which this theory has been generally expounded, it is far too vague and far too full of gross economic inaccuracies to be accepted as it stands. In order to illustrate the real meaning of the phenomenon in question it will be convenient to consider a country which is isolated from other countries. In such a country a sale of stock cannot take place unless a buyer is forthcoming within that country. The currency which the sellers get into their possession the buyers must part with. If the buyers have drawn this currency out of the general circulation, it is natural for this currency to be again restored to the market by the sellers. In that case the supply of means of payment in the market remains unaffected. A surplus of purchasing power can only arise if fresh currency is created to enable buyers to pay for the stocks that are for sale. Now, that is exactly

8

what happened during the War. In Germany, for instance, fresh currency was continually created and placed at the disposal of the Government, and they used it for purchasing raw material and unfinished goods, live stock, and other supplies needed for the War. The sellers thus obtained possession of a surplus of currency, and when this currency was placed on the market the supply of funds available for short term loans became plentiful. As a consequence the interest rates on short term loans were forced down, and this could be regarded as a reason for the Reichsbank keeping its discount rate low. This view of the matter has, in fact, been energetically supported by the Reichsbank, which, during the first period of the War, continually reverted to an emphatic assertion as to how satisfactory was the position of the German money market. " By a reduction in stocks, by the necessary limitation of production, and by a restriction of foreign trade," to quote the bank's *Zweite Denkschrift* for the period November, 1914, to April, 1915, " a considerable amount of capital was set free, so that a plentiful supply of floating capital was available on the money market. The favourable situation on the market accordingly rendered it possible to satisfy without difficulty private capital requirements, and likewise brought about the brilliant success of the first War Loan, and the still more brilliant success of the second. Further, it permitted the Board of the Reichsbank to take the unusual step, shortly before the end of the year—on the 23rd December, 1914—to lower the bank rate—namely, from 6 to 5 per cent., a rate which not only had been frequently applied during the peace years immediately preceding the War, but had even very often been exceeded —the last time being from the 14th November, 1912, to the 12th December, 1913." This way of presenting the matter has manifestly contributed very largely towards misleading public opinion. The extremely plentiful supply of money was, in fact, brought about neither by a reduction of stocks nor by any other changes in domestic economy, but simply by the creation of fresh currency from the side of the Reichsbank and the Government. It was, therefore, the financial administration's own monetary policy which brought about this superabundant supply of means of payment, forced down the interest rates, and, according to the Reichsbank's own statement, rendered possible its particularly low bank rate. If this rate were represented as a result of a particularly favourable development, this may possibly be accounted for by the necessity for keeping up confidence in war-time; but such a representation of the case is nevertheless incorrect, and this fact must be generally realised if any clear understanding of cognate questions is to be arrived at. It is also, as a matter of fact, very misleading to speak of considerable capital being set free through the sale of stocks. The floating capital of a country, from a realistic point of view, simply consists of stores of raw material and half-manufactured goods, of live stock, and of similar supplies of real commodities as come within the process of production. To describe a reduction of these supplies as an increase in the available floating capital seems to be a rather dangerous confusion of ideas.* The principal function of currency is just this, to serve as an instrument for deals in the goods which make up the floating capital. A reduction in this floating capital should properly bring about a corresponding reduction in the quantity of currency. The notion that the real capital which is consumed in the household of an isolated nation is exchanged there for a corresponding amount of

* If the quantity of the means of payment has been increased in connection with such a reduction, we can only regard this increase as all the more serious.

currency, which, so to speak, takes the place of the consumed capital, is absolutely false.

Such false ideas have naturally not been confined to Germany, but have been vigorously propagated also in the other belligerent countries as well as in neutral states. It is only the circumstance that Germany, relatively speaking, completely fulfilled the conditions of an isolated country which makes the case of Germany particularly applicable for clearing up the point at issue. For a country which has intercourse with abroad the case is more complicated. Holland, for instance, during the War sold out on quite a large scale supplies to abroad, and received gold in payment. In this case there actually took place an interchange of exported supplies and imported gold. The sellers of the supplies came into possession of gold or of bank balances, which represented gold. The market became plentifully provided with means seeking investments at short term, and the interest rates were forced down. In this case, too, however, the cause was an abnormal supply of currency. The difference is that this currency now consisted of gold which flowed in from abroad, and which could not be prevented from flowing into the country as long as the latter adhered to an effective gold standard and did not increase its paper currency so as to enable it to compete successfully with the influx of gold.

The very hypothesis on which the argument here discussed is based—namely, that stocks have been sold out—shows itself, on examination of actual facts, to have been considerably exaggerated. A complete selling out of stocks should imply that the entire industrial process of the nation was stopped, and all further production ceased. This has certainly not been the case anywhere. In the belligerent countries, it is true, some branches of production had to be very considerably cut down, but in compensation therefor other branches of production underwent a quite abnormal expansion. A private concern may have sold out its stocks in order to take up some kind of war industry, but its capital has then been at once utilised for procuring new stocks, and no reduction in the total amount of stocks belonging to the community has thereby taken place. If we have regard to the enormous development of war industries, we shall certainly find the common estimate of the reduction in stocks to be highly exaggerated, if industries as a whole are taken account of. Far more considerable would seem to have been the reduction in floating capital in agriculture, particularly in the case of certain countries.

As explained above, raising the discount rate has for its purpose a stricter limiting of the demand for capital, so that the demand may be levelled down to the supply of fresh savings. However, this limitation of demand will generally not prove effective until rates for long term loans have also been raised. The question arises, therefore, What influence has the bank rate on the other rates ? Clearly the bank rate can only exercise an influence over the rates for long term loans if the bank rate is maintained for some length of time at a certain level. Investors then have a choice between placing their capital in repeated short term loans or in one longer term loan, and the rates for these different kinds of loans must consequently become adjusted to one another. The connection between the rates for long and short term loans is strengthened by the use of long term bonds as security for short term loans. Raising the rates for these short loans lowers the market value of the bonds, and this reduction will approximately correspond to the increase of the short loan rate, if this higher rate is expected to last for any length of time.

From this it follows that an effective limitation of

excessive demands for capital can generally only take
place by applying a higher discount rate for a longer
period. A central bank which really aims at a definite
restriction of unusually heavy demands for capital must
therefore consistently maintain a higher discount rate,
and preferably should announce beforehand that it
intends to do so. Had the central banks at the very
outset of the War raised the discount rate sufficiently
high, and had they announced that they proposed to
adhere to such a high rate as long as the War lasted,
they would certainly have found that all other rates of
interest had fairly soon come up to a corresponding level,
thereby effectively limiting the demand for capital. But
nowhere have the central banks displayed any such clear
idea of what the situation required. Their discount
policy has been vague and vacillating, and has therefore
failed to effect that increase in rates for long term loans
which circumstances necessitated. In Sweden the effective interest for public and industrial bonds during the
first years of the War was below the discount rate.
During the prosperous years 1915–1916 rates for long
term loans stood at a level between 5 and 5½ per cent.
It was not until towards the end of 1917 that the rates
for long term loans began to rise, and this was clearly
influenced by the increase of the bank rate—which took
place much too late—at the end of 1917. When in 1919
the Riksbank went down to 6 per cent., the rates for
long term loans were brought down slightly below that
figure. After the raising of the discount rate to 7 and
7½ per cent., the rates for long term loans were brought
up to about a corresponding level. If we consider this
development it is incontrovertible that the Riksbank
could have exercised an effective influence over the rates
for long term loans, if it had right from the beginning
consistently applied a higher discount rate and announced

that it proposed to abide by that rate as long as the War lasted. During the years 1915–1916 a bank rate of 7 per cent. would have been fully justified, and, had it been consistently maintained, would undoubtedly have brought up the rates for long term loans to a corresponding height. Thus the regulation of the capital market would have become quite otherwise effective.

The result of keeping bank rates too low has turned out exactly as might be expected. In the belligerent countries, however, it is not possible to attribute these effects directly to the too low bank rate. As has been pointed out above, the belligerent Governments' demand for funds has brought about a creation of artificial purchasing power which has certainly been fairly independent of the bank rate. As a regulator for private industry the discount rate in the belligerent countries proved to have an ever more and more limited significance, as industry to an ever increasing degree came under State control, and as thus the use of capital became almost entirely regulated by Government requirements. However, the low discount rate has doubtless played an important part in misleading public opinion on the real situation in the capital market, and has given support to a financial administration anxious to assure the public that there was a plentiful supply of money, and that there could not possibly be any question of a depreciation going on. It is not in the least to be wondered at that a public whose economic reasoning was brought up on such a doctrine were quite at a loss when they at last discovered how enormously the value of their money had depreciated, and found themselves, in view of this catastrophe, faced with the task of re-establishing a sound monetary system.

The official doctrine that the discount rate was ineffective under the abnormal conditions of the War, and that the central banks could not control the development

of the value of the currency, now proved disastrous.
With the low rates to which they had grown accustomed
the banks were reduced to complete ineffectiveness in
face of the period of speculation which broke out after
the conclusion of peace, and in face of the unreasonable
demands raised at this time for funds for public purposes.
The consequence was an additional inflation and a rise
in prices far exceeding that caused by the War. But this
also caused the final overthrow of the official doctrine
that the rise in prices was merely a consequence of the
War and its claims and of the scarcity of commodities
which it created, and the public began to realise that an
actual depreciation in the value of money had taken
place and was still going on.   Even now it was to be a long
time before wider circles of the public realised the decisive
significance of the discount policy for the maintenance
of money at a stable value.

In the neutral countries the false discount policy
naturally had a more direct influence on the development
of industry. When capital can be obtained at too low
interest rates, the productive forces of a nation will
be directed on too extensive a scale to the production
of fresh real capital, and the satisfying of immediate
requirements of consumption will receive a set-back.
Money is expended on new buildings, new factories, and
new machinery, and both labour and raw material are
drawn upon for such purposes out of all normal proportion.
The machinery by which this conversion of national
economy is worked is the whole system of prices. In
consequence of too low interest rates credits granted will
exceed available savings, and will thus partly be based
on artificially created currency. The increased nominal
purchasing power forces prices up, and this rise in prices
produces an extensive limitation of consumption on the
part of the broad strata of the population which do not

manage to get their incomes increased in like proportion. A certain amount of productive forces are thereby set free, and it is these which become available for the increased production of real capital. Such a process may be observed at any time of prosperity, but during the War it assumed quite abnormal proportions.

This false application of the forces of industry which a weak discount policy directly brought about has been highly intensified by the influence which the adhesion to low interest rates exercised over foreign purchasing power in the neutral countries. The belligerents' demand for credit has naturally been stimulated by credit being kept unnaturally cheap. It may, of course, be said that the belligerents would never have been discouraged in their demand for credit merely by higher interest rates. But it is obvious that a neutral country which applied particularly high rates would have become less attractive as a market for borrowers, and could thus have more easily avoided having to meet extensive demands for credit. Moreover, too low rates in the neutral country naturally make people more disposed to grant the belligerents credit, or to allow accrued balances to remain abroad. This has naturally had a particularly important bearing on export industries and shipping. A high discount rate during the first years of the War would certainly have induced the neutral exporters and ship-owners very considerably to limit their granting of credit to the belligerents. A third point which has undoubtedly been affected by the too low rates has been the importation of bonds. By repurchase of their own bonds and by importing other securities as mentioned above the neutrals during the War placed enormous sums at the disposal of the belligerents. This movement could certainly have been considerably restricted if interest in the neutral countries had been kept at a higher percentage than was actually the case. Thus there can be no doubt but that the low rates in the neutral countries largely contributed towards increasing the quantity of the purchasing power in the neutral currencies placed at the disposal of the belligerents. As, against this growing purchasing power, there was no corresponding increase in real capital, this purchasing power, to the extent to which it was used on the neutral market, must bring about a rise in prices. In this way, too, then, the weak discount policy has helped to force up the level of prices in neutral countries. At the same time, also, the productive forces in these countries have to an unproportionate degree been directed towards producing whatever the belligerents desired to purchase, as well as towards increasing the real capital required for such production. The satisfying of the requirements of the country's own population was thus restricted in a corresponding degree. The neutral nations' contributions to the war costs of the belligerents were thus procured by a general forcing down of those nations' standard of living.

All this time the central banks in the neutral countries gave earnest assurances that no depreciation in money was taking place, that the rise in the general price level was due to all other possible causes, and that in any case the central banks were not responsible, since they possessed no means of exercising any influence over the course of events.

Dr. Vissering, the head of the *Netherlands Bank*, in his above-mentioned article in the *Economic Journal* (June, 1917), attempted to prove that no inflation existed in Holland. In support of this assertion he declared (on p. 164) that there had not existed so much money as to cause the money rate in the market to drop, when all the same he had shown some pages previously how the

private discount rate had at times been forced down to
1 per cent., and for a short interval even dropped to
½ per cent., and how the Government had managed to
place three to six months' treasury bills at rates varying
from 1·7 to 3·9 per cent. He has proved that the Stock
Exchange accepted monthly loans against an interest
rate of 2 to 4 per cent., and that long term loans were in
several cases reduced to an effective interest of 4½ per
cent. and even considerably lower. If there is one clear
sign of inflation, it must be that such interest rates could
have been in force at a time which saw such enormous
demands for capital as we are discussing here. This inflation, as we have seen in the foregoing, was undoubtedly
to a large extent forced upon the Netherlands Bank by
the influx of gold from abroad; but this cannot justify
a denial of the existence of inflation. The abnormal
increase in the Netherlands Bank's gold stock, bank-note
circulation, and balances of accounts current would
naturally, according to Vissering, have been a sign of an
inflation of money, yet, says he, in spite of these facts,
the direct consequences of inflation, which in the first
instance would be a general rise in prices and a fall in the
Exchanges, were not present. Vissering denies that a
general rise in prices occurred in Holland. In the light
of the index figures which the statistical central bureau
of Holland has just published, this assertion appears
somewhat doubtful. As stated above, the average index
for wholesale trade prices, if the index for 1913 is reckoned
at 100, was 149 for 1915 and 234 for 1916—the year
whose conditions Vissering's remarks most nearly concern. Vissering, on the whole, seems to want to deny the
existence of inflation in the case of other countries as
well. He says: "In all countries the circulating medium
increased to an extraordinary degree—the same phenomenon, that is to say, as we have observed in the Nether-

lands. . . . Has the increase of fiduciary money sent up prices to such an extent ? I do not think so." After this there follows an attempt to explain the rise in prices along the usual lines: increased demand and reduced supply of goods for sale—an explanation which may well seem curious when one adopts the standpoint that no general rise in prices has occurred. In support of this attitude Vissering further maintains that prices of certain materials—of bricks, for instance—did not rise very much. "Side by side with this a great increase took place in the circulation media, because the circulation media were so much more required for cash payments than had previously been the case. This fact is, however, entirely independent of other factors, and has, in my opinion, had but little influence on the increase of the prices. A general inflation of money would have raised all prices." Further on he says: " But if then the prices of goods have risen owing to other causes, and the increase of fiduciary media in itself does not imply inflation, why should one conclude that the value of gold has depreciated merely on the ground that a greater sum of gold is at present required to purchase quantities of certain kinds of goods, whereas, on the contrary, other useful goods have not so risen or have even dropped in value because the demand has temporarily diminished ?" This quotation will probably be sufficient to show the general character of the views of the situation held by the head of the Netherlands Bank, such as they were at the beginning of 1917. Upon a closer study of the document quoted, one comes across much that is seriously obscure on points of a fundamental character. The later statement on the monetary problem after 1914, which Dr. Vissering submitted in his inaugural speech at the Brussels Conference, has hardly contributed to make the subject clear.

In its annual reports the Board of the *Danish National*

Bank has time after time reverted to the extraordinary conditions obtaining in the monetary sphere. In the 1917 Report (covering the banking year 1st August, 1916, to 31st July, 1917) it remarks upon the speculative mania which, particularly in the summer of 1916, in spite of all warnings, overstepped all reasonable bounds; upon the keen buying and selling of landed property at high prices; and upon the high cost of living. Nevertheless, during the whole of the bank year the discount rate was 5 per cent., and the bank rediscounted bills to the private banks at ½ per cent. below the prevailing discount rate— that is to say, at 4½ per cent. The bank, however, refuses to recognise any connection between this bank policy and its effects. " The consequences of the scarcity of commodities and the plentifulness of money are a rise in prices and high cost of living. No country in the world has evaded it, nor been able to do so." " The credit which the national bank has had to grant to abroad, or the gold which it has had to take over, has been forced upon it to the extent rendered unavoidable by the surplus of exports over imports, and the bank would have no right whatever, even if it were able to do so, to refuse its co-operation in this adjustment of the nation's balance. The high cost of living essentially brought about by the abovementioned causes has involved an increase in the quantity of notes : this increase, therefore, in the case of Denmark is, strictly speaking, an effect of, and not a cause of, the high cost of living." In the 1918 Report mention is made of the plentiful supply of money, which is regarded as partly due to a realisation of commercial stocks and cattle, combined with the impossibility of procuring by importation of commodities the renewal of stocks which regular normal trade requires.

That selling to abroad might result in growing balances abroad is natural enough. But why it should, therefore,

be necessary also to increase the quantity of Danish notes
is not quite clear. The bank says, of course, that it was
compelled to grant credit to abroad; but have not the
demands for credit from Denmark been considerably
enhanced by the unreasonably low discount rate of
5 and 4½ per cent. which the bank maintained even in the
years 1917–1918, in spite of the prevailing abnormal
dearth of capital? The real explanation is that in
Denmark, as everywhere else, people were so blinded by
the abundance of money that they could not realise the
existence of an actual dearth of capital. In the 1918
Report it is further remarked: " Speculation on the Stock
Exchange has continued unabated, and the abnormal
purchase of landed property has increased . . . the
existence of plenty of money has been particularly manifested in the amount of share-issues, which during the
banking year have totalled about 400 million kroner. . . .
Whether all this money will prove to have been well
utilised when the coming time of peace alters existing
conditions may well be doubted; and the bank has been
considering whether raising the discount rate would not
have been appropriate as a means of restricting the
extensive issue of shares. However, there were important
grounds for opposing this. For even if it cannot be
denied that the raising of the discount rate would at least
have proved a kind of warning not to go too far—in
Sweden and Norway the discount rate was raised with
this end, among others, in view—yet its effective result
would have been extremely doubtful, if the rate of
interest was not to be raised to such a height as to endanger
legitimate business (*inter alia*, producing new buildings);
besides, the normal grounds for raising the rate—viz.,
dearth of money, did not exist; rather the contrary was the
case, and therefore that discount rate was retained which
most European countries had kept to."

The reference in this connection to the low discount rates in other countries gives the impression that these rates are regarded as true expressions of the situation. Pointing out the "legitimate" requirements of business is characteristic. When at any time during the War people set about limiting credit, their motive in all countries was the need for checking speculation. It never occurred to them that the real meaning of the limitation of credit is simply the check thereby obtained on the demand for funds for producing real capital. The raising of the discount rate in a neutral country would only be of real use by restricting production for purposes of export, by restricting industrial expansion and the building operations connected therewith, and in general by limiting the demands for capital to what people could afford—*i.e.*, to the amount of the country's available savings.

On the 2nd January, 1919, the Danish National Bank raised its discount rate, which ever since the 10th June, 1915, had been 5 to 5½ per cent. In the 1919 Report this is remarked upon as follows: "It was not to be expected that speculation could be stopped, that consumption could be altered and prices reduced, by raising the discount rate. In times like the present the general, slightly varying, changes in the discount rate are hardly sufficient to cope with the violent fluctuations in the business world, and the powerful mechanical influences of buying and selling, etc. People have everywhere realised this during the War, or at any rate have everywhere acted in conformity with this view." During 1920 circumstances at last compelled the bank to go up to the fairly satisfactory rate of 7 per cent. (on the 17th April). In its 1920 Report it is declared in reference to this that the method is a doubtful one, and that " account has to be taken of the difficulties caused to savings banks and such institutions by a very high discount rate, of the fall in the bond market, of the obstruction to building operations, and to other valuable sources of livelihood." Again, in the Report for 1921, the bank maintains its theory : " It is our opinion now, as it was during the War, that the discount rate has not the same influence on industrial life as it used to have, because the variations in exchanges and prices have in the last few years been so wide that interest rates have had but little significance."

Certainly the bank has displayed no interest in trying to unravel the thread of circumstances affecting the mechanism of money, but rather has expressed the opinion that the complicated character of the situation rendered such an attempt impossible. In 1917 the remark is made that " one cannot control the particularly complicated and kaleidoscopic conditions here under discussion." In 1920 the bank writes: " No direct conclusion can be drawn from the relation between the circulation of notes and the height of the discount rate, exchange rates, and level of prices—either one way or another; they are undoubtedly all correlated, but in what sequence and how powerfully they influence one another seems, as in the case of all complicated economic phenomena, practically impossible to determine."

If everyone had been satisfied with such a spirit of resignation, where should we now have stood in knowledge of the monetary revolution after 1914 ?

As to the view of the *Bank of Norway* on the monetary conditions, it may suffice to recall what was said in that bank's Report for 1916. The hope is there expressed that the unsound speculation, of which mention had already been made in the previous Report, may have reached a climax in the course of 1916. Immediately afterwards it is announced that the bank's total lendings amounted to more than twice those of the previous year— viz., 1217·3 million kroner for 1916 as against 573·5 million kroner for 1915. Then comes the following passage: "This considerable increase in the bank's business must not be regarded merely as a consequence of the expansion of industry, but the reason must also be sought in the rise in the general price level combined with the fact that the sale of commodities, both for import and export, is now effected to the greatest possible extent against cash. Further, the extraordinary measures taken to preserve our neutrality play a not unimportant part in the circumstance under discussion."

The Board of the Bank of Norway do not appear to have realised that what was actually taking place was a sharp depreciation in the value of the monetary unit in Norway. Still less does it seem to have occurred to the Board that this depreciation might have some connection with a discount policy which found it the right course during such a critical period to reduce the discount rate as low as $4\frac{1}{2}$ per cent. (on the 29th May, 1916), and to continue this low rate right up to the 18th October of the same year.

In *Sweden*, too, the altogether too low interest rates had allowed the demands for capital by far to exceed available savings. Capital was required on an unprecedented scale, both directly for industrial expansion at home and still more for export. Since current savings could not satisfy these demands for capital, an artificial purchasing power had to be created by more and more bank currency being made available. This was done to a large extent by granting credits to abroad. Foremost in this granting of credit was the Riksbank; its holdings in foreign exchange were increased to an altogether abnormal degree during the years 1915–1916. This item, which on an average for 1913 amounted to 98·8 million kronor, had, by the 31st December, 1915, been raised to 178·5 million kronor, and on the 31st August, 1916, reached its maximum

9

height of 236·4 million kronor. At the same time the total of the bank's domestic lending had gone down, and on the 31st August, 1916, amounted to only 58·5 million kronor, against 139·4 million kronor, which was the average for 1913. If we take the last day of August, 1913, as the basis of comparison, we find that foreign currencies rose from 92·5 million kronor to 236·4 million kronor in 1916, while at the same time the total lending at home sank from 134·2 million kronor to 58·5 million kronor. Thus, by purchasing foreign currencies on an abnormal scale, the Riksbank had created such a quantity of means of payment in Swedish kronor that the home market was well supplied without having recourse to the Riksbank even on a normal scale for loans and discounting. The Riksbank's note circulation had thereupon risen from 214·5 million kronor on the last day of August, 1913, to 345·5 million kronor on the corresponding day of 1916— an increase of 131·0 million kronor.

At the same time, also, the amount of the private banks' credits to abroad had assumed very large dimensions. Debts and bills outstanding used to show on a yearly average before the War a balance in favour of abroad, but after the outbreak of the War this debt was soon wiped out, and was converted into a claim which rapidly grew and reached its maximum at the end of 1918 with 467·1 million kronor. If we calculate the balance at the Riksbank in a similar way—that is, exclusive of foreign Government securities—we find that the total of foreign balances of all Swedish banks combined, which on the average for 1913 amounted to 69·8 million kronor, rose to a maximum total of 609·0 million kronor by the end of February, 1919.

The purchasing power of Swedish kronor which was thus placed at the disposal of foreign countries gave a false direction to the whole of Swedish industrial life.

The productive forces of the country were applied to meeting foreign requirements to an excessive degree, and the Swedish nation's own supply was therefore neglected. The concrete manifestations of this distortion of Swedish industry have already been discussed in a foregoing chapter.

The low discount rate has, without doubt, contributed to the abnormal expansion of credit-giving to abroad. Hereby and through the direct influence it has had upon the direction given to Swedish industry, the low discount rate has created artificially prosperous conditions, characterised by a steady rise in prices, and consequent violent speculation, combined with immense industrial expansion calculated to meet the abnormal claims of the War period, without due regard to what might normally be required in the way of industrial products during a future time of peace. While this period of expansion was continued year after year, and showed more and more serious symptoms, the Riksbank kept to a low discount rate, disclaimed all responsibility for whatever might happen, declared that the discount policy had now lost its effectiveness, discovered all sorts of possible and impossible explanations for the rise in prices, and trotted out their favourite statement that the situation was so abnormal and so complicated that, strictly speaking, one could know nothing about it, and that at any rate on the part of the Riksbank nothing could be done.

As early as in 1915 we find Mr. Moll, the head of the Riksbank, stating in an article in an economic review (*Ekonomisk Tidskrift*) that he did not believe that " raising the interest rate would act as a hindrance to the import of Swedish securities now going on. It is an old experience here that quotations of industrial stocks, and even of bonds, are particularly insensible to alterations of the bank rate. That the quotations would feel the

influence of a rise in the bank rate still less at the present
time than under ordinary circumstances is a recognised
fact." In the light of the experience which has now
been acquired, it is evident that this idea is absolutely
false. Further on, in the same article, Mr. Moll says:
"Tightening the discount screw has no longer any effect
outwards; it merely makes credit scarce at home." It
is just this effect of making credit scarce which was badly
needed, and it certainly could not have failed to exercise
its influence outwards as well. In his article, "The
Riksbank and the High Cost of Living " (*Ekonomisk
Tidskrift*, 1917), which is a reply to my book "Dyrtiden och
Sedelöverflöd " ("The High Cost of Living and the Excess
of Notes "), Mr. Moll tries to acquit the Riksbank of the
charge of having, by creating a superfluity of purchasing
power, brought about the high cost of living, and for this
purpose he employs the method of piling up in a most
confusing way all possible factors which might be supposed
to have an influence on prices, and explains that "account
must be taken of the complex conditions that continually
affect the formation of prices. . . . That an increase
in the note circulation can cause a raising of the price
level is obvious, but equally obvious is it that raising the
price level may occasion an increase in the note circulation." The independent factors Mr. Moll desires us to
take into consideration are "the general variations in the
conditions of production and the scarcity of commodities
which influence prices, and the difficulties of transport
which stand in the way of price adjustment between
different countries." Mr. Moll goes on to say: "In every
country imported commodities grow more and more
scarce, and this inevitably leads to higher prices. Thus, in
important spheres of economic life there exist—apart
from money—factors tending to raise prices. These
further affect the nearest situated spheres according to

the principle of the endless screw, not in like proportion, but with a power irresistibly making for higher prices. The contributory factors in this complicated process—including the note circulation of the Riksbank—are dependent on one another and on the process as a whole. . . . We have been struck by the international price-wave which the Riksbank has been unable to resist."

Mr. Moll often returns to his favourite subject, the Swedish currency's dependence on gold. I have shown in the foregoing how short the period really was during which this dependence existed as a reason for the rise in prices. Depreciation of the Swedish currency during the early part of the War, as I have many times pointed out, is not explained by this dependence on gold; still less can its dependence on gold in any way excuse the enormous inflation which followed upon the gold exclusion, and which actually brought the Swedish krona far below its gold parity.

In this same article it is said that the Riksbank had met representatives of the central banks of Denmark and Norway to discuss the question of discount policy. On this subject Mr. Moll writes: " The object of raising the discount is, of course, to reduce the note circulation. But people are unanimous in the opinion that raising the discount rate under present circumstances would not have this effect, for the reason that in business calculations the question of interest plays a far less important part than it would under normal conditions. . . . Raising the interest rate would not have the slightest effect on the granting of credit to abroad. . . . Similarly, a few per cents. higher discount rate would have little power to check the importing of bonds. In this kind of trans-action, too, people count on such a margin of profit that the discount rate in force for the time being is not a deciding factor. On the other hand, a rise in the interest

rate would prove an increased burden in the innumerable
cases where people are dependent on credit, but where
there is no possible chance of benefiting by war conditions.
Under these circumstances the Scandinavian banking
world has not considered it advisable to propose a rise
in the discount rate." No one nowadays can doubt that
the Scandinavian central banks were entirely wrong in
this matter. There can be no question but that if the
Riksbank had fixed a high discount rate, and had announced that it proposed to adhere to that rate as long as
the War lasted, or as long as there prevailed a tendency
towards an increase in the note circulation, the value of
the Swedish currency would have been maintained far
better than was actually the case. There are, of course,
always cases of demands for capital on which a moderate
rise in the discount rate has no effect; but there are, on
the other hand, " innumerable cases " which are on the
boundary line, and there a rise in the discount rate has
some effect. In this respect the discount rate is exactly
like other prices. It is unreasonable to suppose that a
rise in price would not be an effective means of limiting
the demand for an article just because there are wealthy
persons who do not have to worry about what that
article costs. And it is, as experience ought to have
taught us by now, an extremely dangerous policy to
endeavour, out of regard for those who should really be
forced by a rise in prices to restrict their buying, to keep
the price below the level demanded by the situation.

It was much to be feared that the mass of foreign
currency on the Riksbank's hands would cause considerable losses to the Riksbank, should the steady process
of depreciation of foreign currencies continue, and in my
book just quoted I had uttered a warning against the
serious danger the Riksbank was incurring in investing
its resources in this way, and had laid particular stress on

the inadvisability of the Riksbank's keeping secret the
exchange rates at which this foreign money was entered
on the books. To this Mr. Moll replies that the Riksbank
had never made a practice of publishing these rates.
" The present juncture is hardly a suitable one at which
to depart from this practice. Very large sums on these
currencies have been written off during the War. In
the Riksbank the opinion is held that by the end of
the War the amounts written off will prove sufficient."
Mr. Moll states that he has hereby placed my " principal
charges against the Riksbank in the light in which they
appear, judged from a practical point of view." Just
how practical these points of view were anyone can now
see for himself, having before his mind all the economic
misery which inflation has brought upon the country.
If anyone considers this argument to be too far-fetched,
at any rate the unprecedented losses which the Riksbank
itself has suffered on its foreign currencies will no doubt
offer a striking proof that the practical judgment shown
by the management of the Riksbank was no more highly
developed than its theoretical insight. Amongst the
items of expenditure incurred by the Riksbank may be
found an item " expenditure on foreign business and
depreciation on foreign currencies." Under this heading
the following amounts are written off:

1918	..	..	..	13·3	million kronor.
1919	..	..	..	15·8	,,	,,
1920	..	..	..	45·4	,,	,,
1921	..	..	..	12·9	,,	,,
			Total	87·4	,,	,,

Besides this there appears on the account for 1920
" Depreciation on bonds, etc.," a charge of 10·5 million
kronor. I was therefore not altogether unjustified in
my demand when on the 2nd October, 1916, I asked for

an immediate inventory to be made of the Riksbank's
assets, and it may be safely said that it would have been
to the great advantage both of the country and of the
Riksbank itself if the serious warnings uttered by me
on the question of the Riksbank's foreign currency
holdings had induced Parliament to enter upon a public
examination of the situation.

THE EXCHANGE RATES

THE wide variations in the intrinsic values of the various currencies has necessarily involved a complete disorganisation in the exchange rates. The ancient bonds between the different monetary units had been sundered, and the relations between their values, which we had been accustomed to regard as definite and invariable, had been substituted by quite different ones, which in their turn were changing from day to day. Indeed, the world's commerce now had to reckon with a number of free paper currencies, independent of one another, and each continually changing in value, while their mutual exchange rates appeared to have no firm foundation. That such an exceptional change in familiar conditions should also produce an exceptional confusion of public opinion was but natural. Here practical experience was of little use, and the lines along which the analysis of exchange rates had previously been carried out were not suited to the new conditions. People naturally endeavoured, as long as possible, to adhere to the idea that this was a question only of temporary disturbances, and that the exchange rates must inevitably revert to their former levels as soon as the disturbing factors had disappeared. But when the course of developments gradually compelled a revision of this point of view, the feeling got the upper hand that the world's monetary system was in a state of complete chaos.

The discussion on the variations in exchange rates and their true explanation, which has been going on the whole world over ever since the outbreak of the War, has been chiefly characterised by a remarkable lack of clearness on the question as to what really determines the exchange rate between two independent currencies. People have pointed to the variations in supply and demand, but have never got to the real gist of the problem, for the simple reason that people have never realised, or not even desired to realise, that the very object of this supply and this demand—the thing bought and sold—was in itself something different from what it used to be. If a commodity sinks to a third of its former price because its quality has deteriorated to that extent, one does not look for the reason of the reduction in price in a variation of supply and demand! But when it is a question of money the public, with incredible tenacity, sticks to the idea that a krona is still a krona, and a pound a pound, whatever one may do with the currency in question. It was this idea which beyond all else precluded the public from obtaining a true insight into the significance of the dislocation of the exchange rates. The first question that has to be unravelled, if we are to gain a clear idea of the exchange problem which the War has bequeathed to us, is this: What is the principal reason for a foreign currency being in demand, and what effect has an alteration in the intrinsic value of that currency upon the demand for the same?

The putting of this question has brought me to the following line of argument: Our willingness to pay a certain price for foreign money must ultimately and essentially be due to the fact that this money possesses a purchasing power as against commodities and services in that foreign country. On the other hand, when we offer so and so much of our own money, we are actually offering a purchasing power as against commodities and services in our own country. Our valuation of a foreign currency in terms of our own, therefore, mainly depends on the relative purchasing power of the two currencies in their respective countries.

Here, then, we have the first and most elementary ground on which the exchange rates between two countries are determined. But this ground is not in itself sufficient. It presents a solution of the exchange problem in only a first and quite rough approximation. The possession of a foreign currency does not imply that one has, within one's own country, direct disposal over those commodities and services which may be purchased for that currency in the foreign country. The way to obtain such a power of disposal may offer various difficulties which cannot but affect the valuation of the foreign currency. Even under the more stable conditions which obtained before the War it might well have happened that one's money, after being changed at the ruling rates of exchange, possessed a somewhat higher purchasing power in the one country than in the other, and thus the exchange rate was not a fully reliable indication of the intrinsic value of the different currencies. As will be more fully explained in the following enquiry, differences in the two countries' economic situation, particularly in regard to transport and customs, may cause the normal exchange rates to deviate to a certain extent from the quotient of the currencies' intrinsic purchasing powers. In view of the complicated nature of the problem it is hardly possible to calculate this exchange rate theoretically.

Given, however, normal free trade between two countries A and B, a certain exchange rate will establish itself between them, and, apart from slight fluctuations, this rate will remain unaltered so long as no variations take place in either of the currencies' purchasing power, and no obstacles are placed in the way of trade. Now should an inflation of A's currency take place, and consequently its purchasing power be reduced, the value of A's currency in the country B will necessarily fall in like proportion. Should at the same time B's currency have undergone inflation and its purchasing power have been reduced, clearly the valuation of A's currency in B will, as a consequence, rise in a corresponding degree. If, for instance, the inflation in A has reached the ratio of 320 to 100 and the inflation in B the ratio of 240 to 100, the new exchange rate (taking the quotation of A's currency in B's currency) will be three-quarters of the old rate. Thus the following rule: When two currencies have undergone inflation. the normal rate of exchange will be equal to the old rate multiplied by the quotient of the degree of inflation in the one country and in the other. There will naturally always be found deviations from this new normal rate, and during the transition period these deviations may be expected to be fairly wide. But the rate that has been calculated by the above method must be regarded as the new parity between the currencies, the point of balance towards which, in spite of all temporary fluctuations, the exchange rates will always tend. This parity I call *purchasing power parity*.

Owing to the excessive supplies of means of payment, the purchasing power of the various currencies during the War has been greatly reduced, although in very different proportions. Consequently the purchasing power parities have undergone very considerable variations, and are now entirely different from those parities which obtained before the War. If one looks at the exchange rate problem from that point of view, there can no longer be any reason for believing that the world's exchanges will ever return to their former parities. These former parities have as a matter of fact lost their significance, they possess now a pre-eminently historic interest, and can no longer in any respect be regarded as normal. The continual references that are made to them are a serious obstacle in the way of a clear understanding of what has really happened to the currencies of the world. In statistics it is likewise only misleading to keep up the old practice of converting foreign money on the basis of pre-War parities. It is of the utmost importance, both theoretically and practically, that we make ourselves fully acquainted with the fact that normal rates of exchange nowadays are something entirely different from what we were formerly accustomed to regard as normal. In the system of independent paper currencies now in practice the normal rates of exchange are determined by the purchasing power parities.

Such is the simple representation of the meaning of purchasing power parity and its significance for present monetary conditions submitted in my first Memorandum to the League of Nations. It is of importance to observe that the purchasing power parity is here calculated on a basis of the fall in the value of money since 1914. Consequently we start from a rate of exchange which has existed at a certain equilibrium of international trade—a rate, therefore, which in its time has been normal. From this rate of exchange we arrive at the rate which must now be regarded as normal by taking into consideration the degree of depreciation which the value of the monetary unit has undergone in both countries. In doing so, to be exact, we must presuppose that no other changes have taken place. If in each country prices are unaltered in their relation to one another, but have only undergone a common rise, then there is nothing to prevent our supposing the balance of trade between the countries to be unaltered. The equilibrium of the exchanges must, then, have been dislocated in the manner shown by the ratio of the deterioration of money in the two countries. If, on the other hand, the different prices have moved in their relation to one another, this circumstance may possibly in itself have affected the equilibrium of international trade and have caused some dislocation of the equilibrium of the exchanges. However, the depreciation of money which has taken place since the outbreak of the War has been so tremendous and has gone to such different lengths in the different countries, that the dislocation of the exchanges brought about thereby must have quite paramount importance. We are therefore justified in taking into account in the first place only this dislocation—that is, in calculating the new purchasing power parities solely on the basis of the relative depreciation of money in the different countries. These parities in any case represent roughly the new equilibrium of the exchanges, and it is manifestly both correct and unavoidable first to determine this equilibrium and then to take into consideration such deviations therefrom as may possibly be caused by other factors than the depreciation of money.

The conception of purchasing power parity having once been admitted, there has appeared a certain disposition further to simplify the problem of the exchanges. People want to determine by direct means the quotient of the purchasing power of money in the respective countries, and to regard this quotient as the normal level of the exchange rates. But the problem is not so simple. It is only if we know the exchange rate which represents a certain equilibrium that we can calculate the rate which represents the same equilibrium at an altered value of the monetary units of the two countries. Now the exchange rates prevalent during the gold standard régime before the War manifestly corresponded on the whole to a certain general equilibrium of international trade. If we suppose this equilibrium to have been unaltered—or at any rate not so altered as to disturb the exchange rate—then, on the basis of the exchange rates ruling before the War, and with our knowledge of the degree of inflation of the different currencies, we can calculate the purchasing power parities which are to be taken as the normal exchanges between the paper currencies of to-day. This is how I have proceeded in my representation of the theory of purchasing power parity.

However, it is evident that the exchange rate between two countries must always fix itself in accordance with the price level in either country so that a certain amount of trade between them becomes possible. That sentence in itself is quite useful. It makes it clear that trade between two countries cannot, as is frequently imagined, be nullified or even hindered through the level of prices in one of the countries being high. This disadvantage is indeed invariably adjusted by the exchange of that country falling in proportion in international value. Conversely, it follows from this that a country cannot increase its power of competition in other countries by lowering its general price level. For this lowering of the price level simply means increasing the value of money in the country, and that will be followed by a corresponding increase in the international value of the currency in question. This implies a fall in the value of foreign currencies as expressed in the currency of the country concerned. Thus it is evident that the lowering of the general price level in the country will not have produced any increased power of competition in foreign markets. Of course, an alteration of the price level can hinder exports (or stimulate them, as the case may be) during the interval that may possibly elapse before the exchange rate has had time to adapt itself to the new level of prices. But then it is a question of a lack of adjustment between exchange rate and purchasing power parity—a subject to which we shall revert later on.

The classical doctrine that the international exchange of commodities is determined by relative costs of production appears particularly simple when we consider the trade between two countries, each with its own independent paper currency, from the point of view just stated. However the level of costs of production in the two countries may turn out, the exchange rate between them will always so adjust itself as to render possible an exchange of commodities between the countries. A country, therefore, in respect of its power of competition on foreign markets, cannot be inferior in all spheres just as it cannot be superior in all.

In judging the value of a country's money, a foreign country will naturally not only go by trade prices, but also by the height of wages. For the foreign country can buy labour for the money in question, as, for example, by having raw materials worked up in that country. But even if the country utilises home-acquired raw material to make its export products, nevertheless the latter's value represents, to a considerable extent, labour expended on them. The level of wages in the country, therefore, is always a very important factor—in the long run may be the predominating one—in determining the international value of the country's currency. This point is of particularly great practical importance for the policy of Labour. It is of very little use forcing up nominal wages if a corresponding reduction in the international value of the country's currency is thereby caused. For this implies a proportional rise in the prices of all imported commodities consumed by the working classes. In this respect the last few years have produced a number of very striking experiences.

An important consequence of the doctrine of the dependence of the exchange on the purchasing power parity is also this, that a rise in prices in a foreign country can never cause a rise in prices at home. The rise in prices in the foreign country is compensated for by valuing the foreign currency at a lower rate. Naturally, however, this is only done on the assumption that the country's own currency is not at the same time itself depreciated. If this currency is kept unaltered in its value—*i.e.*, if the country itself is not provided with means of payment capable of supporting a rise in prices —then an inflation in foreign countries will merely express itself in a fall in the value of the exchanges of those countries. A great deal of nonsense has been and is still being written on this subject. In particular has it been a favourite theme of the central banks to speak of the general rise in prices abroad as a factor which with irresistible pressure has forced on a rise in prices in their respective countries as well. People have got into a way of talking of " international waves " of rising prices, and by such phrases have suggested the idea of something inevitable under whose protection the central banks might free themselves from responsibility for the values of their respective currencies. There can be no doubt but that this very idea of the inevitability of the international movements of prices has had a real influence, and has contributed towards spreading price movements from country to country. But there can be no doubt either that it would have been possible essentially to resist these influences on a country's price level by a stable and determined monetary policy which clearly recognised the fundamental truth that a country with an independent paper standard is alone responsible for the internal purchasing power of its currency.

Naturally enough, the political and economic revolutions which have taken place since 1914 have to some extent altered the equilibrium of trade between countries, and it is therefore possible that a certain dislocation of the exchange rates could have taken place even if inflation had been equally high in the different countries. The purchasing power parities which are now calculated on the basis of the equilibrium of international trade existing in 1914 cannot, therefore, as submitted above, be expected to be fully exact. If a peace could be brought about which in essentials restored the production and trade of Europe to what they were before the War, nevertheless the conditions for the international exchange of commodities would probably not have altered to such an extent that any considerable dislocation of the exchange rates would have been necessitated on these grounds. The most suitable basis, therefore, on which to estimate the relative values of the currencies, and especially of the rates which will come to be the normal ones in future, will probably be found to be that of the purchasing power parities which are arrived at by converting the exchange rates before the War exclusively on the basis of the inflation that has taken place in the different currencies.

It is clearly, then, of the highest importance to possess as accurate data as possible on this inflation. What was said in a previous chapter as to the importance of a uniform method of calculating the rise in prices in different countries, and as to the urgency of having reports on this rise in prices published and compiled immediately after the end of each month, gains all the more in force when we find that such reports are the only approximately sure means of gaining any idea as to the relation between the internal values of the different currencies, and thereby as to the parities which, in spite of all temporary fluctuations, may be considered to mark the true equilibria of the exchange rates.

DEVIATIONS FROM PURCHASING POWER PARITIES

DURING the earlier phases of the War, when international trade still enjoyed some freedom, the real exchanges used fairly closely to coincide with the purchasing power parities. But later the severe restrictions on trade between the different nations often caused these rates to differ considerably from the parities. If the trade between two countries is more obstructed in one direction than in another, then the currency in that country whose export is relatively more hindered will fall in the other country below the purchasing power parity. This result is only one simple consequence of our general view of the exchange rate as an expression for the value set upon a means of procuring foreign commodities: if they are by artificial means rendered more difficult to obtain, then the actual value of the foreign exchange must fall. There are many instances of such abnormal deviations in the exchanges. Thus inflation has without doubt been far less severe in the United States than in Sweden, and the dollar has retained much more of its former purchasing power than the Swedish krona. The purchasing power parity must, therefore, have risen decidedly above the old parity of kr. 3·73 for the dollar. But, during the period of the most severe war-time restrictions of American exports to Sweden, the actual rate fell far below the old parity, the mean monthly rate for November, 1917, being as low as kr. 2·55. As soon as the restrictions were removed the dollar exchange rose to a height corresponding to the purchasing power parity, and even, for a short time, above it. The explanation of the temporary undervaluation of the dollar is to be sought in the absence of any immediate employment for dollars in Swedish possession, as also, of course, in the risk involved in keeping the dollar, speculating upon the prospect of its future use.

The restrictions of which we have to take account in this connection may be of various kinds. Absolute prohibition of export, prohibition covering a system of licenses, rationing of export, export duties, measures adopted for maintaining higher prices for foreign buyers than those payable on the inland market, etc., are samples of the methods applied during the War, and in many cases retained even now. They .all tend to a corresponding depression of the international value of the currency of the country applying them. If this were fully realised the ardour for practising such methods would probably cool very considerably. The restrictions may also take the form of artificial hindrances or natural difficulties hampering transport from the country A to the country B more seriously than the transport in the opposite direction. The result will be some undervaluation of the money of A in that of B.

This will also be the natural result of any import-restricting measure in B. The import prohibition on luxuries applied in latter years in several countries, and intended to improve the equilibrium of trade, tends to raise the international value of the currency in that country which thereby limits its imports. If there exist other tendencies threatening to force the currency below its purchasing power parity, they may possibly be counteracted by a restrictive policy of this nature. From the point of view of the country which closes itself to the import of luxuries the matter can be explained by the circumstance that foreign money loses part of its value as soon as it cannot be utilised for procuring foreign luxuries; from the point of view of the foreign country the matter is regarded thus, that import prohibitions make it more difficult to procure the currency of the country in question.

We can imagine several other factors capable of reducing the international value of a currency to a point below its purchasing power parity. But if there exist no special obstacles to the export of commodities from the country in question, then every underestimate of the country's currency will naturally cause an increased international demand for its commodities which must tend to counterbalance the depreciation of its currency. For as soon as a country's currency is undervalued compared with its purchasing power parity, it will be of peculiar advantage to buy this currency, and to employ the money thus obtained in procuring commodities from that country. The stimulus thus applied to demand will necessarily very soon raise the price of the currency to the level of the purchasing power parity. Where no extraordinary restrictions are laid on the country's exports (or on imports from that country to others), the influence of any other causes forcing the exchanges below the purchasing power parity can only be of a temporary nature.

Nevertheless, it is of practical importance that we should know these causes and the nature of their influence. A depreciation of currency is often merely an expression for discounting an expected fall in the currency's internal purchasing power. The world sees that the process of inflation is continually going on, and that the condition of State finances, for instance, is rendering a continuance of the depreciation of money probable. The international valuation of the currency will, then, generally show a tendency to anticipate events, so to speak, and becomes more an expression of the internal value the currency is expected to possess in a few months, or perhaps in a year's time.

The value of a currency may also be depressed below the purchasing power parity by speculations in exchange. The authorities have made an energetic use of this explanation for depreciation, and speculation in exchange has been made the scapegoat for the rise in foreign exchanges or for the fall in the international value of the home currency, in just the same way as speculators in commodities have been accused of causing the general rise in commodity prices within the country. An impartial judgment, however, would most certainly find that the speculation in exchange implies, on the whole, a levelling down of the fluctuations of the exchanges, and not an intensification of them.

By far the most important of the depreciating factors now under discussion, however, is the practice of selling at any price a country's exchange in other countries in order to procure funds in their money. This method of procedure has reached such lengths during the past few years, and has been such a prominent feature in the international monetary situation, that particular attention must be paid to it.

The case of Germany offers the best means of studying the whole problem. As noted in a previous chapter, the German mark has for years been sold to abroad on an ever-increasing scale at any price obtainable. When the central Government, the municipalities, the banks and business enterprises were in dire need of foreign means of payment, and it did not seem possible to procure it in any other way, the country was beguiled into thus getting money on its currency. The demand for reparations later compelled Germany to have recourse to this method of financing its needs on such a scale that it degenerated into an absolute swindle.

We must regard the process as a substitution—and a very very poor one at that—for the more regular course, that of obtaining foreign loans. When lenders were not forthcoming, Germany turned to a new class of investors, speculators in exchange, and in place of high interest rates offered them the advantage of an exceptionally low exchange rate. Of course, the speculators suffered severe losses when the rates gradually fell. But fresh ranks of speculators were always ready to believe that " the bottom had been reached "; some speculators, indeed, have actually made large profits.

Obviously this process had to lead to a depreciation of the German mark below its purchasing power parity. This means that the German mark on the world's market was forced down to a price considerably below what it should have fetched in view of the purchasing power it possessed on the German home market. At certain periods this depreciation has doubtless been very considerable. In particular the payment of reparations on the 31st August, 1921, and the decision which followed shortly afterwards as to the partition of Upper Silesia, have caused an exceptional fall in the international value of the mark, and thereby a particular, violent undervaluation of the German currency; so also have the immense demands of the Reparations Commission in the early part of 1922.

Doubtless, under such circumstances, it would have been very advantageous for foreigners to procure German marks with which to make purchases on the cheap German market. If this could have been done unrestrictedly, then practically everything could have been exported from an impoverished Germany, and often with very large profits. For Germany itself this was, of course,

an impossible situation. The country was simply driven
to preserve its scanty supplies of provisions and raw
material by preventing their being exported. As to
other commodities, Germany endeavoured to defend
herself from buyers desirous of availing themselves of the
low exchange value of the mark by raising commodity
prices against these foreign buyers—at times by hundreds
per cent. Such measures, however, according to what
has been said above, must have the effect of permanently
forcing down the international value of the mark below
its purchasing power parity. They imply a particularly
arbitrary behaviour towards foreign countries. Germany,
indeed, has in the first place exported marks, and the
buyers of these marks have reckoned on the value of the
mark being kept up by the purchasing power of the mark
within the country—*i.e.*, on their being able to buy commodities from Germany at prices ruling in Germany itself.
When Germany afterwards one-sidedly raised the prices
of exports, she thus arbitrarily deprived foreign possessors
of marks of a considerable part of the value of their marks.
If a debtor arbitrarily writes off his debt to one-half or
one-third of its original value, the character of such a
proceeding is evident to everybody, probably even to the
debtor himself. What is done by means of the German
regulation of exports and export prices is fundamentally
the same, even if for a time the true meaning underlying
this policy was successfully disguised. It is nothing else
than a sheer swindle to sell time after time marks—*i.e.*,
claims on German commodities—and afterwards to refuse
to honour these claims with more than a fraction of the
quantities of commodities to which they originally
amounted. But it is only by means of such a swindle
that the victors' unreasonable demands on a conquered
Germany have up till now managed to be paid. Thousands
of people in all countries of the world have been ruined

in order that these reparation claims might be fulfilled. It is time that the world learnt to see through all this business, and no longer allowed itself in this way to be sucked dry for the benefit of the countries claiming reparations. Germany's debts to abroad must be so limited that Germany herself can pay them.

Of course, it has not been possible for Germany to prevent the enormous amount of purchasing power placed in the hands of foreigners from being turned to a certain extent against Germany, and from making itself felt on the home market in forcing up prices for domestic buyers as well. Even within Germany itself the deplorable State finances have produced a steadily increased inflation. For both these reasons the internal purchasing power of the German mark has gradually sunk lower and lower. The *Frankfurter Zeitung's* index figure, which was still at 1 123 for January, 1920 (100 representing the middle of 1914), and for January, 1921, was at 1·606, has since then, probably, principally as a consequence of the reparations payments, been forced up to 3·596 for January, 1922.

In the same degree as the internal purchasing power of the mark has sunk its purchasing power parity has naturally gone down in countries with an unaltered currency. Nevertheless, the mark is still undervalued on the international market, although on a very varying scale. To this undervaluation of the mark the lack of confidence in its future, of course, largely contributes— this lack of confidence being caused by the experiences the world has reaped in the matter of the internal and external depreciation of the mark. If the reparations had been framed from the beginning on an economically judicious basis, and if a successful attempt had consequently been made to uphold confidence in Germany's future, the international value of the mark could have

risen to the level of its internal purchasing power. Then
it would not have been necessary for Germany to keep
on treating foreign buyers in a different way, and conditions would have allowed of a stable equilibrium of the
German exchange. Now Germany has been driven so
far along the road to ruin that it will certainly meet with
exceptional difficulties in attaining anything like stability
in the value of the mark, and in any case stability will
only be reached after a very considerable reduction in the
internal purchasing power of the mark.

The example of Germany shows quite clearly the
disastrous effects of an attempt at wholesale selling of
a country's currency to speculative buyers abroad.
Although this example is certainly the most striking one,
the method of procedure has by no means been confined
to Germany. Other countries which have been tempted
to follow the same course should now realise the necessity
of checking this mad career in good time.

Our calculation of the purchasing power parity rests
strictly on the proviso that the rise in prices in the
countries concerned has affected all commodities in a like
degree. If that proviso is not fulfilled, then the actual
exchange rate may deviate from the calculated purchasing
power parity. If the rise in prices in the country A, for
example, has affected in a particularly high degree those
commodities which that country exports to B, the consequence must be that the A exchange in B is depressed
to a value somewhat below the purchasing power parity
calculated on the basis of the alteration in the general
price level in A. This result is, indeed, merely a simple
consequence of our conception of the exchange rate as
an expression of B's valuation of what it can purchase for
A's currency. After the armistice coal prices in England
were for quite a long time considerably higher than would
correspond to the rise in the general price level. This

circumstance has probably been one of the chief reasons for the pound being depressed during that period to an international value which, as far as can be judged from available statistics of prices, was slightly below that which would have corresponded to its internal purchasing power. This at any rate seems to be the most probable reason for the low quotation for the pound in Stockholm during that period.

If it is thus evident that a particularly violent rise in the prices of a country's export goods has some influence on its exchanges we must nevertheless not draw the conclusion—which has, indeed, sometimes been drawn —that new normal equilibria of the exchanges should be calculated simply and solely on the basis of the prices of export commodities. The principal error in such a view lies in this, that, if export commodities have risen in relative value in the exporting country, they have probably in the importing country also risen in desirability, and therefore in value, as compared with other commodities. The higher price of the export commodities, therefore, need not necessarily cause the value of the exporting country's exchange to be reduced on a like scale. Further, it must be borne in mind that, if considerable relative dislocations of prices have taken place, export commodities in general are no longer the same as they were before the War, and that consequently " price indexes of export commodities " scarcely admit of calculation. Even the method I use for calculating the new normal equilibrium of the exchanges on the basis of the rise in the general price level in both countries suffers, of course, from some degree of uncertainty, where relative dislocations between the prices of different commodities have taken place to any considerable extent; and it may be necessary in the matter here shown to take particular note of this disturbing factor. But our method of calculating the normal equilibrium of the exchanges has nevertheless the advantage of giving us that rate which will be normal if normal conditions are ever re-established in the world in the sense that international trade becomes somewhat similar to what it was before 1914. Only a continuous study of the real movement of the exchanges can clearly show how far the purchasing power parities calculated on a basis of the rises in the general price level in the different countries are an expression for the equilibrium to which the exchanges are tending. As long as such deviations from the calculated purchasing power parities as the real exchange rates show can be satisfactorily explained on such grounds as are mentioned above, and as long as the real exchange rates in important cases approximately agree with the purchasing power parities, then there is no reason to assume that any considerable dislocation of the equilibrium of the exchanges has taken place, other than that which has been caused by alterations of the general price level.

I still regard, therefore, the purchasing power parities calculated on the above-mentioned grounds as the normal exchange rate. If the actual rate for a country's money is lower, then I say that the money of that country is undervalued. If the rate is higher, then the money is overvalued.

As long as the exchange rate is in this sense normal, it will be just so high as it must be in order to permit of normal trade between the countries concerned. The fact of this exchange rate being considerably higher or considerably lower than it used to be before the War has in this respect no significance. The public, nevertheless, stubbornly adheres to the opinion that the exchange rates of pre-War times should somehow or other still be normal, and describes the exchange rates as "high" or "low," according to their position as compared with pre-War rates.   This is highly misleading.   It is the purchasing power parity calculated on the rise in the price level in either country that nowadays represents the normal level. The public's mistaken idea on this point, however, governs the official view as well and even stamps its mark on legislation.   The Safeguarding of Industries Bill, passed in England in August, 1921, starts from the assumption of a depreciation of foreign currencies in comparison with the pound sterling, and the application of the law is made dependent on this depreciation amounting to at least $33\frac{1}{3}$ per cent. of the pre-War parity.   Such misconceptions are rather the rule in public debates on matters of commercial politics in all countries.   In reality the purchasing power parity represents an indifferent equilibrium of the exchanges in the sense that it does not affect international trade either way.   Thus a country's export is not checked by low rates of exchange, provided only these rates correspond to a high price level abroad, or a low level at home; nor, on the other hand, is export particularly stimulated by high foreign exchange rates, so long as they only correspond to the relative purchasing power of the different currencies.   Similarly, low prices of foreign currencies do not mean the encouragement of import from abroad or keener competition for the home producers, so long as these rates are merely a true expression for the purchasing power parity of the foreign currencies. On the same hypothesis high prices of foreign currencies do not in any way act as a check on import.   In reality the terms "high" or "low" exchange rate have no significance in themselves; if they are to be used at all they must clearly refer to the truly normal rates—i.e., to the purchasing power parities.

It is likewise obvious that every deviation of the true exchange rates from the purchasing power parities must cause considerable disturbances in international trade.

The export from A to B must be largely checked if B's currency is valued lower in A than what would correspond to the general price level in B compared with the price level in A. At the same time the import from B to A would be artificially stimulated by such a valuation. Indeed, both these influences would tend to raise the value of B's currency in A, and to restore it to the purchasing power parity, which shows that this parity is the true equilibrium of the exchanges.

In reality, however, this restoring of the equilibrium may take a long time, especially if the forces which keep the rate down are powerful and are continually at work. And this period may have a very disturbing effect on trade and industry in both countries. Usually the country which has had its currency undervalued is regarded as the one that suffers, and the difficulties of its position are perfectly apparent. When these difficulties reach a climax they make it practically impossible to import even the most essential articles of consumption and raw material. Actually, however, the country whose currency is overvalued is in no better position, as such a country is exposed to a new kind of dumping of the most inconsiderate and arbitrary sort, while at the same time its export is largely restricted. The majority of European countries have experienced much inconvenience from the exceptional undervaluing of the German mark, while Germany itself has had to undergo all the difficulties and peculiar disturbances of a country exposed to an abnormal undervaluation of its currency. On a smaller scale deviations of this sort from the purchasing power parities have occurred in several other cases, and have, of course, involved international trade in like difficulties. Both practically and theoretically it is of special importance closely to follow such deviations, and to account for their causes. We have to remove them if we are to avoid the awkward consequences of exchange deviations from the normal. Other protective measures against these consequences are never effective, and besides involve fresh interference, which renders it still more difficult for international trade to recover any degree of stability.

The whole world is now discussing how to prevent the ruinous competition which the serious undervaluing of the German mark makes it possible for Germany to force upon all markets. We have seen that Germany itself is trying to compensate for the mark's undervaluation by raising export prices above those on the home market, wherever such an increase is possible without Germany thereby endangering its power of competition abroad. But at the same time Germany's neighbours are taking steps, or are discussing the question of doing so, to close themselves to imports which, owing to the undervaluation of the German mark, are too cheap. All steps of this kind have this common fault, that they intensify the undervaluation of the mark, making it constant, and they consequently to a certain extent counteract themselves. *One* country might by means of high differential tariffs against German imports possibly succeed in protecting its industrial life from the extraordinary competition which the undervaluation of the German currency provokes. But if a majority of countries act in the same way, the consequence must be so violent a depression of the international value of the German currency that Germany's power of competition is restored. At bottom this is very natural. The principal cause of the underestimation of the mark exchange lies in the reparation claims of the Allies. If these claims are to be fulfilled, Germany must export on an enormous scale, and must find a market for its goods by means of an adequate reduction of prices. The consequence of this must be a very serious disturbance of the existing conditions of production and trade. The only way to avoid these undesirable consequences is, without doubt, to reduce reparation claims to reasonable proportions.

The United States Customs Commission have recently published the results of their investigations into the depreciation of the exchanges and its influence on international trade ("Depreciated Exchange and International Trade," Washington, 1922). These investigations are entirely based on the idea of purchasing power parity, and contain, *inter alia*, very valuable calculations of the purchasing power parity for the English pound, the French franc, and the German mark in relation to the dollar in a monthly average from January, 1919, to September, 1921, for which period are also given the averages for the exchange rates on the three said countries actually quoted in New York. From this it may be seen that a considerable overestimation of the pound and the franc took place at the beginning of 1919, when the system of officially supporting the rates during the War had not yet been abolished. Afterwards the actual rates of these currencies fall, and during 1920, particularly in the case of the franc, stand considerably below the purchasing power parity. During 1921 the pound rate fluctuated round about the purchasing power parity while the franc rate on the whole lay some points per cent. below it. As to the mark rate, the calculations show a very considerable undervaluation during 1920; during the first six months of 1921 the mark rate stood at about two-thirds of the purchasing power parity, but after that a very considerable depreciation again made itself felt. It is striking that the undervaluation of the foreign exchanges is influenced by the violent rise in prices which took place in the United States at the end of 1919, and which reached its culminating point in May,

1920, only to be followed later by a still more violent fall in prices. The actual exchange rates apparently did not succeed in immediately adapting themselves to the exceptionally violent internal depreciation of the dollar which took place during the latter part of 1919 and the first quarter of 1920.

The American investigations prove that in the case of standard commodities on the world's market the prices in the different countries are to a great extent so adjusted to the exchanges that even the violent international under-valuation of certain currencies fails to bring about any abnormally low prices on these commodities. On the other hand, there are a quantity of more special commodities whose prices are far from being adjusted to the international exchanges, and which for that reason Central Europe in particular is in a position to sell at an abnormally low price in dollars. Generally speaking, an American importer can buy in Germany for one dollar commodities which are worth two dollars in America. The report further shows, by means of interesting statistical data, that the German producer has a considerable advantage over others in the competition on the world's market in consequence of the low wages in Germany, which have by no means risen in proportion to the fall in the mark rate. The advantages to German competition, however, are in no way so great as one might suppose in view of these facts; for on the one hand there exists in Germany a serious scarcity of a number of commodities, and on the other hand the export prices of many commodities are higher than the home prices, while in some cases export is entirely prohibited.

The report concludes that the creating and administration of a customs tariff to counteract the low exchanges would be attended by serious difficulties. The adjustment of these exchanges to the equilibrium represented

11

by the purchasing power parities is very different in the case of different countries, and even in the case of different commodities in the same country. Specific protective tariffs would therefore have to be applied in view of this, and, further, would have to be constantly revised in accordance with the process of adjustment between prices and exchanges.

In its theoretical principles this otherwise excellent report contains one vague point, in so far as it still supposes the idea of purchasing power parity to be based on a comparison between the absolute height of the price level of one country and that of another (pages 11 to 12 in the report). According to the theory stated above, there is no need whatever to presuppose that the parity rate of exchange exactly corresponds to the quotient of the absolute price levels. There may be a certain difference, in which case the same relative difference must be expected to remain after both currencies have undergone inflation. The American report, however, gives certain figures which seem to prove that the difference between the exchange rate and the quotient of price levels before the War, particularly in the case of England and the United States, has been almost negligible.

POPULAR MISCONCEPTIONS

THE theory of exchanges here expounded has from the very beginning met with violent opposition, and though this has begun to be gradually overcome, yet there still exist in the general conception of problems concerned such considerable remnants of the old false ideas that a critical examination of these opposed ideas may perhaps be necessary, in order to gain absolute clearness on the subject.

Just as, during the first years of the War, people tried to insist that no internal depreciation of the currency had taken place, and sought therefore to explain away the rise in prices within the country, so everything possible was done to explain away the low internationa valuation of the country's own currency. This valuation was in no way to be taken as a proof of any actual decline in the internal value of the country's own currency, and therefore other often very curious grounds of explanation of the weakness of the exchanges were invented.

In so doing people completely forgot that the low valuation abroad seldom expressed anything like the absolute depreciation of the currency: as the foreign currencies were also depreciated, the absolute depreciation of the home currency must be far greater than that depreciation, which was expressed in the exchanges.

Among the popular explanations of weak rates " profiteering " in exchange has always held a prominent place. It was asserted that speculation within the country forced up the prices of foreign exchange, and also that enemy countries, by means of certain kinds of cunning manœuvres whose *modus operandi*, however, could never be fully explained, forced down the rate of the home currency on the world's market. It is now easy to realise that all such factors taken together have had very little influence, as a whole, on the development of the exchanges. Occasional disturbances may perhaps have been caused in this way, but it cannot be doubted that the exchanges should remain for the present where they are now, even if their development had never been affected by any malicious speculation. However, the incorrect analysis in this case has been by no means a purely theoretical error. Indeed, on this analysis a number of most obstructive measures have been based, such as regulation of exchange, the establishment of centres for exchange business, compelling private individuals to sell foreign exchanges, etc.—*i.e.*, measures analogous to the price control by which attempts were made within the country to prevent the falling internal value of the currency from becoming apparent. Even if such interference in exchange business in certain cases and in certain particular respects may have been of some use, it is likewise evident that it proved to a great extent ineffective, in so far as it was a question of preventing the depreciation of money from becoming apparent in the exchanges, but that, on the other hand, this interference represented a very serious obstacle to the universally desired re-establishment of international trade. The attempts at public control of exchange transactions must also be held responsible for having provoked illicit trade in exchange, which has had an extremely demoralising effect and often reached such a pitch as to render State control completely ineffective.

Another very popular explanation of the unfavourable exchanges has been the adverse trade balance caused by the War or by abnormal post-War conditions. A thorough criticism of this explanation is only possible in conjunction with the theoretical discussion of the exchange problem to be dealt with in the next chapter. But here a few words will suffice to prove the actual incorrectness of the explanation in question. When people declare that a low international valuation of their own currency is not due to an internal depreciation of the currency, but only to a temporary deficit in the trade balance, they must mean by that that the currency is substantially undervalued on the world's market. Now, such an undervaluation is, of course, possible to a certain extent, if the export from the country is restricted while its import is comparatively free. But has such one-sidedness in the obstacles to free trade really asserted itself in the case of countries with weak exchanges ? If external obstacles are in question, then the answer will most probably be that import, let us say in the case of the Central Powers, has been rendered more difficult than export. The Allies' blockade of Germany during the War could, therefore, not cause any undervaluation of the German mark. In so far as any undervaluation has actually taken place, especially since the War, it has been due to Germany itself, as pointed out above, having put a check on exports. Apart from this undervaluation the fall in the mark has obviously been caused by the internal depreciation of the value of the mark currency. The same is the case with all other currencies. A poor trade balance cannot in itself induce an undervaluation of a currency, for such an undervaluation would immediately lead to a large increase in exports, which would restore the balance, provided no special obstacles were placed in the way of exports.

Even in this case the incorrect explanation has not exclusively had the character of a theoretical error, but has led to far-reaching practical consequences in the form of attempts, with the aid of State control, at effecting an adjustment of the trade balance by which it was hoped to improve the international quotation for the home exchange. It is not known that these attempts have been able to show any useful results, and in any case the international valuation has largely followed the internal value of the currency in its downward tendency without succeeding very far in being kept up by trade regulations. The very fact that the measures based on the popular theory of the bearing of the trade balance on the exchanges have to a great extent proved ineffective should be a powerful reminder to the great majority of the public as to the unreliability of the theory in question.

So long as people refused to admit that a real internal depreciation of money had taken place, they manifestly closed the door to a true insight into the causes of the variations in the exchanges. They sought to account for these variations by temporary conditions, and were thus forced to draw the conclusion that the exchanges must return to their normal levels, which were still taken to mean the pre-War rates. This idea was very widespread, especially during the first years of the War, and has indeed exercised a strong influence over public opinion. Even experienced and intelligent bankers for a long time found it difficult to get rid of the idea that the pre-War rates were normal levels to which, by some secret natural power, the exchange values must eventually be restored as soon as peace came in sight. It was this same idea which, at every new fall in the rate of this or that currency, induced the public to believe that " the bottom must have been reached." Unheard-of losses have been incurred in this way in the last few years by people who all too readily accepted the official doctrine regarding the causes of the depreciation of the exchanges.

It having now turned out that the exchanges have not by any means returned to their old parities—nor indeed do they show the least tendency to do so—there should certainly be sound reason for a complete revision of the entire shallow conception of the exchange problem that has been generally accepted, to the world's immense harm.

If the point of view were insisted upon that the internal value of money has not been reduced, then some other explanation had to be found for the rise in prices within the country. This, too, was attributed to temporary circumstances or to external conditions lying outside the scope of the country's administration of its own currency. The simplest way, then, was to blame the rise in prices in foreign countries for the rise in prices at home, and this explanation has, as a matter of fact, been vigorously exploited in the official doctrine in various countries. When, however, it is a question of countries with free paper currencies, this explanation is not feasible. Then, a rise in prices in a foreign country should have no other effect than that of the country's currency being quoted so much lower that the prices on goods imported therefrom remain unaltered. If the influence of the rise in foreign prices is carried further, it is a sign that it has found support in an independent domestic inflation.

When a country has depreciated its own currency, prices of foreign currencies have naturally been forced up thereby. This increase in the value of the foreign currencies has then been taken as an explanation of the rise in prices within the country. This extraordinary confusion of ideas has been only gradually seen through by the uncritical public. It is clear, however, that a rise in the price of the currency of country B can never be a reason for a rise in prices in country A, so long as the exchange rate is a true expression for the relative

purchasing power of both currencies. Only if the B
currency were quoted above the purchasing power parity,
and in that sense were overvalued, could the high price
of this currency have any influence to raise the prices
in country A. But even this influence would not be
able to raise the general price level unless it had the
support of a more plentiful supply of means of payment—
i.e., of an inflation. If, for example, the German exchange is now internationally undervalued, then the high
prices of foreign currencies will tend to make the imports
which Germany requires more expensive and, in so far
as the internal supply of means of payment is adjusted
to this price increase, these high prices of foreign currencies will also contribute to a general rise in prices
within the country. This simply means that the undervaluation of a country's currency has a certain tendency
to correct itself, *inter alia*, by means of the price level
within the country being raised so that the purchasing
power parity is brought nearer the actual exchange rate.
However, disregarding those cases where an overvalua-
tion or an undervaluation of a country's currency takes
place, and, further, presupposing that the exchange rates
correspond to the purchasing power parities, we see that
it is impossible to accept the circumstance that foreign
exchanges have a higher price now than before the War
as being responsible for the price level in the home
country having been forced up.

A basis of explanation akin to the above has been the
increased difficulties of import. The view has been held
that the increased freights, other countries' export prohibitions, and the belligerents' blockade measures, must
have enhanced the prices on imported commodities and
thereby contributed to the rise of the general price level
within the country. This explanation has certainly,
more than any other, been viewed by the general public

as self-evident and indisputable. Nevertheless, it is obvious that all difficulties of import can only have had the effect of aggravating the scarcity of commodities. Had the supply of means of payment within the country been adjusted to the increased scarcity of commodities, no rise in prices would have been necessitated. Supposing the supply of means of payment to be unaltered, we have to reckon with a rise in prices proportionate to the scarcity of commodities. The real influence of this scarcity has been dealt with more closely in a previous chapter.

RELATIONS TO EARLIER THEORIES ON THE EXCHANGES

We must now take a backward glance at the development of the theory of exchanges and explain the relation in which the representation here given stands to the earlier scientific analysis of the exchange problem, as also to the general theory of money which I have developed in earlier works.

The first theory of exchanges of a scientific character was probably that given by Ricardo in the chapter on foreign trade in his work, "Principles of Political Economy." The subject which interests him, however, is not directly the exchanges, but the distribution of the precious metals in the case of free commercial intercourse between the nations and the different value of money dependent thereupon in the different countries. By the value of money, therefore, he means the purchasing power of gold (or silver) against commodities. At an earlier stage in the history of the community, says Ricardo (p. 82 of McCulloch's edition), when every country's products are much alike, the value of money in the various countries is principally regulated by their distance from the mines from which the precious metals are derived; but at a more advanced stage, when different nations win the advantage in particular manufactures, the value of the precious metals mainly comes to be regulated by pre-eminence in these manufactures. If England and Poland both only produce grain and products comparable thereto in respect of transport, then

Poland, which lies further away from the gold countries than England does, and which must consequently send its products a longer distance in order to procure gold, will be worse off for this metal than England. Gold will therefore have a higher value in Poland than in England—that is to say, the price level will be higher in England than in Poland. If, however, Poland should succeed in producing a commodity which was much sought after and which possessed a high value in a small volume, then Poland would obtain an increased quantity of gold in exchange for this commodity, and the commodity prices in Poland would then rise. The difference in the distance to the gold countries would probably be more than compensated for by the advantage of possessing an exportable product of high value, and money would come to possess a permanently lower value in Poland than in England. If, conversely, England had the advantage in capability and machinery, that would constitute an additional reason, apart from the question of proximity to the gold countries, for gold being less valuable in England than in Poland and for the price level in England being higher. The difference in the value of money will not find its expression in the exchange rate; bills can still be quoted at par, although prices are 10, 20, or 30 per cent. higher in the one country than in the other.

Already from these extracts from Ricardo's proposition we find that what he is discussing, according to our manner of expressing ourselves, is the case of two countries having the same metallic currency. If we can disregard the costs of transport of the metal from the one country to the other (and, strictly speaking, also all expenses connected with the conversion of the one currency into the other), then the exchange rate will be at par. It can then be no question of a theory of exchanges. Analysis will concentrate instead on the position of the price level in the

different countries. It is thus manifestly true that the
price level must be higher in that country which finds
it easier to export its products, whether this is due to its
products being particularly in demand in other countries
or on their being easy to transport. This result coincides
with what has been previously observed as to the deviation
of an exchange rate from the purchasing power parity in
a case where the transporting of commodities from the
one country to the other is rendered more difficult in
the one direction than in the other. If the obstacles
placed by freightage in the way of trade between the
two countries are less as regards exports from the one
country than as regards exports from the other country,
then the exchange rate can remain at its metal parity,
in spite of the higher price level of the first-mentioned
country. The higher price level compensates for the
advantage in respect of export, so that a balance is
reached.

This is also Ricardo's argument. He further develops
it in his chapter on the taxation of wages (p. 138). If
trade in precious metals is entirely free and money can
be exported without charges of any kind, then the
exchanges must remain at par. On the basis of this
argument Ricardo finally draws various conclusions which
in reality contain much of what a true theory of exchanges
should contain. But his results naturally come to be
expressed in a different form. One has to bear this in
mind when studying Ricardo, especially if comparisons
are to be drawn between the conclusions Ricardo comes
to and those which are the result of a direct investigation
of the exchanges.

Ricardo emphasises the point (p. 138) that if a country
has adopted a paper standard its exchange rates may
deviate from par in the same proportion as the quantity
of its currency is increased beyond the amount which

would be retained by the country if it had a metal standard and trade in that metal were free. Ricardo means that the increased quantity of currency would cause a corresponding rise in the price level: If England, by introducing a paper standard or by depreciating its metallic currency, were to get 20 million pounds in circulation instead of 10 million, then all prices would be doubled and the exchange rate would be at 50 per cent. against England. By this is clearly meant that an inflation of money must bring about a fall in the international value of the currency proportional to the reduction in its internal purchasing power. Ricardo further proves that the assumed rise in prices in England would not imply any obstacle to export; indeed, the higher prices would be compensated for in the case of the foreign buyer by the lower exchange rate on England (p. 139). These observations are made by Ricardo, however, as being a side issue of the subject. His main interest lies in showing that, with a metal standard and exchange at par, each country receives by virtue of its foreign trade a certain definite quantity of money, and that the value of the money, or what we call the general price level, may vary in the different countries in consequence of the different supply of money available. If the sending of money from one country to another involves certain charges, the exchange rate may deviate from par. Within certain limits, therefore, fluctuations in the exchange rate are possible. But these fluctuations are an independent factor and have nothing to do with the purchasing power of money in different countries. It is therefore quite natural for Ricardo to draw the following conclusion, which he formulates on p. 84: " When we speak of the exchange rate and the relative value of money in different countries, we must not have in mind the value of money in relation to commodities in any of those countries. The exchange rate is never determined by the relative value of money in relation to grain, cloth, or any other commodities, but by the value of one currency in relation to another." It is not at all to be wondered at that a conclusion thus formulated outwardly offers fairly violent opposition to the conclusion one comes to when studying the exchange rate between two countries, each possessing an independent paper standard.

Ricardo's representation of the subject is influenced by the historical conditions under which he wrote. It was still in his time a moot question whether the English currency during the Napoleonic Wars was depreciated or not. It was natural that the study of the currency problem should primarily be directed to a study of the metal currencies, and that a paper currency would thus be regarded simply and solely as a deviation from the normal state of affairs. At any rate Ricardo clearly did not think he had any reason, in the course of his studies of the problem, to proceed from the assumption of a system of independent paper currencies. Besides, at a time when freightage was so heavy in proportion to the value of commodities, as was still the case at the beginning of the nineteenth century, the difference in the purchasing power of money in different countries, caused by differences in transport charges, must naturally come to the fore as an essential element in the currency problem.

For those desirous at the present day of studying the currency question the material conditions are quite different. Since all countries have been reduced to paper standards, and since up to the present only one, the United States, has resumed a gold standard, it is natural to choose a system of free paper standards as the primary subject of our investigation. It is also natural now to give the freightage between countries a secondary place in the investigation. In my earlier expositions of the theory of international exchanges I have therefore started from the consideration of two countries standing in lively and extensive commercial relations with one another and having no freightage or customs duties between them, so that the costs of transporting commodities from one to the other are practically nil. We then arrive at the result that the exchange rate between the countries is determined by the quotient of the purchasing power of money in either country. I have thus endeavoured to take as my starting-point a case where the conditions are so simple that the fundamental cause underlying the value of the exchange rate is immediately apparent, and a theoretical calculation of the exchange rate is possible. Strictly speaking, such a calculation cannot even then be worked out, for the reason that we have no exact common measure for the price level in the two countries. We can, of course, assume that a certain representative quantity of commodities must cost the same in both countries, if the exchange rate between their currencies stands at its equilibrium. But this statement is exact only provided one and the same quantity of commodities can be considered representative of the total quantity of commodities turned over in either country. This is naturally the case if both countries have practically identical conditions of production. But then, again, no trade can take place between the two countries as long as the exchange rate stands at its equilibrium. An exchange rate can, of course, still exist, as travellers between the two countries need to exchange the one currency for the other.

If we are to get nearer to reality we must give up any attempt at directly calculating the exchange rate between two countries with given conditions of production and trade, but must instead start from a given equilibrium at a time when the exchange rate is presumed to be known, and on the basis of this rate calculate that rate which corresponds to the same equilibrium if an inflation of the currencies has taken place without any change having otherwise occurred. This method, which I have always applied in my treatment of the present currency problem, is clearly both justified and natural in an investigation primarily concerned with explaining the causes of the alterations which the exchanges have undergone after a given date at which they are assumed to have represented a normal equilibrium.

Writers who, after Ricardo, have treated the exchanges generally adopt Ricardo's representation of the problem as their starting-point and build on the foundations which he laid. They assume the case of two countries with the same metallic standard. The equilibrium of the exchange rate is then given by the metallic parity, and thus the investigation can only concern the different position of the price level in the different countries. According to Stuart Mill the price level in any country is determined by that country's ability to buy its imports, and particularly the precious metals, at a low value ("Principles of Political Economy," book iii., chapter xxi., para. 3). Even in the case of the same metal standard, however, a certain variation in the exchange rate is possible. The limits of this variation are set by the points where an export or import of the metal begins to pay—that is to say, by the "gold points," if the metal in question is gold. The problem is then to find out the factors which, within these limits, determine the exchange rate. Mostly, people, in discussing this problem, have been content to refer to the effect of supply and demand in the market for foreign bills. Foreign means of payment, just like any other commodity, must have a price determined by the situation of the market. Mill devotes some lines to an analysis of this market, and points out that a deviation of the exchange rate from par affects international trade in a direction which must counteract the deviation, and thus represents a corrective to it. He also points out that granting credit involves a possibility of payments being postponed, and this naturally alters the situation on the market.

A paper currency is regarded even by Mill merely as a depreciated metal standard. The actual exchange rate in the case of such a depreciated currency is the result of two factors: the "real" rate, which follows the alterations in the balance of payment, and the "nominal" rate, which is determined by the amount of the depreciation of the currency below its metal parity (book iii., chapter xxii., para. 3).

Goschen, in his work "The Theory of the Foreign Exchanges" (third edition, 1864) largely adopts the same point of view as his contemporary Mill. The principal subject for consideration is the exchange rate between two countries with the same metal standard. A depreciation of the currency causes a premium on gold, and prices on foreign bills rise in proportion to this premium in exactly the same way as prices on any other purchasable article (p. 102).* If, however, gold cannot be sent as means of payment, this ground for determination does not exist. Prices of foreign currencies will then depend entirely on supply and demand; if the demand for bills exceeds the supply, theoretically there is no limit whatever to the price of bills (p. 74; *cf*. pp. 71–72). Goschen

---

* With every issue of inconvertible money a progressive rise, proportionate to the depreciation of the currency, would un-avoidably take place (p. 101).

The bills of a given country fluctuate in value in proportion to the extent to which the prices of all purchasable articles—bullion included—are affected by the depreciation of the currency (p. 69).

seems, therefore, to have been of the opinion that the problem in this case is undetermined. Thus he has hardly undertaken an exposition of a theory of exchanges between free paper currencies.

In the case of currencies maintained at their metal parity, the exchange rate is determined, according to Goschen, by the balance of payment—that is to say, by the supply of and demand for bills. But the balance of payment is itself affected by the granting of credit, which in its turn is necessarily affected by the interest rates. The study of the effect of money interest upon the immediate balance of payment, and thereby upon the exchanges, seems to represent Goschen's most important contribution to the solution of the exchange problem.

The popular conception of the problem has in a great measure been governed by the idea that the exchanges are determined by supply and demand, and that the whole problem is exhausted by this simple statement. This view of the question has been pronounced self-evident, as something requiring no further examination, and the door has thereby been closed to any deeper insight into the true nature of the problem. People have stopped at the formula: If there are more buyers than sellers of foreign exchange, the rates must rise. But how this rise in the rates can remedy the disproportion between supply and demand people have not deemed it necessary to think out. Still it is clear that equilibrium must be effected, and that the manner in which this is done is of fundamental importance for the exchange problem. We have to find out by what means equilibrium may be attained, and especially, of course, what rôle the exchange rates themselves play in this respect. Even in the question of how the price of a commodity is determined, a simple reference to " supply and demand " is an entirely unsatisfactory answer. It is not sufficient to say that the price of a commodity rises if the demand for it exceeds the supply. Equilibrium must be attained, and the price has the function of limiting the demand, or stimulating the supply, so much that the demand can be satisfied by the supply. It is by this condition that the price becomes determined. In the theory of exchanges it is a matter of finding out how the corresponding machinery functions with regard to the regulation of the market for foreign exchanges.

Thus a rational theory of exchanges must start from the condition that a steady equilibrium exists in a country's balance of payment towards other countries, and in the first place the question arises: By what means can such an equilibrium be maintained? In my lectures on money I have for many years put the problem in that way, and my representation of this side of the exchange problem, as given in " Theoretische Sozialökonomie " (§§ 60 to 62), contains a summary of the results I have arrived at along these lines. We find that occasional deviations from the even balance of payment call forth counteracting forces which restore the equilibrium. This takes place automatically, for the simple reason that engagements to pay, as they fall due, must be fulfilled somehow. Even so, a dislocation of the exchange rate from the normal position can take place; but so long as the normal position itself is not disturbed this dislocation is usually quite limited. Its effect is always an intensification of those reacting factors which produce equilibrium in the balance of payment.

The theory of exchanges, however, has quite another side, which altogether escapes attention when the problem is considered only from the point of view of the effect of supply of, and demand for, foreign money. I allude to the question of how the normal position itself is determined. The question cannot be cleared up unless we go further and answer the question why a certain price is paid for a foreign currency. A generally applicable reply to this question can only be given if we keep in mind a system of free paper currencies. Only a theory which has been built upon such a broad basis could serve as a starting-point for an explanation of the revolution in the international exchanges brought about by the War. Here it was primarily a question of profound internal alterations in the values of the currencies—alterations which must also be reflected in dislocations of the exchanges far more extensive than the ordinary fluctuations round a fixed equilibrium. The nature of these alterations could obviously best be judged by proceeding from a theory of money which saw in the purchasing power of money against commodities the basis of the value of money.

Even since 1904 I had built up the whole theory of money on the conception of money as an abstract scale of counting, in which certain means of payment—they may be of any physical quality whatsoever—have current paying power, and where the value of the unit is determined by the scarcity of the community's provision with these means of payment. I had thereby abandoned the untenable popular conception of a gold standard as a standard in which a certain weight quantity of gold is the unit of value, and I had in place of that represented the gold standard as a free standard in which the price of gold within certain narrow limits is fixed. This had led up to the idea of the gold standard being a special case of free standards. For the theory of exchanges this had the consequence that the representation commenced with the case of free independent standards, and that the problem of exchanges in a gold standard was to be conceived as a special case of the general problem. For such a theory of exchanges it was evident that the actual reason for certain prices being paid for foreign currencies must be found in these foreign currencies having a certain purchasing power as against commodities. I had thus arrived at the general conception of the nature of the problem of exchanges, which is expressed in " Theoretische Sozialökonomie " in the following words: " The reason why bills on B are in demand in the country A is that they represent purchasing power on B's market. This purchasing power will obviously be valued higher, on the one hand, the lower the general price level stands in the country B—in other words, the higher the value of money is in that country—and, on the other hand, the higher the general price level stands in A itself."

This fundamental view of the problem proved particularly useful when it was necessary to find one's bearings amidst the violent disturbances in the established exchanges which the War occasioned. It was a long time before the public properly realised that the gold standard was really done away with, and that what we had to deal with was, therefore, a system of free paper standards with no internal connection with one another. Consequently a long time also elapsed before the truth entered into the public mind that there was no fundamental cause underlying the values of the separate currencies other than the limitation of those means of payment recognised as valid in each particular standard. It was a very slow process paving the way for a conception of the new exchange rates as an expression primarily for those new relations between the internal values of the currencies which the different degrees of depreciation of money brought about. Right from the very beginning of the War, however, my efforts at solving the exchange problem have been along these lines. The idea that the new exchange rates must essentially be determined by the dislocation of the old exchange rates, which must be a consequence of the different degrees of inflation the various currencies underwent, is further developed in certain works which I published in 1916 and 1917. What I then called the "theoretical exchange rate" corresponds exactly to the idea denoted by the term "purchasing power parity," which I later introduced. During the first years of the War the only available price index was that for England. Elsewhere, as, for instance, in Sweden and Russia, the degree of inflation could be judged according to the increase in the note circulation. But otherwise I had to calculate this degree of inflation with the help of the actual exchange rates, and with the use of the known figures regarding the rise of prices in England. Later on, the calculation of price indexes becoming more universal, it was possible to establish independently the height of the general price level in different countries, and thus to make a real calculation of the purchasing power parities, though, owing to the nature of the material available, this was somewhat uncertain. By placing the actual exchange rates beside the purchasing power parities thus obtained, it has also been possible to establish the amount of any deviations from the purchasing power parities that may have taken place.

The actual term "purchasing power parity" I introduced at a later date (*cf.* my article, "Abnormal Deviations in International Exchanges," in the *Economic Journal*, December, 1918).

Although this term has attained by now fairly general use in economic literature in different languages, a theory of exchanges which primarily judges the exchange rates by the alterations which the internal purchasing power of the currencies has undergone has hardly yet fully penetrated the public consciousness. Even when people have gone so far as to declare the whole theory to be self-evident, or else want to assert that they have entertained the same conception of the exchange problem all along, more often than not it transpires that the conditions on which the theory must rest, or the limitations to which it is necessarily subject, have not been fully realised, nor are its consequences thoroughly grasped, as, for instance, with regard to the influence of exchanges on international trade. Sometimes, too, the theory is urged so far as to become pure dogma, the very possibility of exchanges deviating from the purchasing power parity being denied. In opposition to such a point of view, I would express the opinion that it is necessary constantly to follow the actual development, and to see how far it is in accordance with the main lines of a rational theory of exchanges, as here expounded, or whether further factors come in which require special analysis.

On the other hand, there still exists stubborn opposition to the theory of the dependence of the exchange rates on the purchasing power parities. People firmly adhere to the vague theory of supply and demand, or content themselves with declaring that the whole situation is so unclear, and is influenced by so many factors, that it is impossible to know anything with any certainty !

As a rule these views appear in such a vague and confused form that any criticism of them involves the difficulty of finding definite points of attack, and is, therefore, not very profitable. However, even a false idea is capable of making very valuable contributions towards arriving at the solution of a doubtful question, if the idea proceeds from a trained thinker. An unusually good example of this is offered by the proposition on the exchange problem which Mr. Keynes gives in passing in his latest work, " The Revision of the Treaty " (p. 93).

Keynes maintains the old idea that the exchange rate is
determined by the balance of payment, and consistently
therewith represents a fall of the international valuation
of a currency as a result of supply exceeding demand. It
is hard to understand how he can hold to this idea, when
he even emphasises the statement which is the basis of
every rational theory of money, that there must exist
equilibrium between sale and purchase, and that, too,
as he says, for every day (see note on p. 95). However,
Keynes declares that when the international value of a
currency falls in consequence of an internal inflation, it is
owing to inflation, by strengthening the purchasing power
within the country, bringing about an increase in imports
(or alternatively a reduction in exports) which disturbs
the equilibrium of the balance of payment, thus raising
the prices of foreign currency. Such a point of view
cannot be accepted. The increased purchasing power
within the country represents purchasing power increased
outwards only, so long as the corresponding lowering of
the international valuation of the country's currency
has not yet had time to be affected. Keynes' assertion
rests upon the assumption that the internal fall in value
always precedes the external. Experience offers hardly
any support to such an assumption. It seems to be at
least equally usual for the sequence to be reversed. We
must manifestly claim this of our exchange theory, that
it shall explain the alterations in the exchange rate,
both in the one case and in the other, and more especially in the case where the international valuation closely
follows the alterations in the internal value of the currency,
as indeed it must do, provided no particularly disturbing
factors intervene. On the last-mentioned assumption
there must obtain, day by day, complete equilibrium on
the exchange market, and still the constant inflation
will bring about a constant lowering of the international

valuation of the currency. Then the possibility of reference to a preponderating number of sales is precluded, and we are compelled to realise the gist of the exchange problem, out of which the whole of the present enquiry has proceeded—namely, that the international value of a currency is primarily determined by its quality—that is to say, by its internal purchasing power.

In those quarters where special interest is paid to the restoration of the gold standard people have sometimes conceived the doctrine of determining exchange rates by the purchasing power parities, as if it were in some way opposed to the principle after which the exchange rates between gold currencies are normally determined, and, therefore, also to a certain extent as opposed to the whole idea of striving to restore a gold standard. Of course, no such opposition exists. It is impossible to revert to the old gold standard without the purchasing power of money, in the different countries which do so, being restored to the same proportions as those which obtained before the War. The re-establishment of a constant exchange rate between countries with a gold standard does not depend primarily upon these countries possessing a gold standard, but upon the purchasing power of their currencies being kept on a certain level adjusted to the gold standard. Thus the fundamental condition for fixed exchange rates, even in a gold standard, is a fixed ratio between the internal purchasing powers of the currencies. A country desirous of keeping to a certain gold standard, therefore, will find itself compelled to keep to a certain definite purchasing power in its currency, and the chief significance of the gold standard really lies in this, that in a manner that is at once apparent it confronts those responsible for the country's monetary policy with this necessity. If the currency's purchasing power as against commodities should fall considerably below what it ought to be, then demands for gold must arise, since gold, at any rate in the rest of the gold countries, still retains its purchasing power as against commodities. Against such demands for gold accumulated gold reserves are of no use whatever. The redemption of the country's currency with gold can in the long run only be sustained if the purchasing power of the currency is kept at its equilibrium. Thus the possibility of returning to the old gold standard or of adopting a new and lower gold standard depends on the level at which the internal value of the country's currency can be stabilised in relation to the purchasing power of the gold currencies—that is to say, for the present, the purchasing power of the dollar. The stabilisation of the purchasing power—i.e., of the general price level—cannot be avoided; the exchange rates will always be primarily dependent upon the internal purchasing power given to the currencies. It is a thoroughly false idea that the gold standard would in any way free us from the necessity for such an administration of credit, and in particular of bank rates, as will enable a definite purchasing power in the country's currency to be maintained. On the contrary, such administration of a country's monetary system under normal circumstances is an inevitable condition for the maintenance of a gold standard. It is of importance that full light be thrown on this point when we enter upon a closer study of the problem of restoring normal monetary conditions in the world.

INFLATION AFTER THE WAR

ACCORDING to the prevailing theory, the rise in prices was only to be regarded as a result of the War, and it was thus to be expected that the armistice would have been followed by a reduction in prices. When normal conditions returned, the price level should, strictly speaking, go back to its pre-War standard. This has been the general opinion as to the future development. Indeed, to begin with, a general, though very moderate, downward movement of the price levels actually occurred, if we disregard countries completely ruined; but this movement lasted only a few months. During the course of 1919 renewed inflation appears everywhere, forcing up the price level, in some countries far beyond the maximum previously reached.

In Sweden the fall in the price level was comparatively considerable. The index of wholesale prices, which during the War reached a maximum of 370 (October, 1918), rose after a slight fall in November to 372 for December, 1918. During 1919 there takes place a gradual decline to a minimum of 307 reached in October. But after that begins a new rise in prices, bringing the price level up to a maximum of 366 for June, 1920, which is practically the same as that for the month of the armistice, but somewhat lower than the previous maximum figure. Here is manifestly a process of pure inflation which absolutely cannot be accounted for by any references to the peculiar difficulties of the War period.

In England the reduction of prices was of still shorter duration. From 231 for November, 1918, the price level goes down to a minimum of 212, reached as early as March, and from the second half of 1919 the index number (all this according to the *Economist:* the figures being reduced to 1913=100) is considerably above any reached during the War. The rise in prices continues until the spring of 1920: the *Economist* shows a maximum for March of 310, and the *Statist* a maximum for April of 313.

In the United States the decline in prices is only slight. The index number (according to the Bureau of Labor) falls from a maximum of 206 for November, 1918, to 197 for February, 1919—*i.e.*, by less than 5 per cent., but rises again to 207 for May and June, with which the index number for the month of the armistice is thus again reached. By July the figure is already 219, and after that takes place a rise in prices which brings the index number far above the pre-War maximum. The highest point is reached in May, 1920, with the figure 272.

In France and Italy, after some slight fall in prices during 1919, a very violent rise occurs. The new maximum for France is reached in April, 1920, with the figure 588, as against 366 for November, 1918, but in Italy not until November, 1920, with the figure 670, as against 409 as the average for 1918.

Generally speaking, the fall in prices was scarcely greater than would probably be caused by the improvement in the supply of commodities, which was the result of the restoration of free international communications. In the case of Sweden this factor has been of special importance, as Sweden's supply of commodities during the latter part of the War was particularly restricted. As to other countries, the fall in prices hardly amounts to more than 5 to 10 per cent., and may therefore well

be accounted for by a more plentiful supply of commodities. Ultimately, of course, the discount. policy
has determined the movements of the price level during
this period also. So long as the idea prevailed in the
public mind that peace would necessarily bring with it
a fall in prices, and make sellers more ready to dispose
of their stocks, while holding buyers back, a fall in prices
was possible even with a relatively low bank rate. If,
however, we want to find out how it was that the price
level in Sweden during 1919 went down so much more
than it did in England, we cannot overlook the fact that
the Swedish Riksbank kept its discount rate at 7 per
cent. up to the 24th April, then at $6\frac{1}{2}$ per cent. up to
the 12th June, and from the 13th June at 6 per cent.,
while during the whole of that time England maintained
a rate of 5 per cent., and not until the 6th November
went up to 6 per cent. That the obviously far too low
discount rates of the Bank of England during 1919 proved
exceptionally effective first by restraining the tendency
of prices to fall, and then as a powerful factor in causing
a rise in prices, is as indisputable a fact as it is instructive.

The new rise in prices which takes place during 1919
and reaches a climax in the course of 1920 has altogether
the character of a new inflation. As to the causes of
this inflation, we must first of all remember the waste that
went on everywhere in State administration. During
the War politicians had got used to the idea that the
Treasury had inexhaustible resources, and it was hard
to rid oneself of such an idea at a period when such
extraordinary demands were made upon State finances
from all quarters. The many public needs set back
during the War demanded urgent attention, without
much regard being paid to the possibility of procuring
means to satisfy them. Expenditure was covered either
directly, by having recourse to the banks, or by taking

up loans which the banks were to a great extent called
upon to effect, or, again, by means of taxation, which
likewise involved a continued creation of bank currency.
In particular business enterprises were called upon to
pay enormous taxes, but their liquidity had become more
and more unsatisfactory, so that they had to have
recourse to bank credit on a large scale to enable them
to pay their taxes.

The democratic advance which was a result of the War
has shown in all countries a tendency to increase State
expenditure. It naturally takes some time before the
new elements making for power succeed in gaining an
adequate knowledge of the real economic situation so
that they may be induced to exercise the necessary
restraint in the matter of expenditure. England gradually managed to cut down very considerably the building
programme, which far exceeded the country's financial
powers, and even in other respects succeeded in reducing
to more reasonable proportions demands which reluctantly
acquiesced in limiting within the bounds of what was
economically possible the carrying out of schemes
previously promised to the public. In other countries
with a less strongly developed tradition for sound economy
the necessary limitation of calls on the public purse has
been more difficult to effect. It has naturally been most
difficult in countries where a political revolution has
taken place. The revolutions in Europe after the War
have everywhere involved an inflation which has more
or less placed the earlier war-time inflation in the shade.
That this was so in the case of the Russian revolution
is obvious to anyone, but it concerns also to a serious
extent other countries where a revolution with similar
tendencies got the upper hand for any length of time.
The figures denoting the inflation in Hungary and Finland are instructive on this point. In Germany the

revolution provoked an increase in the quantity of notes far exceeding that required by the War. But in this case the unprecedented extortions of the victorious Powers have so largely contributed to the unsound increase in State expenditure that it can never be worked out exactly what significance either of these factors has had. For the end of February, 1914, we can reckon the total circulation at 5·27 milliards of marks. Germany probably had five times this amount by the beginning of October, 1918—that is to say, immediately before her final defeat. After that the figure was already ten times greater by February, 1920, and fifteen times greater by April, 1921. Thereafter the pace was still further increased, so that by the end of the same year the circulation was already twenty times greater. It seems clear that the Allies' demands on Germany during this last phase is the one predominating cause of this excessive inflation.

If we disregard those countries whose State finances have been completely ruined by the War and its consequences, we can more easily discover what causes other than the demands of State finance were decisive in bringing about a revival of inflation during 1919. One factor of very general significance has been the craving for raw materials and food which was universally felt after the scanty conditions under which people had been living before. As soon as vessels were available there began a vigorous importation of raw materials. There was apparently a general idea that there would be an unprecedented scarcity of commodities, and that it was worth while paying any amount in order to be assured of getting what one wanted. In consequence of this prices for certain groups of commodities were forced up to a level which far exceeded that reached during the War. Thus the index numbers of the *Economist* (referred to 100 for 1913) show very considerable rises during the latter part of 1919 and throughout 1920. For the group including grain and meat the index number for 1918 was 216, but rose afterwards to a maximum of 267, reached in October, 1920; for textiles the index number for 1918 was 284, but rose afterwards to a maximum of 465 for March, 1920; for minerals the 1918 index number was 166, but by October, 1920, had reached 252; the group of sundry commodities, which *inter alia* includes timber, showed a rise from 231 for 1918 to 290 for March, 1920. We find similar conditions if we consider the rise in prices in the United States; here, too, the highest price increase reached was in the case of textiles, which as early as 1918 had risen to 239, but continued to rise right up to 356 in February, 1920; while for timber and building material the prices rose from 151 in 1918 to a maximum of 341 in April, 1920. In Sweden the prices for food and agricultural requisites had already risen so high during 1918 that only insignificant further rises could take place. On the other hand, the price index for coal and coke rose to 1,252 in June, 1920, as against an average of 856 for 1918; the index number for pulp rose to 788 in May, 1920, as against an average of 300 for 1918.

The keen competition for commodities which prevailed on the world market, particularly during the latter half of 1919 and the first half of 1920, is clearly seen in the exceptional increase in import figures both in the case of the European countries and of the United States. As for Sweden, imports on the whole showed a considerable increase in comparison with 1913. This increase is best brought out if the value of imports is calculated at the 1913 prices and is expressed in percentage of the value of the 1913 imports. Such a calculation is being made at the present time by the Commercial Board

(Stockholm) on the basis of foreign trade statistics, which, however, do not embrace the whole of foreign trade. The index number we thus arrive at lies in the beginning of 1919 considerably below 100, but reaches that figure by May. Thereafter it remains well over 100 for all months up to September, 1920, with the exception of November, 1919. The index number reaches its maximum in July, 1919, with 181. The average index number for 1919 is 109·2, and for 1920, 123·4. For 1920 the value of the whole of Sweden's imports amounted to 3373·5 million kronor, whereas exports were only 2293·6 million kronor, so that there was an enormous surplus of imports amounting to 1079·9 million kronor.

An index number calculated by a similar method for the foreign trade of the United States (*Federal Reserve Bulletin*) shows that the imports for both 1919 and 1920 were somewhat above 171, as compared with 100 for 1913; for August, 1919, and for the first four months of 1920, the imports were considerably more than double the normal quantity, and the maximum was reached in March, 1920, with the figure 247·2. The increase in exports was relatively far smaller. The balance of trade, however, was the whole time favourable to the United States, but exports went on such a large scale to Europe that the balance of trade with other parts of the world showed a deficit. This was particularly the case with regard to South America and the Far East. In payment for the excess of imports from these countries the United States had to ship gold and silver. The net exports of gold to South America during 1919 amounted to 87 million dollars, and during 1920 to 94 million dollars. The net export of gold to the Far East amounted in 1919 to 205 million dollars and in 1920 to 156 million dollars; to this, however, must be added a net export of silver of 199 million dollars in 1919, and 92 million dollars in

13

1920. During 1919, therefore, the net export of precious metals from the United States to the Far East rose to 404 million dollars. The figures give a good idea of the abnormal extent of the United States' imports of commodities from the parts of the world in question.

None of the grounds of explanation just mentioned, however, suffices for a true explanation of the general rise in prices that took place after the War. Without a corresponding increase in the supply of means of payment neither the increased demands of State finance nor the hunt after commodities would have succeeded in producing this general rise in prices, which in its very essence, in this as in all cases, is a monetary phenomenon.

The different countries' provision of nominal purchasing power has been determined by the general credit policy of their respective central banks, and particularly, of course, by their discount policy. One would think that the price-raising tendencies here under discussion in conjunction with the violent speculation which everywhere followed as a consequence of these tendencies, and, as far as European countries are concerned, the extremely dangerous development of the trade balance, must have proved for the central banks a sufficiently powerful motive for a vigorously restrictive discount policy. If ever the raising of the bank rate was called for it was certainly so in the spring of 1919, when, under such conditions as then prevailed, clear signs of a fresh expansion of credit began to appear. The Bank of England, however, as has been pointed out before, kept to the discount rate of 5 per cent., which had been introduced on the 5th April, 1917, for over two and a half years—in fact, right up to the 6th November, when the rate was raised to 6 per cent. This rate was in force up to the 15th April, 1920, when it was raised to 7 per cent. The Bank of France remained at 5 per cent. right up to the 8th April, 1920, when it raised its bank rate to 6 per cent. The Bank of Norway, which at the beginning of 1919 had a discount rate of 6 per cent., found by the 9th May, 1919, that the time had come to lower this discount rate to $5\frac{1}{2}$ per cent., which rate was kept up to the 18th December of the same year, when the 6 per cent. rate had to be resumed. The Danish National Bank had at the beginning of 1919 a discount of 5 per cent., which, however, was already raised by the 3rd January to $5\frac{1}{2}$ per cent., where it remained right up to the 7th October of the same year, when it was raised to 6 per cent. Sweden's Riksbank, which commenced the year with the reasonable rate of 7 per cent., as has previously been recorded, thought it proper to reduce its discount rate twice during 1919—namely, on the 25th April to $6\frac{1}{2}$ per cent., and on the 13th June to 6 per cent. Not until the 19th March, 1920, did the bank return to 7 per cent., while on the 17th September of the same year, when the commercial tide was already on the ebb, the bank raised its rate to $7\frac{1}{2}$ per cent. The Netherlands Bank kept its discount rate unaltered the whole time at $4\frac{1}{2}$ per cent., but on the 19th October, 1920, increased its interest on loans by 1 per cent.

It is plain from the above figures that the central banks of Europe judged the situation absolutely incorrectly. They did not come to realise the necessity of raising the discount rate until the far too generous provision of purchasing power had already brought about a new inflation which, in a way, went even further than the inflation during the War. Besides, the first hesitating steps towards raising the discount rate were insufficient for checking the rise in prices which had been set in motion. Obviously the prevailing doctrine of the ineffectiveness of the discount rate under the extraordinary conditions of the time contributed in large measure to the remarkable weakness of the central banks' attitude during this period. But this entire doctrine was to prove utterly false by the very inflation which resulted from the excessively low discount rate.

The discount policy has been carried out in precisely the same way in the United States. Right up to the late autumn of 1919 the Federal Reserve banks maintained a minimum discount rate of 4 per cent. This minimum rate was not brought up to $4\frac{1}{4}$ per cent. until November. It was thus not until the country had lost hundreds of millions of dollars in gold, and that too in a month when the price level had been forced up to 230, that it was considered time to proceed to raise the discount rate, and even then the rise of the minimum rate was confined to a modest $\frac{1}{4}$ per cent., whereas for certain other rates it reached $\frac{1}{2}$ per cent. The consequence of this belated tightening was that the discount later on had to be raised all the more vigorously. The New York Federal Reserve Bank, which during the whole of 1919 had maintained a discount rate for thirty to ninety days' commercial paper at $4\frac{3}{4}$ per cent., raised this rate to 6 per cent. on the 21st January, and to 7 per cent. on the 29th May, 1920. Thus these rises came just about two months later than the corresponding rises in London. The main portion of the discount pressure came in this way to be applied on the wrong side of the wave of prosperity, which actually reached its culminating point with the price level at 272 in May, 1920. To anyone reviewing the course of events in the United States during 1919 it is evident that the far too generous discount policy is ultimately responsible for the most serious inflation of the dollar currency which took place in the latter half of that year and the beginning of the following year. The cause of the Federal Reserve banks maintaining their manifestly too low discount rates, in spite of the very

obvious signs of a new inflation, is one connected with
State finance. This is expressly stated several times in
the official organ of the American central banks system,
the *Federal Reserve Bulletin*. What has characterised
the development since the end of June, 1919, as the July,
1920, number says on p. 662, is the attempt to prevent the
Federal Reserve banks' portfolio of Government securities
issued for war purposes from being augmented, and the
successful alteration of the discount rate from the low
stabilised level necessitated by war conditions to the
higher level corresponding to commercial conditions, and
reflecting the efforts of the system to control the expansion of credit and its corresponding endeavours to induce
its members to set a limit to excessive or non-essential
advances of funds. In a report laid before the Board of the
banks in October, 1919, it is declared that " the fact that
Government financing is on a descending scale seems not
to require such a degree of uniformity in Federal Reserve
bank rates as prevailed during the War, when the Liberty
Bond rate necessarily overshadowed all others and
practically dictated uniformity." In the editorial article
in the November, 1919, number it is said that the
Treasury's reduced demands on the market foreshadows
the approach of the time when the financial operations
of the Government will cease to be the important factor
in shaping Federal Reserve bank policies. A review of
all the conditions in the banking situation has confirmed
the Board in the view that in the application of its
discount policies an advance of rates should no longer
be deferred. It was this idea which led the Federal
Reserve banks in November, 1919, to raise the discount
rate, as mentioned above. In the editorial article for December, 1919, occurs the following passage: " The usual
method of restricting the undue use of the rediscounting
privilege is to advance rates. This policy would have

been put into operation several months ago, except for
its bearing upon Government financing." The Treasury
had sold more than 20 milliards of dollars' worth of
various war securities, and the banks had given loans
on the security of this paper with the consent of the
Federal Reserve Board. This fact " materially altered
the policy which would otherwise have been adopted by
the Board." The maintenance of a relatively low rate,
however, it goes on to say, in order to support *bona fide*
subscribers to Government bonds, gave an opportunity
for other borrowers to obtain funds for private purposes
at relatively low costs.

The common assumption that the bank rate had lost
its effectiveness under the abnormal conditions of the
time finds frequent expression in the *Federal Reserve
Bulletin*. These statements, however, cannot possibly
make much impression when placed side by side with
such admissions as have been quoted above. In its
review of the financial year that came to a close in June,
1920, the *Federal Reserve Bulletin* of July, 1920, further
directly states that " the general conclusion to be drawn
is unmistakably to the effect that the operation of credit
control through higher discount rates has had a marked
success." How far it would have been possible for the
Federal Reserve banks to raise their rates earlier to a
level required by the economic situation in the country
cannot be discussed here, as the question is one of the
political problems of war finance. But no observer who
judges the matter objectively can doubt that, if it had
been possible from a political point of view to effect a
sufficiently substantial rise in the discount rate immediately after the armistice, it would have effectively
prevented the rise in prices which afterwards took place.
The obviously far too low discount rate maintained
during the whole of 1919 has at any rate fully manifested

its effectiveness by the enormous rise in prices that was
its immediate result. The steps taken later to raise the
discount rate also proved effective, as we shall see, but
they were over a year too late, and therefore failed to
prevent the inflation which reached its climax in the
spring of 1920.

The all too weak discount policy adopted by the
United States has without doubt had a strong influence
upon Europe. As the internal value of the dollar was
so considerably reduced, the internal depreciation of the
European currencies in operation at the same time did
not stand out in so serious a light as it would otherwise
have done. In Europe it was possible with some success
to put the blame on " the international rise in prices "
and thereby detract public attention from the renewed
process of inflation which was going on. Further, with
a sound monetary policy in America, a policy which would
have maintained unaltered the internal value of the
dollar, the dollar exchange rates would have risen in
Europe in a far more disquieting way than was now the
case. Thus, even from that point of view, the monetary
policy of the United States during 1919 contributed
towards lulling Europe into a sense of security, which
was inevitably followed by a particularly rude awakening.

The new process of inflation also brought about a new
depression of the value of gold. From the outbreak of
the War until the 1st April, 1917—that is, about the time
when the United States entered the War—the gold stock
of the United States was increased in round figures by
1,200 million dollars. Between April, 1917, and June,
1919, the alteration in the gold stock was but slight, as
the import of gold from the Allies stopped when the
United States, after their entrance into the War, provided
their Allies with commodities on credit, and when, in the
autumn of 1917, export prohibition of gold was intro-

duced. The monetary gold stock of the United States is
given in the monetary statistics for the 1st June, 1919,
as 3,092 million dollars, as against 1,891 million dollars
for the 1st July, 1914.   Trade statistics show net imports
of gold from the 1st August, 1914, to the 10th June, 1919,
inclusive, at 1,101 million dollars.   When, on the 9th June,
1919, prohibition on gold exports was removed, the United
States were consequently especially well equipped to
withstand any possible loss of gold.   However, this loss
of gold proved, from the point of view of other countries,
very considerable.   For the remainder of the year the net
loss amounted to 321·3 million dollars.   During the first
quarter of 1920 an additional net loss of 102·8 million
dollars took place, so that the total net loss from the date
of the removal of the prohibition on the export of gold
up to the 1st April, 1920, amounted to 424 1 million
dollars.   As pointed out in a previous chapter, this heavy
loss of gold was mainly due to the enormous imports of
commodities from the Far East and South America.
Gold flowed in ever larger quantities from Europe, or else
from South Africa via Europe.   The total amount of gold
imports during 1919 and the first quarter of 1920 amounted
to 111·6 million dollars. The total export during the
same period, however, went up to 506 1 million dollars.
In 1919 an amount of 29·8 million dollars went to Spain.
But otherwise the export of gold has almost exclusively
served to pay for the United States' surplus imports from
the Far East and South America.   As against the considerable export of gold to Mexico there was a far heavier
import of silver from Mexico, and as this silver was also
exported to the Far East, the export of gold to Mexico
can likewise be regarded as having served to pay for the
surplus imports from the Far East.
   A supply of gold to these markets on such a scale as
the above could not but exercise strong pressure on the

value of gold, which naturally would cause a corresponding increase in the prices expressed in a gold currency.

In spite of the considerable reduction in the internal value of the dollar which took place during the period June, 1919, to May, 1920, the dollar nevertheless still retained a relatively higher value than the European currencies, which at the same time underwent a new inflation—in part even more violent than that which took place in America. The result was that gold was able to continue its migration from Europe to the United States. When, afterwards, the lively trade conditions no longer obtained in countries exporting raw material, and the world found itself fairly well provided with raw material, the gold export from the United States to those countries ceased. The balance of gold in the United States became fairly even during the middle of 1920. Thus, in spite of its falling internal value, the dollar had fully maintained its parity with gold. As, thanks to the enormous stock of gold previously accumulated, the United States were in a position to satisfy all gold requirements arising in the world, it was nowhere possible for gold, disregarding transport costs, to possess higher purchasing power than it did in the United States. In other words, the value of gold was depressed to the level at which it stood in America, and this value was determined by the value of the dollar. During this post-War inflation period the United States assumed a unique position which is really exceptionally striking. It is a singular phenomenon for a currency which, owing to an internal inflation, sinks in value thus to be able to draw down gold with it in its fall. And it is scarcely to be wondered at if the world had difficulty in at once realising exactly what was happening during the period of inflation with which we have just been dealing. In April and May, 1920, when the prices in England and America reached their highest level, the average quotations in London for fine gold were 105s. and 107s. 5d. respectively per ounce troy, which was certainly considerably above parity (84·96s.), but was nevertheless far less than earlier quotations had been, and was, therefore, not particularly disquieting. The fall in the value of gold, during this period just as much as during the War, seems to have caused the inflation in Europe to appear in a less serious light than it would otherwise have done.

REFORM PROGRAMMES

THE danger of a continued creation of artificial purchasing power has, of course, to some extent been observed everywhere during the inflation period, and the different means have been discussed which could conceivably render possible a return to more normal conditions. The first serious attempt, however, at shaping a real plan for the restoration of normal monetary conditions was probably made in England, where as early as January, 1918, the Cunliffe Committee was appointed to examine the different problems likely to arise during the period of reconstruction with regard to the currency of the country and foreign exchanges, and to recommend such measures as would be necessary for restoring normal conditions. On the 15th August, 1918, the Committee issued its first report, in which was evolved a comprehensive scheme for the adoption of measures considered necessary to re-establish in the country a sound monetary system. The main point of this scheme was that the gold standard must be restored without delay. For this purpose the Government should refrain from taking up fresh loans, and, if possible, also begin paying off its debts. Besides this, however, the Bank of England, by raising its discount rate and making it effective, would have to prevent the export of gold to abroad, and, further, all speculative expansion of credit.

The main interest of the Committee, however, was directed towards bringing about, by means of legislation, the restriction of the circulation not covered by gold reserves. To promote this object the Committee suggests in the first place accumulating as much gold as possible in the Bank of England. Therefore, an internal gold circulation must not be re-established, all banks, on the contrary, having to transfer their remaining gold reserves to the Bank of England. The normal minimum to be aimed at for the gold reserves is placed at 150 million pounds. Until this sum is reached, and has been successfully maintained for at least one year in a satisfactory situation for foreign exchanges, the uncovered note issue would have to be cautiously reduced. If by this means the uncovered note circulation was reduced in one year, its maximum for that year was to be fixed as the legal maximum for the following year, exceptions, however, being allowed to take place in case of necessity. The final fixing of the amount of uncovered note issue was not to take place until the exchanges proved to be functioning normally at a minimum gold reserve of 150 million pounds.

Towards the end of 1919 the Committee submitted its final report, in which it adhered to its original plan. The proposed rule for restriction of the uncovered note issue within a maximum corresponding to the maximum of the preceding year was immediately accepted, and has consequently been in force from 1920 inclusive. However, this restriction was rendered possible, at any rate at the beginning, mainly by increasing the gold reserves and not by reducing the total note circulation.

The average of paper circulation (Bank of England notes and currency notes) for January, 1918, amounted to 257·16 million pounds. In November it rose to 359·26, and in December to 382·16 million pounds. In January, 1919, the average circulation was 380·96 million pounds; in January, 1920, 421·95; and in January, 1921, 461·06 million pounds. The highest monthly average was reached for December, 1920, with 472·97 million pounds. In estimating this rise due account must, of course, be taken of the transfer of gold from the private banks to the Bank of England, as proposed by the Committee, and afterwards carried out. It may be considered beyond doubt, however, that the total circulation underwent a quite considerable real increase after the Committee issued its first report. In any case, as was shown in a previous chapter, the rise in prices went on, inasmuch as, according to the *Economist*, the price index rose from 227 in November, 1918, to a maximum of 310 for March, 1920 (100 for 1913 being taken as basis). That it was possible in spite of this to effect a considerable increase in the central gold reserves was due partly to the compulsory transfer of gold from the private banks, partly to the fact that the Cunliffe Committee's proposal to re-establish the effective gold standard was not carried out.

In the light of this experience the weakness of the Committee's report becomes quite apparent. It was all very well to urge the restoration of the gold standard, and the regulations by which the Committee hoped gradually to arrive at a fresh limit to the uncovered note contingent may in themselves have been well thought out. But for this ultimately more formal side of the question the Committee had failed to devote close attention to the far more important problem as to how a fall in the general price level could be brought about, and what would be the consequences of such a depression of prices for the industrial life of the country, as well as for the State finances. Nor has the Committee fully brought out the international character of the problem. It has not sufficiently emphasised the all-important fact that the value of gold was depressed by the general inflation. Its statements as to the extent of the English inflation are, therefore, somewhat vague, and it has not adequately explained how far a reduction in the general price level would be necessary for the restoration of the gold standard. This question could not be answered unless at the same time the development of prices in the United States was taken into consideration, and consequently a deliberate policy aiming at the restoration of the English gold standard was not possible without the co-operation of the United States. It is true that the Cunliffe Committee expressed the opinion (on p. 9 of its first report) that " it is probable that after the War world prices will stand for many years, if not permanently, at a greatly enhanced level." This prophecy evidently implies that the value of gold would remain low, but the Committee did not enter upon any close analysis of the import of this prophecy nor, indeed, of the factors which would determine the future purchasing power of gold. Neither seems the danger of an unnecessarily increased competition for gold between the central banks to have been predominant in the mind of the Committee as the fundamental feature of the problem of restoring the gold standard which it has in reality proved to be.

The deflation programme of the Cunliffe Committee was, by its very nature, primarily a programme concerned with State finances. How great are the difficulties which the fulfilment of this programme would necessarily involve has recently been represented in an English financial organ (Barclay's Bank *Monthly Review*, December, 1921, p. 4), from which I cannot deny myself the pleasure of quoting the following lines:

" The first essential to such a policy is the cessation of Government borrowing, and the imposition of taxation sufficient not only to meet outgoings, but also to provide a surplus for the reduction of national indebtedness. Clearly this is only practicable during a period of prosperity, yet the report contained nothing in the nature of a close analysis of the position which would arise with a slump in trade. This is the more curious as effective monetary deflation must, in the long run, tend to depress industry, since a steady and persistent fall in prices necessarily diminishes and discourages trading activity. So long as industry is booming and a sufficient volume of taxation can be gathered without prejudice to production, the policy outlined by the Cunliffe Committee can, within reasonable limits, safely be commended. But if trade depression becomes sufficiently acute, monetary deflation will sooner or later be impossible, because of the Government's inability to collect sufficient from the profits of industry to meet all outgoings. If the policy is persisted in after the time for it has passed, a grave danger arises, for the payment of taxation will then involve trespassing upon the capital, and this, by retarding trade recovery and reducing the nation's productive capacity, will accentuate the very evils it is desired to cure."

The report of the Cunliffe Committee had this significance for England, that it fixed at an early stage the idea that the aim of the monetary policy should be the restoration of the gold standard. The limitation of the uncovered note issue carried out on the proposal of the Committee has been a continual reminder of the necessity for keeping the circulation within reasonable limits. The report, however, has not offered much guidance for the practical fulfilment of the proposed deflationist programme. Nor, indeed, have the results achieved been very satisfactory. More than four years after the appointment of the Committee their principal demand—the restoration of the gold standard—is still unsatisfied, whereas the depression which could be foreseen as a consequence of the deflation policy has set in, and has shown itself to be of an extremely serious character.

It is consistent with the spirit of the English that they

have not allowed themselves to be discouraged by the
difficulties they have had to meet, but steadily hold to
the purpose in view, declaring their readiness to do so
should it take five or even ten years to accomplish. But
this strength of purpose would have been of considerably
more practical value if it had been combined with a more
clear insight into the nature of the problem, its national
as well as its international scope, and with a sure conception of the character of the methods by which the end
in view could be attained.

A wider view of the monetary problem in its entirety
has been expounded by Lord D'Abernon, who, in a speech
in the House of Lords on the 26th November, 1919,
deprecated the superficial ideas current, and, as may be
gathered from the short abstract given below, expressed
points of view conducive to a real and tenable explanation.

He had previously requested of the Government information as to production, price movements, note issues,
etc., in different countries, in order to be able to show
whether the causes of the high cost of living were to be
found in under-production or in the artificial increase in
means of payment. This information was now forthcoming,* and showed that the world's production of a
number of important articles was only slightly below the
pre-War production. From this D'Abernon inferred that
the general rise in prices could not be accounted for by
reduced production. The world supply of commodities
during 1918 amounted probably to at least 90 per cent.

* Statements of Production. Price Movements and Currency
Expansion in Certain Countries (Cd. 434). Part of the material
is reprinted in the *Economic Journal* for December, 1919,
which adds the following remark to the point: "The actual
statistical relation between volume of currency, prices, and rates
of exchange is in so close a conformity with the predictions of
theory, as to surprise even theorists, having regard to the many
disturbing factors of the present time."

of the 1913 standard. But the quantity of means of payment became five times greater during the War. The rise in prices, therefore, must essentially be due to the far too plentiful supply of means of payment. This conclusion is further strengthened by the fact that prices in the various countries have risen in close conformity with the excessive issue of paper money.

Lord D'Abernon was also able to show with the material supplied by the Government the impracticability of the popular conception of profiteering as a cause of the rise in prices. In reality, as is clear from the English investigation, the profits have been by no means so great, nor have had such a general significance, as has been supposed.

The different rises in prices in the different countries have, in their turn, been the cause of the enormous dislocation of the exchanges we are witnessing to-day. The usual explanations which try to put this dislocation down to international indebtedness, or to the alterations in the international trade balances, are entirely indefensible. If the percentage of metal in the standard of a country were reduced by half, it would be apparent to everyone that the exchange rates of the country could not remain unaltered. But the result will be exactly the same if a country with a paper standard suddenly doubles the quantity of its notes. Here lies the essential explanation of the alterations which exchange rates underwent during the War. The alterations in the internal values of the currencies represent such an overwhelming cause of dislocations in the exchanges that every effort to improve the exchanges by increasing exports or reducing imports is as equally effective or useful as trying to stem the rising tide by causing by means of artificial puffs of wind a reverse ripple on the surface of the water ! This powerful overthrow of a hitherto commonly cherished

14

delusion was received by the House of Lords with loud acclamations.

D'Abernon further declared that the data just published completely upset the theory on which most Governments of the world had hitherto acted. It was, therefore, necessary to find a new basis to work on. Six months of suitable control of the world's means of payment would do far more towards reducing the cost of living than what had been accomplished during the last three years under food-control commissions and courts dealing with profiteering, or by appeals showered on producers and consumers to increase production and cut down expenditure. If England only had adequate control over the means of payment, she would be able to get rid of all her troublesome restrictions on the import of goods as well as the prohibition against the export of money. The evil of the high cost of living was by no means sent by Providence, but was provoked by direct measures adopted under a policy which might be reversed.

This problem permeated all others, and so long as it was not dealt with from the right points of view all efforts at reform in other directions were in vain. The mismanagement of money is by far the most powerful and most threatening of all causes of social unrest. But here we have one obvious course to pursue.

Lord D'Abernon proposed that a new and impartial commission be appointed to report on the causes of the high price level and on the influence upon it of the monetary policy; and further, that the Government should take steps to summon an international conference to discuss monetary conditions and prices. Viscount Peel answered on behalf of the Government that these proposals should be laid before the Government. He acknowledged the correctness of D'Abernon's view of the problem, and emphasised the exceptionally wide range of the question at issue.

Among the more important documents treating of the currency problem during this period must also be mentioned the " Economic Declaration " of the " Supreme Council," dated the 8th March, 1920. This declaration, among other things, lays stress upon the fact that the depreciation of gold is due to considerable quantities of gold having been set free within Europe and having flooded other countries. No close analysis, however, is made of this phenomenon, nor are the consequences drawn with regard to the restoration of the gold standard. It is recognised that the collapse of the exchange is, at least in part, a result of the reduced purchasing power of sundry currencies; nevertheless, the idea is still maintained that the exchanges are essentially dependent upon trade balance. An adverse trade balance is regarded as a reason for the value of a currency in terms of other currencies falling below the level determined by the relation between the internal purchasing powers of those currencies. It is pointed out that such an undervaluation of a currency enhances the prices of import commodities and thus tends to make food and raw materials in the country concerned still more expensive. To remedy this an increase in exports is recommended. Before such an increase becomes possible a temporary equilibrium must be established with the help of private commercial credits accompanied by the reduction of all non-essential imports to an absolute minimum. The declaration finishes by recommending a policy of deflation to be made effective by—

(a) Cutting down current State expenditure to what can be covered by income;

(b) Imposing such additional taxation as may be necessary with a view to this end;

(c) Consolidating short term loans by the aid of loans payable out of the savings of the nation;

(*d*) An immediate curtailment of the note circulation, followed by a progressive reduction.

The declaration contains no discussion of the difficulties which such a policy would involve or of the ultimate end to be aimed at by adopting that policy.

Of particular importance for the further treatment of the exchange problem was the International Conference which met in Brussels in the autumn of 1920 at the invitation of the League of Nations. The copious materials collected for this conference, the various reports and memoranda submitted, and the discussions held there, form together a source of knowledge of the exchange problem that will always be extremely valuable to anyone desirous of gaining information on this subject. The Conference's resolutions, however, are hardly framed in such a way as to offer much guidance for a positive work on the readjustment of the world's monetary systems. Still, in a negative way, the resolutions at times make quite important contributions to the subject, as when the opinion is expressed, for instance, that " neither an international coinage nor an international unit of calculation would serve any useful purpose or remove any of the difficulties from which international exchange suffers to-day "; or when " all attempts to limit fluctuations in exchange by imposing artificial control on exchange operations " are deprecated as " futile and mischievous." That strong emphasis is laid upon the necessity for the limitation of armaments, for a ruthless cutting down of other expenditure, and for an effective co-operation between the different countries, as well as upon the necessity for affording the greatest possible amount of freedom from State interference in home industries, and of encouragement to international trade, was a happy expression of the sound ideas entertained on these questions by the leading financial experts of the world. In certain respects, indeed, these pronouncements have also had some effect upon the development that followed, but in other respects, and particularly with regard to honest co-operation between the nations and to the freedom in international trade, this cannot, unfortunately, be said to have been the case.

With regard to the actual currency problem the Conference report is not very enlightening. On the essential points its statements are extremely vague. While declaring, on the one hand, that " it is highly desirable that the countries which have lapsed from an effective gold standard should return thereto," it states, on the other hand, that " the reversion to, or establishment of, an effective gold standard would in many cases demand enormous deflation "; nevertheless, it fails to draw from this the obvious conclusion that such a deflation must be avoided and that, therefore, the parity of the currency with gold must be placed considerably lower than it was before the War. The report instead makes the very vague statement: " Deflation, if and when undertaken, must be carried out gradually and with great caution; otherwise the disturbances to trade and credit might prove disastrous." No answer is given to the fundamental question as to what should really be the object of such a process of deflation. Instead of saying clearly and honestly that a great deflation must be avoided, the Conference thinks fit to recommend that the process of deflation be gradual, a recommendation which at bottom is nothing more than an evasion well suited to those who will not look difficulties in the face. Also it seems to be imagined that such a gradual deflation could be effected by increasing the wealth on which the currency is based. Further, as means for effective deflation are recommended the gradual paying off of public debts, higher rates of interest, and a sort of rationing of credit.

With the question of how inflation has affected the value of gold and what influence a policy of deflation and the steps necessary for restoring an effective gold standard would be likely to have on the value of gold, the Brussels Conference hardly dealt at all.

In the resolution the only statement made on the subject is this: " We cannot recommend any attempt to stabilise the value of gold, and we gravely doubt whether such attempt could succeed. . . ." The matter, however, was referred, for closer investigation, to the Financial Committee afterwards appointed by the League of Nations.

The preparations for the Brussels Conference were going on just at the time when the post-War inflation process above described reached a climax, and when several European countries were giving themselves up to an inflation which was bound to lead to the complete ruin of their monetary systems. Under such conditions it was natural enough that the Brussels Conference should devote its chief attention to the necessity of putting an end to the inflation which was going on everywhere, and also that its resolutions should strongly emphasise this necessity. If by the side of this the analysis of the difficulties and dangers attending the coming process of deflation were neglected, then in view of the circumstances such neglect may in some measure be excusable; but none the less it has undoubtedly proved very injurious to the ensuing development. In just such a situation as occurred in the autumn of 1920, would an authoritative pronouncement as to the main lines of the monetary policy to be pursued and as to the object and means of this policy have been more than ever urgently needed.

In an article in the *Economic Journal* for March, 1920, ("Further Observations on the World's Monetary Problem"), I expressed the opinion that a process which aimed at reducing prices to their former level would probably ultimately prove still more disastrous than the process of inflation had been. The prospect of a long period of falling prices would kill all enterprise and hamper the process of reconstruction. Further, an increase in the value of gold would for many countries aggravate the difficulties of reverting to a gold standard, and very seriously increase their already overwhelming financial burdens. It was therefore natural that the world should desire to prevent any further rise in the value of gold.

In opposition to the then prevailing idea that deflation could be attained by such increase in production as would bring it on a level with the provision of means of payment —*i.e.*, without any reduction of already existing means of payment—I showed that this was bound to be a very slow process. With a normal rate of progress of, let us say, 3 per cent. per annum, it would take thirty-one years to overcome an inflation indicated by the index number 250, and wellnigh thirty-eight years for the supply of commodities to correspond to the supply of means of payment in a country where the inflation had reached the index number of 300. To continue to reduce artificially the world's provision of means of payment for such a long period would obviously be quite out of question. " Besides, the continual fall in the general level of prices which would be the result would, of course, hamper all enterprise and cause a severe economic depression. Under such circumstances it would be vain to expect that normal progress of the world's production on which the whole plan rests."

To this reasoning the objection has been made that the world has gone through long periods of falling prices before without progress being thereby checked. Reference has particularly been made to the period 1873 to 1895, when a marked scarcity of gold brought about a very considerable fall in prices. But this period is, in fact, also to a great extent a prolonged period of depression, during which the constantly sinking price level manifestly proved a very serious obstacle to enterprise. Sweden, which is particularly dependent for her exports on the continuous creation of real capital in the world, suffered severely from this depression, and during the period in question the conditions of Swedish industrial life were extremely difficult. Of course, enterprise will not be entirely paralysed at such a time, as it is always expected that the fall in prices has reached the bottom. It is obvious that depression must become still heavier if it is announced in advance that it will continue until a certain low price level is reached. A programme of this kind must in reality provoke such a depression that a violent fall in prices is inevitable. A slow and gradual process of deflation is therefore an impossibility—a fact of which, indeed, the most convincing proof is to be found in the tragic experiences the world has suffered since the middle of 1920, when a process of general deflation was actually started. It must not be denied, however, that a country which has gone through a period of inflation can, under exceptionally favourable conditions, accommodate itself to the too large volume of means of payment with which it has supplied itself. This may be said to have been the case with the United States after the Civil War; but then, during the subsequent decades, the country also acquired an uninterrupted supply, both of immigrant labour and of European capital, and at the same time had at its disposal its own undeveloped natural resources, of which it could now make use with the help of these newly acquired productive forces. At present such an expansion can certainly not be expected in many countries !

In my first Memorandum laid before the International Financial Conference in Brussels I uttered a warning against any attempt at further deflation. I pointed out that the way to cause a deflation must be, firstly, by imposing additional taxation for reduction of the means of payment; and, secondly, by a severe restriction of credit, particularly by aid of high rates of interest. The former method could not offer much prospect of success at a time when most countries had serious difficulties to contend with in getting their taxation to meet current expenditure. The latter method would certainly prove effective, but, at the same time, was bound to have a very depressing influence on industrial life and business enterprise. Such being the means of a process of deflation, the practical possibility of carrying out the deflationist programme would manifestly be rather limited, and its complete realisation would certainly show itself very little desirable.

As to the analysis of the deflationist policy which I submitted at the time, I must refer the reader for closer details to my above-mentioned Memorandum. I cannot, however, refrain from recalling here one aspect of the deflationist programme which I brought out in that book—namely, its influence on gold. In chapter xii., "The Gold Question," I explained how the problem of the stabilisation of the dollar exchange in Europe would be further complicated if the United States raised the value of its currency by a process of deflation. It would obviously be to the interest of all countries desirous of stabilising their dollar exchange that the United States should not engage in any monetary policy aiming at an increase in the internal value of the dollar: " It is desirable that one country should take the lead by fixing the internal value of its money, and it seems natural that this country should be the United States." If the world was to revert to a gold standard it would be a common interest to the world to prevent gold from again rising in value.

The hope for the stabilisation of the internal value of the dollar was not to be fulfilled. During 1920 there was carried out in the United States a process of deflation which eventually resulted in a violent fall in the general price level, and consequently a corresponding rise in the purchasing power of the dollar, and thereby also in that of gold. This process having severely complicated the exchange problem for other countries, it has naturally attracted lively attention throughout the world. Now, afterwards, people in the United States have wanted to make out that the fall in prices was spontaneous, and that no deflationist policy—that is, a process aiming at raising the internal value of the dollar—had ever been deliberately pursued. This, however, can hardly be true, for it would then prove extremely difficult satisfactorily to account for the fall in prices. That a currency can in so short a time undergo such a radical change in its internal purchasing power is necessarily a phenomenon of a monetary nature which we must be able to explain. If one contends that no deflationist policy was ever pursued, one must be prepared to bring forward other factors of a monetary nature capable of having produced that peculiar result. As this would certainly prove very difficult, at any rate the most natural course is to examine the part which the monetary policy of the United States has played in the heavy fall in prices which went on in that country from May, 1920, to May, 1921.

In order to elucidate this matter, it is necessary to go back one year. During the summer of 1919 there were certainly not many in the United States prepared to deny that the will of the nation was consciously directed towards bringing down the price level. It was during this time that the Government campaign against enhanced prices and profiteering was at its height. A widespread organisation had been founded for conducting this campaign, and the Attorney-General, Mr. Parmer, the head of this organisation, issued a communication to all " Fair Price Committees " appointed by the organisation, in which he declared that it was of the utmost importance that prices be lowered, and in which the co-operation of all State and Federal organisations was most earnestly solicited in the attainment of that end. On the 8th of August, President Wilson summoned the Congress to a general session, with a view to giving support to the campaign against the high cost of living and against profiteering. On that occasion the President expressed the opinion that peace prices were impossible, so long as the financial and economic system remained on a war basis.

No one can fail to get the impression that the object of this campaign was to bring down prices to the level of what the President termed peace prices—*i.e.*, pre-War prices. Certainly neither the tremendous agitation thus set on foot, nor the severe legislation especially passed for the purpose, nor the far-reaching organisation to reduce the price level, was capable of directly bringing about any general fall in prices, as the whole campaign started from a false conception of the problem, entirely overlooked its essentially monetary character, and consequently employed wrong methods. But at any rate the campaign probably accomplished this much : it spread the idea far and wide that prices must go down, and that the pre-War price level was the only natural and proper one. Thus, when afterwards the banks of the Federal Reserve system began to adopt monetary measures with a view to deflation, the soil was well prepared, and these measures were, therefore, very effective, apparently much more so than the management of the Federal Reserve system had imagined.

As we have seen in the foregoing, it was not until

towards the end of 1919 that the Federal Reserve banks found themselves in the position of no longer having to give that prior consideration to the war loans which had previously limited their freedom of action, and that they could therefore proceed to raise the discount rates. At first the increase in the bank rates was altogether inadequate, but during 1920 it became so considerable that it was bound gradually to have the intended effect.

Bank administration in the United States, as in so many other countries, has worked on the idea that any restriction found to be necessary ought to be confined to credits " for speculative purposes," and would not need to affect so-called " legitimate " credits. In reality no such distinction is possible. Stern measures designed to reduce speculative credit are almost bound to react in a thousand different ways on the whole of the industrial life of a country, and to reduce the total volume of credit. Still more impossible is it to place an effective restriction upon all credit for speculative purposes without thereby forcing on a general fall in prices. The scheme for suppressing the granting of credit for purposes of speculation must, therefore, in itself have already involved a scheme for reducing the level of prices. That this object formed the gist of the Federal Reserve banks' restrictive credit policy seems only natural; at any rate this policy must have appeared to the mind of the public as a logical continuation of the Government's vigorous campaign for reducing the level of prices.

In its number dated the 1st October, 1919, the *Federal Reserve Bulletin* discusses the problem of the high cost of living, and refers to the measures taken by the Government against the rise in prices. In direct reference to this subject the journal says: " The problem of reducing the cost of living is, however, mainly that of *restoring the purchasing power of the dollar*." (I have taken the liberty of placing these important words in italics, as also two other passages in the following quotations.) " The dollar has lost purchasing power because expansion of credit, under the necessities of war financing, proceeded at a rate more rapid than the production and saving of goods. The return to a sound economic condition, and one which will involve as little further disturbance of normal economic relationships as possible, will be a *reversal of the process which has brought the country to its present pass.* In other words, the way in must be the way out." The journal, it is true, believes that this can be done by increased production and greater economy, and in support thereof quotes a statement made by the Chairman of the Board. But this statement begins with the very characteristic argument that in consideration of Government finance it is not possible to limit the extent of credits, except by a gradual process. This, however, can only be interpreted to mean that when at some future time there is no longer any need for this consideration, a reduction of the volume of credits would be a proper means for restoration of normal conditions. And what is more, the journal adds: "The cost of living problem on its financial side is misconceived, unless it is conceived as the problem of restoring the value of the dollar. To accept the depreciation worked in the dollar by war conditions, and to *standardise the dollar of the future on this basis,* would be to ratify the inflation wrought by the War and the injustices it produced." It can hardly be denied that a very definite programme of deflation is hereby proposed.

The Board has, as is only natural, first of all devoted its attention to the security of the banks of the Federal Reserve system—that is to say, to the necessity for keeping sufficient gold reserves against their liabilities. When the reserve ratio fell in October, 1919 (the 7th), to as low

a figure as 48·3 per cent., the Annual Conference of the
Federal Reserve system came to pay special attention to
the necessity for restrictive measures. They realise the
necessity for a higher discount, but at the same time are
anxious to make it known that there is no desire to impose
an unnecessary restriction on production. The opinion is,
nevertheless, expressed that " some increase in the bank
rate seems the necessary first step in any programme
for the restraint of undesirable credit expansion." However, the raising of the rate would prove ineffectual,
" unless accompanied by a campaign . . . to secure
greater moderation by banks in the extension of credit
for speculative and other undesirable purposes." There
can be no doubt that a restrictive programme was thereby
proposed, which, if consistently and vigorously carried
out, was bound to lead to a fall in prices.

At the beginning of November the Federal Reserve
banks raised their discount rates generally by ½ per cent.
On this subject the *Federal Reserve Bulletin* of the 1st
December remarks as follows: " The advance was slight,
but, interpreted as it was as indicating a change of discount policy, it had a good deal of effect."

In a review of the development of the Federal Reserve
system during the financial year which closed at the
end of June, 1920, the July (1920) number of the *Bulletin*
remarks: " During this latter period the characteristic
phases have been found in the effort to check the growth
in war papers carried by Federal Reserve banks, in the
successful shifting from the low stabilised level necessitated
by war conditions to the higher basis corresponding to
commercial conditions, and reflecting the effort of the
system to control the expansion of credit, and the corresponding attempt to induce member banks to curtail
excessive or unessential advances of funds." It is further
stated in this number that, " beginning with November,

1919, effort was definitely made to control the reserve position through the application of higher rates of discount at Federal Reserve banks "; and that " the operation of credit control through higher discount rates has had a marked success."

It is true that this result was slow in coming. The reserve ratio continued to decrease, and in May, 1920, reached the low figure of 42·6 per cent. But it is in the nature of the case that the effect of reversing the credit policy in this manner should only gradually make itself felt. It should, instead, prove to be all the more powerful. This postponing of the effect has clearly rendered it difficult for the bank administration to review the consequences of their restrictive credit policy, and has resulted in the administration pursuing this policy further than would perhaps otherwise have been deemed proper. At a meeting of the Federal Reserve Board held on the 17th May, 1920, it was recommended to " urge upon member banks through the Federal Reserve banks the wisdom of showing borrowers the necessity of the curtailment of general credits, and especially for non-essential uses, as well as continuing to discourage loans for capital and speculative purposes, by checking excessive borrowings through the application of higher rates." On the 29th May, 1920, the Federal Reserve Bank of New York raised its discount rate to 7 per cent., this " in view of the steady pressure for funds, and by way of emphasising the necessity of continued moderation in rediscount applications."

On the 17th May, 1920, the United States Senate resolved that the Federal Reserve Board should be directed to advise the Senate as to what steps it purposed to take, or to recommend to member banks, to meet the existing inflation of the currency and credits, and the high prices resulting therefrom, and what further steps it contemplated taking or recommending to mobilise credits in order to move the 1920 crop. In its reply dated the 25th May, 1920, the Board said that it had for many months past recognised that the expansion of credit in the United States was proceeding at a rate not warranted by the production and consumption of commodities. The Board had repeatedly exhorted the Federal Reserve banks to endeavour to induce the member banks to avoid an undue expansion of loans, and to keep the volume of their outstanding credits within reasonable limits. At the above-mentioned meeting on the 17th May the Chairman of the Board had declared among other things that "unnecessary and habitual borrowings should be discouraged, and the liquidation of long-standing, non-essential loans should proceed. Banks were cautioned, however, that drastic steps should be avoided, and that the method adopted should be orderly, for gradual liquidation will result in permanent improvement, while too rapid deflation would be injurious and should be avoided."

Here, as it seems to me, is as obvious a programme of deflation as can be found anywhere. Efforts are, of course, made to retain as long as possible the idea that a deflation can be effected gradually, and without hampering productive activities. But this is an illusion which is, so to speak, tacked on to the deflationist policy and has no influence whatever upon its actual consequences. In the *Federal Reserve Bulletin* for June, 1920, the following passage occurs in the journal's review of the preceding month: "Undue storage and the accumulation of goods has been a prolific cause of demand upon banks during the past few months." It is clear from this that the object of the policy of restriction must have been to force goods upon the market. This was, of course, not possible without at the same time bringing about a violent fall

in prices. It must, therefore, have been part of the
Federal Reserve Board's policy to bring down the general
price level. It is true that after the fall in prices has
already set in, the Board time after time expresses the
belief that the bottom has been reached. But in this
it is mistaken. The consequences of its restrictive policy
are more far-reaching than the Board imagines. In
November, 1920, it is declared that "the problem of
complete readjustment now centres around the placing
of goods and accumulated stocks upon a banking basis
corresponding to the new level of prices which has been
established. It may be expected that, as older accumu-
lations are disposed of, and new goods at the revised price
levels take their place, a more normal situation will
gradually develop." This was written with reference
to the price level in October, 1920, which was denoted
by the index figure 225 (Bureau of Labor). At that
time by far the greater part of the fall in prices which
the deflationist policy of the Board was to bring about
had not yet taken place. In June, 1921, the said index
number stood at 148.

Now afterwards, whenever an attempt has been made
to defend the Federal Reserve Board against the charge
of having through a deliberate deflationist policy forced
on the fall in prices, with all its appalling consequences,
it has been particularly pointed out that the fall in prices
took place before the limitation of credits, and that,
therefore, the restrictive bank policy could not have caused
the fall in prices. This argument is absolutely untenable.
The reason why, in a case like this, the reduction in the
volume of bank currency will necessarily be delayed is
natural enough, and will be considered more closely later
on. This delay does not in any way prove that a restrictive bank policy has not been the primary cause of the
fall in prices. By their energetic efforts at curtailing

15

credits, and especially by their high discount rates, the
Federal Reserve banks have brought about an extensive,
and sometimes precipitate, realisation of accumulated
stocks, have severely cut down the demand for capital
for all kinds of new construction and improvements,
and have thus put a very effective check on enterprise.
A policy of this kind always proves the surest means of
bringing down the price level. The reduced creation of
real capital causes less demand for labour and a reduction
in wages. With increasing unemployment and falling
wages there follows a reduction in purchasing power.
Just as the Board expected, the current savings which
accumulated during that period have been utilised for
cancelling a part of the superfluous means of payment.
By its restriction of credit the Board has convinced the
public of its serious intentions with regard to the deflationist programme, and the public have quite consistently refrained from buying, and that to such an
extent that people have talked of a general purchasing
strike. Not until the public had worn out their clothes
could they be induced out of sheer necessity once more
to start buying textiles and boots, which brought about
some improvement in the respective markets. Not until
the lack of housing accommodation became overwhelming,
and the prices of material and labour had fallen considerably, did building operations commence gradually
to assume more normal proportions. People are still
evidently reluctant to effect purchases in several lines of
business, because they either hope or fear for a still
further fall in prices. The common purchasing strike,
both on the part of business enterprises and consumers,
may perhaps be regarded as the immediate cause of the
fall in prices. But this purchasing strike has been a
direct and natural consequence of the restrictive policy
adopted by the bank administration.

Naturally the deflationist policy has aroused keen opposition in the United States, and this opposition has frequently employed arguments which are inadmissible, and against which the bank administration has found it comparatively easy to defend itself. I have in mind especially the criticisms advanced by the farmers. Attempts have been made from that quarter to show that the Federal Reserve banks have held agriculture in disfavour, and have failed to provide farmers with the credits essential for carrying on. Against this the banks have managed to prove that on a relatively very large scale it is just the credit requirements of agriculture that have been best looked after. Though this charge was thus proved to be false, yet it cannot be denied that agriculture was at any rate the industry to suffer most from the bank administration's general restrictive policy. This is partly due to the fact that, owing to the conditions on the world market, the prices of agricultural produce underwent a relatively severer fall than those of other commodities; partly, also, to the fact that agriculture works with a fairly long investment period, and that consequently a continued heavy fall in prices is bound to prove more disastrous for agriculture than for many other industries. What made things worse was that agriculture had previously been encouraged to increase production to the greatest possible extent. The losses which the process of deflation brought upon the American farmers must, indeed, have been enormous, and the indignation felt in agricultural circles is natural enough.

Opposition in the United States reached such a pitch that it found expression in a certain animosity against the entire Federal Reserve system and the centralisation of power which it undoubtedly represents. To an outsider this must seem to be an exhibition of somewhat exaggerated pugnacity. The Federal Reserve system

has, without the slightest doubt, meant a vast improvement in the organisation and effectiveness of the American
banking system. But even a good instrument can be
misused, and when that is the case the consequences may
easily be very serious indeed. Without the centralisation
of the banking system, which was effected just before the
outbreak of the War through the introduction of the
Federal Reserve system, it would certainly never have
been possible for the United States to finance the War
in the very effective manner in which it was now done.
But it must never be forgotten that this war-financing
was only rendered possible by means of an extremely
harmful inflation, which perhaps could not have been
carried out under a less centralised banking system. The
subsequent process of deflation can also be looked upon
as an indication of the effectiveness of the centralised
banking system, but in this case the effectiveness has
manifestly proved disastrous to the country. The mere
effectiveness of an organisation is, therefore, not everything. In order successfully to utilise such effectiveness,
an administration is required to be capable of fulfilling
the most exacting claims; indeed, the greater the effectiveness of the organisation the higher will be the claims on
the administration. In the present case the administration has undoubtedly displayed great technical ability.
But it has been faced with duties of an extraordinary
nature which it has hardly been capable of completely
mastering.

The complaint has been made in the United States that
the Federal Reserve system has been far too closely
dependent upon the political administration of the
country. There is no doubt that this is just the weakest
point in every centralised banking system, and, as the
Brussels Conference clearly brought out, it is of the
highest importance for all countries with a centralised

banking system to free the bank administration to the greatest possible extent from political influences. But that sort of opposition which is at present displayed in the United States seems hardly likely to promote such an object, or to call forth any greater degree of efficiency in the administration.

THE ACTUAL OPERATION AND EFFECTS
OF DEFLATION

THE deflationist policy described in the two preceding chapters has found its way to most other countries, and there, too, has brought about a more or less extensive reduction in prices. Thus, in this case, just as in the question of the post-War inflation dealt with above, we may with some truth speak of an international price movement. But the common trend in the development of the price level which may thus be said to exist in most countries is not due to any necessary connection between the different currencies, but only to certain common tendencies having asserted themselves in regard to the different countries' monetary policy, as also in the ideas entertained by the public as to the economic situation and prospects for the future.

In order to form a true judgment of these internationally operating causes, it is particularly important to keep constantly in mind that the world no longer has a gold standard, but that every country possesses its own special standard. Only in the United States is this standard a real gold standard. In all other countries it is a paper standard in itself possessing a quite indeterminate value. There no longer exists, therefore, any fixed relation between the currencies of the different countries. But, then, neither is there any common measure for prices in the various countries. Prices are determined in each separate country by a nominal unit of measure quite independent of the units employed by other countries.

230

Thus, each country has its own special price level, and in consequence there exists no direct and necessary connection between the different price levels or their movements. Experience has shown that want of clear knowledge on this point has been a fundamental cause of the universal misinterpretation of the nature of the price movement, as well as of the refusal to admit the possibility of pursuing an independent monetary policy and consequently the responsibility for the fate of each individual currency.

If, therefore, there exists no direct connection between the world's currencies of to-day, nevertheless the idea of a future restoration of such a connection seems to have acted as a connecting link between them. Hopes have been entertained in this and that country that the former gold standard would be restored, which practically meant the restoration of the old dollar rate; or at any rate countries have striven to prevent their currency from being debased in relation to the dollar more than it was already. When, therefore, from the middle of 1920 the internal value of the dollar began to be raised, the other countries deemed it to be necessary to raise the internal value of their own currencies in like proportion. In the better situated countries these efforts have called forth a restrictive credit policy, with a consequent fall in the general price level. The very idea of the irresistibility of what was called an international movement of prices has probably contributed considerably towards making the fall in prices international. The universal belief that only the prices before 1914 can be regarded as normal, and that consequently a " return to normal conditions " can only mean a return to the 1914 price level, has also manifestly exercised an important influence both on the business world and on the consuming public —an influence which has naturally facilitated and intensi-

fied the effect of the deflationist policy in reducing prices.
But the predominating factor in the deflation which took
place in countries apart from the United States has,
without doubt, been the considerable rise in the internal
value of the dollar brought about by the United States'
deflationist policy.

That it is nevertheless always the amount of each
separate country's provision of means of payment that
ultimately determines the internal value of its currency
is particularly well brought out by the fact that, simultaneously with the decline in prices now being discussed,
there occurred a very considerable rise in prices in those
countries in which the authorities were not strong enough
to put a check on the constant inflation, but kept on
providing the public with fresh purchasing power.   This
fact seems to offer sufficient evidence that the fall in
prices might have been prevented in other countries also,
if only a sufficiently liberal credit policy had provided
trade with adequate means of payment.   Thus, if there
exists any connection between the processes of deflation
in different countries, it is a psychological and not a
material connection.

After these remarks on the general character and causes
of the heavy fall in prices, we can with greater confidence
proceed to a consideration of the details of this not only
interesting, but also practically important, phenomenon.

In the spring of 1920 it was strongly felt throughout
the world that the rise in prices which had taken
place was unsound, and that the speculation that went
hand in hand with it was without solid foundation.
Everywhere people expected the bubble to burst.   The
ground was thus well prepared for a crisis, and it only
needed to start in one place for it to spread far and wide.
The first collapse occurred on the market for material
supplied to the clothing industry.   The control of this

material which the belligerent Governments introduced during the War began to be given up, and supplies that had accumulated came to be put freely on the market. The Governments themselves realised their war stocks. These changes had a very considerable influence on the wool market. But the crisis affected other articles as well. Large stocks of leather and hides had been accumulated while the disposal of ready-made articles was held back by the high retail prices. On this market there occurred a violent fall in prices which in three months (from April to July) reduced the prices on the American market in some cases by nearly half. Large stocks of silk, especially on the Far Eastern market, had been accumulated on speculation, with the result that everywhere the consumption was very considerably reduced. When the banks stopped advancing funds for this speculation and at the same time the demand for silk fell, the speculation came to grief. The prices of silk dropped by 50 per cent., and a violent economic crisis broke out in Japan. A heavier fall in the general price level than that which then took place in Japan has seldom been witnessed. In March, 1920, the Japanese Central Bank's index for wholesale prices had reached a maximum of 320. This index number fell for April to 300, and for May to 222. Later on, it is true, a slight recovery took place, but for December the price index stood at 206 (index numbers being calculated on the basis of 100 for 1913).

It was natural that this crisis should first react upon those countries which have the most powerful interests in international trade. In England the general price level had, according to the *Economist*, reached its maximum in March, 1920, with the figure 310. Thereupon there followed a retrograde movement which, towards the end of the year, became more and more accentuated, so that December shows an index number of 220. In the United States the price level was reduced from the highest index number of 272, reached in May, to 189 for December. In France the maximum had been reached in April with the figure 588 (*Statistique Générale*) and fell from that figure to 436 for December. Even Germany, in spite of her steadily increasing note circulation, could not help being affected by the fall in prices. The index number compiled by the *Frankfurter Zeitung*, which in April, 1920, reached a maximum of 1,714, dropped to 1,473 for May of that year. In the case of Sweden the maximum was reached in June with the figure 366. However, no noteworthy decline in prices took place before October. In December the index number had receded to 299 (*Swedish Trade Journal*). In Norway the maximum point was not reached until later—viz., in September—with the figure 425 (*Ökon. Revue :* the prices for January to June, 1914, being denoted by 100). The price index afterwards dropped to 377 in December. In Denmark the case was similar. The maximum was reached in October, with the figure 403, and by December the price index had gone down to 341 (*Finanstidende :* the prices for July, 1912, to June, 1914, being denoted by 100). In the Netherlands the decline started from a maximum of 296 for July and fell to the figure 233 for December (*Central Bureau v. d. Stat*).

In December, 1920, the *Federal Reserve Bulletin* expresses the opinion that a turning-point must now be considered to have been reached. The journal says: " Very sharp reduction in prices coupled with heavy decreases in production, extensive unemployment, and business reaction, often involving bank failures, have been the outstanding features of readjustment in former years." The *Bulletin* considers that the present transition period has caused a minimum of such symptoms, and that, although the process is not yet completed, the difficulties are not likely to be further intensified. In spite of everything, the end of the year 1920 must be regarded as " quite unmistakably a turning-point in the process of transition from conditions procured by the War to the normal economic basis of international and industrial life." A similar idea has most likely been entertained in many other places also. Indeed, so long as the whole process was regarded as an inevitable crisis following upon an ordinary phase of excessive speculation, this idea was but natural enough. We must not press unduly such a statement as the one just quoted, and we may have good reason to remind ourselves of how difficult it was in the extremely complicated situation that marked the end of 1920 to obtain a clear view of what was taking place. However, it is not intended here to lay any stress upon showing up that an error of judgment has been committed, but rather upon pointing out the cause of this error of judgment. And that is quite obvious. The Federal Reserve Board entirely overlooked the one factor which in the whole of this great complicated process was itself the principal driving force—the Board's own deflationist policy, or perhaps let us say, rather, the restrictive bank policy which the Board pursued, and which in itself inevitably implied deflation. I am well aware that both the Board and its supporters deny that a deliberate deflation was ever advanced, but what cannot be denied is that from the spring of 1920 to the spring of 1921 there took place a very considerable rise in the internal value of the dollar. Thus far the decline in prices was undeniably a *monetary* phenomenon, and it was just this that was overlooked by the managements of the central banks not only in the United States, but in most other countries. Just as during the period of inflation the central banks of the world would never openly admit that an internal depreciation of money was taking place, so during the period of deflation they have never been willing fully to acknowledge, at least after the harmful effects of deflation began to appear, that deflation was a monetary phenomenon and involved a fresh change in the monetary unit. With such a standpoint it was inevitable that the situation should be misjudged while the deflation process was actually being experienced. This was, however, from a practical point of view, very serious, not to say disastrous, for it caused the American central bank management to maintain their restrictive bank policy, even after it had failed to serve any rational purpose and could only encourage a further altogether aimless increase in the internal value of the dollar.

Other countries who would not willingly see their currency further depreciated in its relation to the dollar had no option but to pursue the same deflationist policy. They did not succeed thereby in effecting any appreciable improvement in their currency in its relation to the dollar, at any rate during the first year—that is, from the spring of 1920 to the spring of 1921. As the value of the dollar determined that of gold, the value of gold rose during this period in proportion to that of the dollar, and therefore, in spite of all deflation, other currencies came no nearer recovering their gold parity during that period than they were before, in fact rather the opposite. As the deflation affected even the best currency it became a kind of race for bringing up the internal values of the different currencies—a race which was devoid of any rational object whatever.

For the first six months of 1920 the English price level stood (according to the *Economist*) at an average of 300, while the American price level stopped at 259. Working on a pre-War parity of 4·86⅔ dollars to the pound sterling, we find that the figures quoted above give on an average for the said period a purchasing power parity for the pound of (in round figures) 4·20 dollars. In May, 1921, the American deflation had reached the point where it remained for practically the remainder of the year. The index figure for May is 151, while the corresponding English index figure is 182. These figures give a purchasing power parity for the pound of 4·04 dollars. During this year, therefore, the value of the pound in relation to the dollar had, in spite of the heavy English deflation, rather decreased than otherwise. It was not until deflation ceased in the United States that other countries succeeded, by carrying their deflation still further, in effecting a relative improvement in their own currency as against the dollar. So the English price level dropped from 182 for May, 1921, to 162 for December of the same year, while the American price level only fell from 151 for May to 149 for December. It is the same in the case of Sweden. When the Swedish price level reached its maximum (for June, 1920) with 366, the American stood at 269, and the purchasing power parity of the dollar was therefore kr. 5·08. In May, 1921, the Swedish price level was at 218, but by December had fallen to 172. The former figure corresponded to a purchasing power parity for the dollar of (in round figures) kr. 5·40, the latter to a purchasing power parity of kr. 4·31. Thus the period up to May, 1921, involved a marked depreciation of the Swedish krona in relation to the dollar, this too in spite of the very considerable deflation that was taking place in Sweden; but from May to the end of the year through continued deflation the Swedish exchange showed a marked improvement in relation to the dollar exchange, which at that time was more or less stationary.

In the restrictive credit policy pursued in the United

States one determining object has the whole time been an endeavour to strengthen to the utmost extent the position of the banks. The main object was to free the banks from all speculative engagements and to restore to them the greatest possible degree of liquidity. But the steady fall in prices resulted in a number of bank credits becoming, as it was called, " frozen." The value of those articles for the purchase or production of which credits had been opened had sunk below the value of the borrowed capital, and the credit could then only be liquidated at a more or less considerable loss, which it eventually fell to the lending bank to cover. So long as the process of deflation went on, new " frozen credits " were constantly being created in this way, and the effort to preserve the security and liquidity of the banks seemed ever to demand a continuation of the policy of restriction.

The fall in prices in America produced a similar effect on the economic conditions in those countries which were buyers of American export commodities. By the time the export commodities had arrived at, let us say, South American ports, the prices had already fallen so low that the buyers could not see their way to take the goods at the contracted prices without thereby exposing themselves to severe losses. The buyers then refused to accept the goods they had bought, and these accumulated at the ports pending some sort of arrangement, possibly subject to a heavy price reduction. These conditions were aggravated by the fact that the different purchasing countries' own staple products were no longer able to obtain a satisfactory American market. Such articles as sugar, rubber, hides, and other materials found but a poor market in the United States, as the accumulation of these commodities coupled with the industrial depression caused a violent fall in prices or else ruined the market altogether. In consequence of this the paying capacity of the countries in question was very soon practically exhausted. In the autumn of 1920 a moratorium, or at any rate a state of affairs practically equivalent to a moratorium, was introduced in Cuba and several South American states. This caused a further depreciation of the currencies of the countries in question on the international market (*Federal Reserve Bulletin*, December, 1920; January, 1921). Finally, several of the currencies thus affected became simply unsaleable, and ceased to be quoted.

Seldom has the truth of the well-known economic saying that a country must buy in order to be able to sell been more clearly demonstrated. When the United States ceased to buy the products of countries possessing raw material, the United States were no longer in a position to export to those countries. A similar state of affairs has indeed very seriously affected the United States in their relations with the outside world in general. After the War they were so situated that their imports were far from sufficient to pay for their exports. The proper investments of capital abroad have not sufficed to cover the balance. In latter years, apparently, a large part of the exports has actually not been paid for, and is now only balanced by a floating debt amounting to several milliards of dollars, of which a very considerable proportion must be regarded as complete loss. The strong protectionist policy which the United States wanted to advance after the War would, of course, only make the situation worse, and particularly, by depressing the exchange rates in America for those countries which make it their business to sell their products to the United States, but are at the same time the principal buyers of American export commodities, would present a constant obstacle to a natural expansion of the United States' foreign trade.

The fall in prices in the United States has thus, in actual fact, failed to benefit exports. The world has here an example from which it should be able to learn something in the way of correcting a very common delusion. In every country during the period of deflation the doctrine was taught that to bring down the price level and to produce more cheaply were the two essential conditions, if a country wished to retain its share of the world market. There can be no doubt that this idea was one of the most potent factors which accelerated the process of deflation. We know that this idea is false. A lowering of the general price level in a country must have the effect of making that country's currency in its international valuation rise in a corresponding degree, so that the situation as regards the foreign buyers of the country's export products remains on the whole unaltered. What the world's trade needs in order to be able to thrive and flourish is stability, a fixed price level in each separate country, and firm exchange rates between the various countries. The process of deflation which has been going on since the spring of 1920 has offered anything but a favourable opportunity for attending to these needs.

The depressing influence which a continued reduction of the price level must be expected to exercise over enterprise has not failed to show itself. Dealers have to the utmost possible extent refrained from activity in anticipation of prices reaching their bottom level, and consumers have likewise postponed their purchases as long as possible in the expectation of being able to buy at cheaper prices. Unemployment on an appalling scale has been the result. In actual fact unemployment, both in the United States and in Europe, has certainly assumed far more serious dimensions than ever before. Each country has suffered not only through its own deflationist policy, but also through that of other countries. As the deflationist policy has naturally to a very great extent paralysed such forms of production as are required for constructional and building purposes, Swedish industry in particular, which happens to be very largely based on supplying material for such purposes to other countries, has been most seriously affected by the depression caused in those countries by the deflationist policy.

THE RETARDED DIMINUTION OF THE CIRCULATION

In various countries the idea has been asserted that the reduction in the volume of means of payment occurred after, and was considerably less pronounced than, the fall in prices, and that it was therefore incorrect to describe the fall in prices as a result of a process of deflation. It is necessary to look closer into this question, first of all finding out what statistics can tell us about this retarded diminution of the provision of means of payment.

As regards Sweden, we can first of all establish the fact that up to the end of 1920 a very close agreement exists between the note circulation and the price level. For the last quarter of 1920 the index for wholesale prices showed (according to the *Swedish Trade Journal*) an average of 325, the Social Board's unweighed index for foodstuffs an average of 323, while my index for the Riksbank's note circulation stood at 322. We find then that, practically speaking, these figures show complete agreement. The violent fall in prices which occurred in Sweden during 1921, however, has not been succeeded by a corresponding decrease in the note circulation. For December, 1921, the *Swedish Trade Journal's* index number is 172, the Social Board's above-mentioned index shows the figure 203, while my index of the note circulation remains at the high level of 258·3. The Social Board's general index denoting the cost of living stood by the end of the year at

216. As regards the level of wages, no reliable figures are yet available. It may be possible that it was still so high as to justify to some extent the high figure for the note circulation. The different price index figures show conspicuous lack of agreement, and apparently do not correspond to any economic equilibrium. It is therefore not possible to determine with any certainty the note circulation which would correspond to the actual level of prices. It is obvious, however, that in this case a very appreciable delay has taken place in the reduction of the note circulation that might reasonably be expected to occur in conjunction with the violent fall in prices.

For reasons explained in the foregoing it is, generally speaking, not possible to determine the total volume of notes now in circulation, as compared with the pre-War circulation, with the same degree of accuracy for other countries as it is for Sweden. If, however, we give up the idea of going back further than 1920, we shall probably find, in the case of other countries as well, quite reliable figures showing the development of the total circulation during 1921. In England the average of the total circulation (Bank of England notes and currency notes) for December, 1920, amounted to 472·97 million pounds. For December, 1921, the corresponding figure is 427·28 million pounds. A considerable reduction has thus taken place. But we find that it is relatively far less than the reduction in the price level, which went on at the same time, and which is indicated by the index figures 220 and 162 for December, 1920, and December, 1921, respectively (*Economist* index numbers, 1913=100).

We observe a similar state of affairs in the United States. The total circulation outside the Exchequer and the Federal Reserve system, as calculated *per capita* of the population at the following dates, amounted to:

	Circulation in Dollars.	Price Index.
1920 1 January	49·81	248
1 July	50·19	262
1921 1 January	51·29	177
1 May	46·57	151
1 July	45·02	148
1 October	42·98	150
1 November	42·41	149

For purposes of comparison the Bureau of Labor's price index for the corresponding months is placed in the table by the side of the circulation index. From July, 1920, to May, 1921, the reduction in prices represents more than 40 per cent., whereas the reduction in the circulating medium is scarcely more than 6 per cent. After May, 1921, however, the circulation was considerably reduced, while the price level remained fairly constant. We may apparently infer from this that, whereas the decrease in the circulation which should naturally accompany the fall in prices has been delayed, an adjustment to a more normal relation as between circulation and price level has now been introduced.

In this connection it may be noticed that during the period of inflation the circulation did not rise at the same rate as the wholesale price index, and should, therefore, not be expected to drop to a similar extent. On the whole, the rise in retail prices and in wages in the United States seems never to have reached the same high level as the wholesale prices, and this would then explain why the amount of means of payment in circulation also failed to reach the point denoted by the index for wholesale prices.

In other countries, too, the circulation during the period

of deflation has declined decidedly more slowly than the wholesale prices.

It seems, therefore, an undeniable fact that the reduction in the community's provision of means of payment during the period of falling prices which commenced in the course of 1920 set in at a later date, and was more protracted than the fall in the price level. This circumstance demands particular attention, and it is important for us to account for the causes which brought about such pronounced disagreement between the price level and the demand for means of payment. In relation to the price level the demand for means of payment during the period of deflation experienced a sharp rise, and it must be possible, at any rate in general outlines, to adduce the causes of this rise.

We must, in the first place, then, find out whether the increase in the demand for means of payment is uniform in the case of all kinds of means of payment. As far as Sweden is concerned I have made such an investigation with reference to the first five months of 1921 (Second Quarterly Report of *Skandinaviska Kreditaktiebolaget*).

In this investigation I endeavoured to ascertain whether the said increase in the demand did not particularly affect such means of payment as might be expected, under the prevailing conditions, to prove peculiarly adapted for being hoarded by the public as a reserve of savings. I arrived at the following conclusion. The smaller notes— *i.e.*, those of 5 or 10 kronor—are less suitable for hoarding purposes, and are naturally primarily utilised in payment of current expenses. Nor would the largest notes, those of 1,000 kronor, come into question, as people in possession of such notes have in most cases a banking account, and are thus not likely to keep amounts which are not required for immediate outgoings. Nor is it probable that funds are kept on cheque account on a much larger scale than prospective payments warrant. The hoarding of means of payment may thus most likely be expected to be confined to notes of medium denominations—*i.e.*, 100- and 50-kronor notes.

Now during the first three months of 1921 notes of 100 and 50 kronor show an *increase*, as compared with the corresponding months of the preceding year, whereas all other means of payment, notes as well as funds on cheque account, show a reduction. The conclusion to be drawn from this is obvious. The volume of means of payment retained for purposes of actual disbursement has decreased. This, then, may also be assumed to have occurred in the case of the 100- and 50-kronor notes which serve this purpose. But, at the same time, a very considerable amount of such notes—say, about 50 million kronor—has been hoarded. If we could separate this part of the circulation we should find that the remainder, the actual circulation, would, like the funds on cheque account, have fairly closely followed the downward tendency of the retail prices. The fall in wholesale prices, however, is far more violent.

It is possible, and perhaps even probable, that similar conditions prevailed with regard to the note circulation in other countries, and it would, indeed, be of great interest to have these conditions closely investigated. Since, at the beginning of the period of deflation, gold currency disappeared from circulation, it ought to be possible to work out satisfactory statistics of the reduction which the volume of the different means of payment underwent during the deflation period.

It is obvious, however, that the retarded decrease in the provision of means of payment is due also to more general causes which affect every kind of means of payment. The sharper the fall in prices, the more obvious has it become that the reduction in the provision of means of payment has simply been unable to proceed at the same rate. The explanation of this is not far to seek. A restrictive credit policy exercises a direct influence on prices, especially, of course, on wholesale prices. Even the mere announcement that restrictions will be made, and that the chief financial administration will use their best endeavours in working a lower price level, may be quite sufficient to hold back possible buyers and induce sellers to make offers; and consequently lower prices would be obtained on such business as may be transacted. Months may pass before these transactions result in an actual delivery of goods, and still longer time may elapse before the bills drawn in cover of these deliveries are honoured. It is, therefore, very natural for the fall in prices, particularly in the wholesale trade, especially if it is violent, to take place considerably earlier than the decrease in the volume of means of payment actually disposed of. Nevertheless, the curtailment of the country's provision of means of payment is the true cause of the fall in prices.

The retarded diminution in the volume of means of payment disposed of which could be ascertained at the latest fall in prices is only analogous to the circumstance that the rise in prices caused by an inflation can occur before the increase in the volume of means of payment has taken place. After the maximum point reached in 1920 the fall in prices was far more violent than the preceding rise, and it is, therefore, hardly to be wondered at if there should arise a fairly pronounced disagreement between the volume of means of payment and the level of prices. The circumstance just mentioned, however, hardly serves by itself fully to explain the considerable difference that existed throughout 1921 between the price level and the diminution in the provision of means of payment.

When analysing the provision of means of payment during the period of deflation, we must realise that the heavy fall in prices itself makes it impossible for old credits to be liquidated in the normal course, instead of which they will remain as more or less " frozen " credits. Not until these credits have been paid by the realisation of stocks or other assets, or until they have been written off as impossible to recover, will they disappear from the banks' records. The advancing of fresh funds during this process must go on as usual, even if on a reduced scale. But any figure which shows in statistical form the sum total of credits advanced at any given stage in such a period of liquidation will give an exaggerated idea of the volume of means of payment actually required for current commercial transactions.

Even the very demand for means of payment, however, will be abnormal under such conditions. Business firms are not able to count with any certainty upon their claims being paid at maturity, and, as was fully proved by the very disagreeable experiences of the last period of deflation, they must face the possibility of orders being cancelled, of goods already sold not being taken away, or even not accepted upon arrival at the place whence the order emanated. Many concerns, therefore, are obliged to keep more cash in hand, or else more funds on cheque account, than would be necessary under normal conditions. Firms or private individuals who are not sure that they are able to renew loans do not pay off instalments on them, but retain the money which would normally have been utilised for that purpose. People in such a position may allow considerable sums to remain on cheque account, or even keep them in their possession in the form of notes, and these funds will then represent an abnormal addition to the demand for means of payment.

This analysis is important, not only because it throws

light on what has actually taken place during the period
of deflation, but also because it makes it possible to deal
with false ideas regarding the nature of the deflationist
process. The idea is indeed quite widely entertained
that the fall in prices which has taken place since the
middle of 1920 has not the character of a deflation—that
is to say, has not been the consequence of a restrictive
credit policy. This opinion is generally based on the
fact that the diminution in the provision of means of
payment occurred later than the fall in prices. That
this argument is altogether inadequate is obvious from
what has just been said. Banks can easily adopt a
restrictive credit policy without succeeding in effecting
thereby any immediate reduction in the total amount of
their credits. If the banks show wise moderation in
recovering old credits, and if the expected reduction in
the total amounts of the credits is thereby deferred, this
must not be accepted as a proof that no restrictions
have been imposed on the granting of credits. The
restriction may actually have been very effective, and
may have been especially instrumental in causing a considerable fall in prices before being reflected in a reduction in the statistical figures showing the total of credits
granted.

Those who still refuse to admit that the primary cause
of the changes in the price level must absolutely be of
a monetary nature have generally laid very great stress
upon the chronological order of the changes in the price
level and the volume of means of payment, and have in
particular sought to make use of the retarded diminution
of the circulation during the period in question as an
argument against the theory which explains this fall in
prices as a result of a process of deflation. It is clear
that these critics have a far too mechanical conception
of the combination of causes underlying a process of

inflation or deflation. The causes of a variation in the general price level are not directly to be found in a variation in the total volume of means of payment employed in business. This total can hardly be directly affected by the banking policy. It is the decrease in the purchasing power expressed in terms of money that is the active factor in deflation, just as the increase in this purchasing power is the active factor in inflation. As we have already seen, the extent of the purchasing power can be largely determined by the financial policy of the State. But in so far as the supply of purchasing power is determined by the conditions governing bank credits, the manner in which these conditions actually affect the desire to make use of credit will have a considerable influence on the purchasing power and consequently on the price level. Thus the primary cause of variations in the general price level is always to some extent psychological in character.

Moreover, it must be pointed out in this connection that anyone who denies that the fall in prices has been a consequence of a process of deflation does not thereby free himself from the necessity of finding an explanation for the lack of agreement between price level and volume of means of payment which characterised the period under review. And, if he seriously means to try and solve this problem, he, too, will probably come to admit grounds of explanation of a character essentially similar to those here given. Furthermore, it remains, of course, for those who will not accept the restrictive credit policy as the true explanation of the big fall in prices which took place in 1920 and 1921 to advance some other explanation of this phenomenon. Perhaps the nearest causal explanation which they can then fall back upon will be the increase in the available quantity of commodities. Indeed, recourse has already been had to this explanation. As, however, up to the end of 1920 the provision of means of payment may on the whole be said to have fairly closely corresponded to the price level, and as what must be regarded in relation to the price level as a superabundance of means of payment did not come into question until 1921, it would have to be assumed that the supply of commodities was greater in 1921 than in 1920.

This was certainly not the case. It is a well-known fact that unemployment was far more extensive in 1921 than it had been in 1920. During 1921 a great number of vessels were laid up, and statistics of exports show on the whole a sharp reduction in the quantity of commodities shipped abroad. Available index figures denoting the volume of foreign trade also indicate a most decided diminution in the total quantity of commodities. As regards the United States, it is especially worthy of remark that the 1921 crop was considerably smaller than that of 1920. The decrease is placed at 10 per cent. for corn, 13 per cent. for hay, 20 per cent. for potatoes, 54 per cent. for apples, 34 per cent. for tobacco, and 50 per cent. for cotton (Barclay's Bank *Monthly Review*, London, December, 1921). It is thus evident that the fact of an increase in the quantity of commodities cannot be taken as an explanation of the unduly heavy demand for means of payment. On the contrary, the decrease in the quantity of commodities during 1921 is undoubtedly a factor which is bound to make the provision of means of payment during 1921 appear still more abnormal.

When it is a question of accounting for what must be regarded, in relation to the price level, as a superabundance of means of payment, people are very often satisfied with a mere reference to the " decreased velocity of circulation " of the means of payment. This reference is in itself practically meaningless. It must be clearly shown in what respects the means of payment have been less utilised, and the causes of such changes must be fully accounted for. An attempt at such an analysis will go to show that it has been conditions of just such a nature as is here intimated that have played a decisive part in what is termed the diminished velocity of the circulation of the means of payment; and that, therefore, the primary cause of this change in the demand for means of payment is really to be found in the very violence of the fall in prices, on account of which the extent of credit and the quantity of means of payment have not yet succeeded in being diminished on the same scale as that on which prices have fallen, or, in consequence of the critical disturbances actually brought about by the fall in prices, have even failed to be reduced at all.

Before leaving these observations on the retarded decrease in the means of payment we may perhaps be justified in pointing out one other factor which may have had, and in some cases has certainly had, a very considerable influence on the phenomenon in question. I have in mind here the export of currencies to abroad mentioned in a previous chapter (p. 42). The funds invested abroad obviously do not serve as means of payment for domestic business, but are, from the latter point of view, rather to be considered as hoarded capital. There seems to be no doubt that an increase of such means of payment invested abroad took place in 1921, and that, therefore, at least in the case of certain currencies, the quantity of means of payment existing in the form of that country's own currency is in reality considerably less than statistical figures give us to understand. This applies not only to good currencies which are used in countries with an unsound currency, partly as means of payment, partly as means for maintaining wealth, but also to bad currencies exported by such countries as a provisional means of payment and secured abroad by speculative buyers of foreign exchanges. Thus a country like Germany may have many milliards of mark notes lying abroad, while the country itself to a large extent has recourse, for instance, to Dutch and Swiss currency notes. It is obvious that in this way the world's total demand for means of payment is bound to rise above the normal. So long as such a use of means of payment continues to be extended, it is not to be expected that the statistical figures for a country's provision of means of payment will decline at the same rate as the price level.

THE PROBLEM OF STABILISATION

IF we regard the process of deflation described in the last chapter from the point of view of the world's economy, it will at once become apparent how utterly aimless it is. It cannot be of the slightest importance if units of money which form the basis of international trade are raised in value. The only quality demanded of a monetary system which is of any importance for promoting the trade and general welfare of the world, is stability. If the War and all it brought in its train turned the world's monetary system upside down, that is no reason for trying to restore the monetary conditions prevailing before the War. They have nothing of an essential character in them. The essential factor was the high degree of stability attained at that time, and it is this stability we should now endeavour to restore. This is, in fact, the only practicable and wise object we can for the present set before us in our exchange policy.

I am well aware that many entertain a different view of the present problem; justice is demanded for creditors of pre-War days who, through the fall in the value of money, have lost some part of their wealth. If, however, we really wish to take up the question of justice in the present case we must obviously regard the question from an essentially broader point of view. Clearly it would not be fair to give those who became creditors in the course of the worst period of inflation increased real claims on the rest of the community. Especially as, during latter years, State debts have assumed proportions many times larger than ever existed before the War, this point of view plays a very important part. It is, therefore, impossible to dispense justice by restoring the value of the monetary unit to what it was before the War. In view of the economic disturbances that have taken place in the world, justice can never be dispensed at all, however we may choose the new value for money. We are confronted here with an unusually graphic example of the tragedy of mankind never being able really to make good the evil they have committed. If once we have come to acknowledge this, we have all the more reason for taking the bitter lesson seriously to heart for the future. If, besides this, we are able to apply some relief where obvious distress has been caused, it is certainly the highest amends we are now able to make. Those who believe themselves capable of dealing out justice through raising the value of money must further bear in mind that the unprecedented losses caused by the deflationist process may easily render many claims absolutely worthless, and that the creditor then gets but little satisfaction out of the value of the monetary unit on which his claim rests having been improved. If any mention is to be made of justice, then some consideration should also be paid to all the heavily engaged business men and other debtors who are being ruined by the process of deflation, as well as to the masses of unemployed who have been innocent sufferers under this process.

I believe, on these grounds, that upon a discussion as to the most suitable level for the value of the new monetary unit the wisest course will be to disregard the point of view of justice and to keep to the purely economic points of view. As in all economics, it is then a question of directing our gaze to the future. We must indeed ask ourselves this question : How can we at the earliest possible

moment restore such conditions to the economic life
of the world as will prevent the world from going
under ? As far as this question affects the value
of money, there can be no other answer than this: We
must, as soon as possible, and with the least possible
friction, restore stability not only in the internal values
of the various currencies, but also in their international
exchange rates. The level at which the value of money
is then fixed is, relatively speaking, a matter of secondary
importance.

As was predicted, the process of deflation has proved
extremely harmful. The general depression at present
prevailing throughout the world is very largely a result
of this process of deflation. The unfortunate part is
that it can never be determined how far deflation may
be responsible for this depression. The mad policy of
militarism that has been pursued ever since the armistice
in November, 1918, and is the cause of true peace not
having even yet been attained, is in itself quite sufficient
to destroy the world's economic life and to bring ruin
and unemployment upon all the nations of the world.
But the deflationist policy alone would have been sufficient to produce much the same effect. Since both these
mistakes have operated in conjunction with one another,
the result has been a catastrophe for which none of the
contributing parties are being immediately called to
account, and in which each one is able more or less
successfully to point to other predominant factors as
being the cause of the general chaos. A particularly
harmful result of the process of deflation is that the
burden of the public debts becomes heavier than the
community can bear. When these debts have assumed
absolutely fantastic proportions, it is bound to be extremely dangerous to attempt a measure tending to
make the unit in which the figures are calculated larger.

But this is exactly what has been done through deflation. It is probable that some of those countries which by 1920 had already become so overburdened with debts that they had reached the limit of their financial capacity have, through the process of deflation which has gone on ever since, been reduced to a state of actual insolvency. And even where this cannot definitely be said to be the case, nevertheless the increasing burden of public debts has seriously endangered the prosperity of industrial life, and, in the long run, even the entire economic life of the country.

It may well be asked what it was that drove the various countries to such an unwise proceeding. The above-mentioned desire to do justice to the creditors of long standing has hardly been a deciding factor. In the case of the European countries which have gone in for a deflationist policy, the object has been, as previously pointed out, the restoration of the gold standard. The formally legal view that notes represent a promise to pay in gold, and that this promise should at some time be fulfilled, has proved to be a very powerful motive. The unsettled feeling that the existing situation was an abnormal one, and that it was necessary to return to a pre-War condition of affairs, has also played a not un-important part in dictating this policy. People generally seem to have considered very little the question as to whether it lay within the bounds of possibility to achieve the restoration aimed at, or as to what measures would best serve their purpose. They have put off looking more closely into these questions under the impression that if only they waited long enough they would be able to settle all difficulties. The belief that a restoration of what people called normal conditions could be brought about through a gradual deflation has, indeed, been very wide-spread. Even one year's experience has been sufficient

17

to show that such a gradual process of deflation is simply
not possible. As soon as a deflationist programme has
been laid down, and the means of carrying it through which
we possess in the bank policy have been put into practice,
a violent fall in prices is the inevitable result. Even if
later on the fall in prices can·be checked by means of
abatements in the discount policy, yet the depression
can never be entirely relieved until confidence in the
currency is once more restored—that is to say, until
industry obtains the assurance that all attempts at depressing the price level will be discontinued.

However, if in the case of countries whose exchange
lay below the old gold parity there may at any rate have
been some idea in endeavouring to raise the value of their
currency, similar efforts on the part of a country whose
exchange was already on a par with gold must be utterly
meaningless. The deflationist policy of the United States
can scarcely be said to have served any wise purpose.
Under prevailing conditions raising the value of the
dollar could only cause a corresponding rise in the value
of gold. Such a rise could not possibly be of any benefit
to the United States, but for other countries, striving to
raise their currencies in value in relation to gold, the rise
in the value of gold simply meant, as has been shown in
a previous chapter, that all their efforts and sacrifices were
made in vain. The result for the world in general was
that it did not come one jot nearer what is of all things the
most important—the stabilisation of the internal values
of the currencies and of the exchange rates between them.

It is in the nature of things that a stabilisation of
the world's exchange conditions must commence with a
stabilisation of the best currency. A race between
countries for raising the internal values of their currencies
must prove utterly useless if the country which has the
best currency also participates. The foremost must

remain steady. As circumstances now are, it is a matter of the highest international interest that the monetary unit of the United States should have a fixed value. Even if the general desire to return to a gold standard could be disregarded, the dollar would in any case hold a leading position in the world's system of payment. Other countries have debts and interest on debts on a vast scale, which they owe to the United States. It can scarcely be regarded as a satisfactory arrangement that the United States have it in their power arbitrarily to increase the real pressure of these burdens of debt through raising the purchasing power of the dollar. Also, in view of the part now being played by the United States in the world's trade, it is, of course, extremely important that the value of the dollar be kept as firmly fixed as possible. It must further be observed that a stabilisation of the internal value of the dollar involves a stabilisation of the value of gold itself, and thereby acquires considerable importance for the whole of the rest of the world's efforts at returning to a gold standard.

Fortunately the interest felt by the rest of the world in the stabilisation of the dollar is in no wise opposed to the United States' own interest. Both for the sake of its internal economic life and of its foreign trade the United States must endeavour as soon as possible to arrive at stable monetary conditions. Since May, 1921, the process of deflation in the United States has practically ceased, and the wholesale price level (according to the Bureau of Labor) has shown a remarkable stability with only very slight movements round the number 150. There are not wanting signs, however, that a rise in prices may be imminent. The Federal Reserve system's percentage of gold cover has been steadily on the increase, and at the beginning of 1922 reached what will appear the rather unnecessarily high figure of 77·2 per cent. (on the

15th January). It is possible that this high percentage
of gold cover will induce the banks to use their gold reserves as a foundation for making large additions to
their bank currency. Indeed they have already gone
in for a considerably more generous credit policy. Then
it only needs the external conditions, especially the
political, to take a turn which may in some degree be
regarded as favourable, for the tendencies towards a new
era of progress to be liberated, thereby bringing about
a rise in prices. It is highly desirable that such a rise in
prices be kept within narrow bounds. The duty of a
sound bank policy which has for its object the stabilisation
of the currency must be to prevent any alteration in the
price level. Above all, a warning must be given against
attempts at utilising existing possibilities in the interests
of State finance: the temptation to create through an
inflation funds to cover expenditure, the financing of
which appears on the order of the day, must be resisted.
Nevertheless, a rise in prices of 10 to 15 per cent. would
hardly in itself be at all dangerous, if it took place in
conjunction with a strong improvement in the total of
American production, and with a restoration of confidence in the future on the part of industry. Outwards
such a slight fall in the value of the dollar would obviously
prove a decided advantage, inasmuch as it would make it
possible for the sounder European currencies at once to
resume their old parities with the dollar, and thereby lay
the foundation for a more general restoration of the gold
standard.

Stabilising the world's exchange conditions must be a
gradual process. The natural way is to begin by creating
what I have called a " centre of stability," by restoring
the old parity between the pound and the dollar, and
maintaining this parity for the future. The great importance that such a progressive step would have in

restoring the world's economic confidence must be perfectly apparent. We should have gained a firm starting-point for a continued effort at stabilising other currencies, and this effort could at once be directed towards connecting them to the given centre of stability. Moreover, the maintenance of a fixed ratio of value between the pound and the dollar would manifestly bring about a certain stabilisation, not only of the internal values of these currencies, but also of the value of gold itself. Indeed, it is clear that the purchasing power of each currency can fluctuate more if the currencies are independent of one another than if they are bound by the condition of their being constantly at a certain parity.

As the objection is made that a stabilisation of the exchange rate between the pound and the dollar cannot be brought about by any external measures, and that experience has already proved the fruitlessness of all such attempts, it is necessary here to lay stress on the fact that the stabilisation at which I am aiming is something quite different from the stabilisation carried out during the War and the months immediately following the armistice. Through the United States Government's sanctioning unlimited credits, firm exchange rates between the dollar and the currencies of the Allies were successfully maintained—" pegging the exchanges," as it was technically called. This policy had to be given up in the spring of 1919, when it became a question of placing the mutual claims of the nations on a commercial basis, and ever since then it has been self-evident that the exchange rate must be determined by objectively economic factors. This is, of course, perfectly true. Any attempt at maintaining an exchange rate which essentially deviates from the purchasing power parity will, in the long run, prove a vain endeavour, and must invariably involve dangerous and disturbing interference with the natural trend of

economic development. The problem appears in quite
a different light if we set ourselves the task of adapting
the internal purchasing power parity of the currencies
to the exchange rate it is desired to maintain, and if to
this end we suitably adjust the internal purchasing power
of each separate currency. Such an adjustment can
always be attained by a suitable bank policy, and it must
essentially be attained if any stability in the international
exchanges is ever to be achieved. Before the War there
existed a very pronounced stability in the exchange rate
between the pound and the dollar, where each currency
had a definitely fixed purchasing power at home. If we
are to restore the old exchange rate, we must restore the
relation between the internal purchasing power of the two
currencies. Regarded absolutely, this purchasing power
can certainly be less than before, provided it is reduced
to a like extent in either country. If, for instance, the
price level in England and the United States could now
be stabilised at the figure 165, then the old exchange rate
between the pound and the dollar could be restored and
maintained. This can also be done, of course, on any
other common price level. But it is certainly most
convenient to choose the price level that can most easily
and most rapidly be obtained on both sides. The main
thing is for stability to be restored as soon as possible.
Whether it is done at a somewhat higher or lower purchasing power for the two currencies is of no consequence.

However, the creation of a centre of stability as is here
proposed assumes a particularly important aspect, when
it is considered that the stabilisation of the value of gold
would be ensured thereby. To enable the world to return
to a gold standard, or, rather, to enable the world to derive
some benefit from doing so, it is essential that the purchasing power of gold in relation to goods and services be
stabilised. With such unprecedented fluctuations in the

value of gold as we have been witnessing during the past few years, a return to a gold standard would hardly be feasible, and, even if it were feasible, would be very dangerous. The value of gold has latterly only been determined by that of the dollar. If it should now come to be determined by the value of the dollar and the pound, at once an essentially higher degree of stability would thereby be assured.

The maintenance of a practically fixed value for gold, however, is a problem of very wide significance. It is true that the value of gold, just as the value of all other commodities, is determined by supply and demand. But it would be quite incorrect to infer from that that we cannot exert any influence over the value of gold. Its supply must on the whole be considered to be dependent on the world's accumulated stocks of gold and on its annual production, which in its turn is in some degree affected by the purchasing power of gold, but is otherwise determined by natural conditions. On the other hand, we can exercise very considerable influence on the demand for gold—that is to say, on that important part of demand which is generally described as the monetary demand. As the use of circulating gold coins has nowadays been generally suspended, this monetary demand almost exclusively consists of the note-issuing banks' demands for gold reserves. An adequate restriction of these demands cannot be said to lie outside the possibility of a rational monetary policy. On the contrary, it happens to be a very important part of that policy which must be pursued if stable monetary conditions are to be restored to the world. The exceptionally large stocks of gold which the United States Federal Reserve banks have attracted to themselves in latter years have meant a rising demand for gold, and thereby an increased value on gold, which, as we have seen, has proved to be one of the

principal causes of the difficulty that has arisen in restoring
the gold standard. If for the future gold is to attain
any stability in value, it is absolutely essential that the
central banks should co-operate with one another in
suitably limiting their demands for gold reserves. These
demands must not be too small, but neither must they be
too large; they must be constantly adapted on reasonable
lines to the market situation, so that a practically unaltered gold value may be maintained. In future this will
actually become the foremost claim on the gold policy of
the great central banks. The very object of their keeping
a gold reserve will be principally the stabilising of the
world's gold market which can be brought about thereby.

The stabilisation of the value of gold requires a co-
operation between the United States, as the possessor
of the largest monetary gold stocks in the world, and
England, as being the old centre for free trade in gold
and the international system of payment, and as controlling the greater part of the world's gold production.
Such a co-operation would naturally be in a high degree
furthered by a realisation of the foremost practical aim—
the restoration of the old parity between the pound and
the dollar. The necessary direction of the attention
towards the maintenance of this parity would subsequently
prove a natural guarantee for a continuance of this co-
operation along the lines here indicated.

For other countries with more or less settled exchange
conditions this policy would open up possibilities for a
restoration of the gold standard. In certain cases, as for
instance in Sweden, Holland, and Switzerland, this could
be done at the old parity. In other cases, again, it would
be necessary to lower the old parity. In either case the
road to the restoration of the gold standard would lie in
a stabilisation of the internal purchasing power of the
currency—that is to say, in maintaining a certain fixed

price level. If this price level could be kept as low as the Anglo-American price level we have assumed here, then the old exchange rate as against the pound and the dollar could be restored, and the country might return to a gold currency at the pre-War standard. Again, if the future stable price level stood, let us say, double as high as the Anglo-American, the new gold standard would have to be content with a gold parity corresponding to one-half of that of the old. This idea of lowering of the gold parity has hitherto been stubbornly opposed. But it would certainly be a very disastrous thing if, in the sequel, when once the external conditions for conversion to a gold standard are present, a nation should, through any false motives of ambition, allow itself to be prevented from taking the decisive step towards restoring that stability in exchange conditions which is still beyond all things both desirable and necessary.

It is evident, however, that this ambition is still an obstacle to be reckoned with. At the Congress held by the International Chamber of Commerce in London in the summer of 1921 I uttered a warning against the dangers of continuing a deflationist policy with a view to raising the currency at some time in the remote future to its former parity with gold. It was clear that the existence of these dangers was far more widely known than appeared from the voting at the Congress. But it is a fact that no country's representatives are willing to admit in public that their country must reduce its currency's parity with gold, even though this may be quite frankly acknowledged in private by persons occupying leading positions in the sphere of banking or general economic politics. In this, as in so many other spheres of post-War politics, public opinion has too long allowed itself to be governed by illusions and phrases. It is high time now to begin to look dispassionately upon the realities we have to reckon with.

In the case of those countries in which the value of the monetary unit has already fallen as low as 1 or 2 per cent. of the pre-War value, and in which the State finances are still being based on inflation, the problem of stabilisation is, of course, an extremely difficult one. Recommendations to cut down expenses in order to establish an equilibrium between expenditure and real income are as easy to give as they are difficult to put into execution. The experience of the last few years seems rather to have taught us that a country that has once really started along the downward path of inflation finds it very difficult to stop, and that inflation and State expenditure have a very pronounced tendency to expand one another, so that the situation grows ever more and more serious.

The ways and means to be adopted in such cases as are here referred to lie in the main outside the scope of a discussion which must be confined to purely monetary problems. The first condition is, of course, the restoration of a real peace, the cancellation of debts due to foreign Governments contracted during the War, or at any rate a reduction of such debts together with as long a respite from payment as will allow the debtor country time to recover its economic soundness and to create a stabilised monetary system. So long as this primary condition fails to be fulfilled a number of European states are bound to continue to follow the way of inflation and thus to fall deeper and deeper into financial distress. Such a constant deterioration in the monetary systems of a whole group of states is, as the experience of the past year should by now have made it fully apparent to everyone, a matter of very serious inconvenience to all neighbouring countries, and indeed to the entire world. International trade is exposed to disturbances of the most violent and incalculable nature, while the whole productive organisation of individual countries is subject to crises involving enormous economic losses and plunging workers in their hundreds of thousands, not to say millions, into unemployment. Politicians and financiers are apt to speak of the present depression as a juncture which, like all critical junctures in the past, is bound sooner or later to arrive at the turning-point. But if the existing state of affairs is primarily due to the adoption of wrong political methods, then there is really no cause to hope for any improvement in the situation until this policy is completely reversed. This is the first condition for a discussion of the economic future of Europe, if it is to serve any purpose at all.

Now, assuming that this external condition had been fulfilled, it would still remain for the countries with unsound currencies to put their internal finances in order. In the majority of cases these countries are probably incapable of solving this problem by their own efforts. It will, perhaps, prove necessary to a certain extent to treat them as colonial dependencies in which foreign capital under foreign administration is contributed for the purpose of re-establishing the system of communications and of encouraging the use of existing natural resources along rational and progressive lines. It is of especial importance for the ruined countries to realise this necessity, and to give their willing co-operation to what is, in reality, the only practicable form of reconstructional work, particularly by establishing such legal guarantees as are an indispensable condition to enable the work to begin. In order to systematise communications it will probably prove necessary on a fairly large scale to organise enterprises adjusted to the fulfilment of economic requirements rather than to political boundaries, which will mean the extension of their activities to several countries at once.

Under such conditions it may be possible to succeed in

putting a stop to inflation, and upon the ruins of the
old monetary system to create a stable monetary system
in which the unit may perhaps be fixed at 10 or 100
of the old units, or at any such ratio. But it is also
possible that the old currency may have to be wholly
abandoned. If it has depreciated to such an extent
that all confidence in it has been lost, and no fixed prices
can be said any longer to exist, then there is very little
purpose to be served in trying to maintain it. The difficulty in connection with the old claims is thus also
disposed of ; they are already practically valueless.
Under such circumstances it becomes a question of laying
entirely new foundations without regard to the old. It
is probable that a country in such a situation will not
be capable of creating unaided a completely new monetary
system. In this, too, the assistance of foreign countries
will be required. Those whose duty it will be to organise
the new monetary system must act quite independently
of the State authorities concerned and of their financial
requirements. Apparently the natural thing will be to
introduce a foreign currency into the distressed country,
or at least to let it serve as a basis for that country's
new monetary system. Such a movement has already
begun automatically. In the distressed countries business is being effected more and more in foreign currencies.
However, in order to attain true success, there is required
an institution which is supported by foreign capital and
a foreign organisation, and has as its direct object the
provision of a serviceable currency for the country concerned. Whether such an institution should eventually
extend its activities to several distressed countries at
once is for the present an open question.

The discussions which sometimes take place as to
which currency is to be chosen for the creation of a new
monetary system for a distressed country are rather

unnecessary, and often quite childish. The only essential is that the new currency shall be administered in such a way that it acquires a fixed value and may thereby be maintained at some definite parity with the pound or the dollar. The stream of projects for world currencies which still flows steadily on has no significance beyond showing how little the public yet understands of the purely monetary purport of the exchange problem.

Such is the problem of stabilisation in its broad outlines. It only remains now to discuss certain features in greater detail. For this purpose I must refer to what I have said concerning this problem in my Memoranda, particularly the second one, and may here only go into such points as are therein discussed, where they appear to require elucidation, or where objections make it necessary for me to give further explanation.

What appears most to have aroused opposition in the recommendations I submitted for stabilising the world's exchange conditions is the idea of determining beforehand for each particular country a certain price level to be regarded as normal and as far as possible to be maintained unaltered. It has been objected that such an aim would be Utopian, and that in any case the note-issuing banks lack the means to carry it through. This argument may well be met with the reminder that it is just such an aim as this that is set up by those who urge a return to pre-War prices, as also by those who, in demanding the restoration of the old gold standard, are in reality asking for a price level corresponding to that of the United States. It may also be worth while pointing out that a country which, while a gold standard still existed practically throughout the world, decided to maintain its currency on a par with gold, in actual fact decided to keep to a certain fixed price level. Such control of the price level is the only way of guaranteeing a currency's

parity with gold. The gold parity requires a certain
fixed price level. Should the price level deviate considerably from this normal level, no power in the world
can maintain the gold parity. Should the country, for
instance, through a too generous credit policy, cause its
price level to rise considerably above the normal level,
then gold must leave the country, and if that fails to
rectify the credit policy, no amount of gold reserves in
the world can be sufficient to maintain the country's
gold standard. It is only a want of clear knowledge
as to the essential character of a gold standard that
induces people to imagine that there is no need to regulate
the price level where a gold standard is concerned.
Perhaps it is not directly apparent, because the necessity
for keeping up payments in gold compels the pursuit of
such a credit policy as will constantly tend to bring the
price level into conformity with the normal level. If
a country has no gold standard, but desires to adopt
such a standard, the only way to do so is by fixing the
price level. Its invariability is the only thing that can
render possible a practically invariable exchange rate as
against countries already possessing a gold currency.

Doubts have particularly been expressed as to the
possibility of officially stating the price level which a
country's exchange policy should aim at fixing. To this,
again, I have only to reply that that is exactly what
one does when one declares the 1914 price level or the
United States' present price level to be the end in view.
It is also what each individual country that went over
to a gold standard in earlier times had to do; it has had
to fix in advance a price level in conformity with the
world's price level. If this idea has not been expressly
stated, it has nevertheless been implied in the terms of
the scheme dealing with the transition to a gold standard.
It is extremely important, especially in the case of a

country pursuing a deflationist policy, to state beforehand the limits to which this policy will go, and the object it is desired to attain. Deflation *ad infinitum*, a constant screwing down of the price level, would be utterly senseless and, of course, utterly disastrous as well. It is impossible for industrial life to recover the necessary confidence unless it is definitely declared that the administration at least has no intention of bringing down prices below a certain fixed level.

From various statements made by bankers and the financial Press, particularly in England, I find that my recommendations have been regarded as representing some sort of contrast to the scheme for reverting to a gold standard. It is declared that the gold standard is the one fixed point, and that England is not going to be lured into abandoning her object—that of restoring the gold standard—by speculations about the fixing of the purchasing power of the currency. Actually there exists no such contrast. The return to a gold standard is quite impossible without effecting a certain stability in the purchasing power of the currency itself.

What makes the problem at the present time so much more difficult and so much wider than it has ever been before is that now some degree of stability must also be arrived at in the value of gold itself before any transition to a gold standard is either possible or desirable. In the first place this presupposes a stabilisation, at a certain index number, of the price level in the United States. As regards England, it presupposes, as has been shown above, the stabilisation of the English price level at the same index number. The very nature of the problem clearly shows the necessity for co-operation between England and the United States. If people assert this to be beyond the bounds of practicability, then they must declare by what means they imagine it to be possible to restore the gold standard in England. In the case of other countries the problem of reverting to a gold standard similarly involves first of all the selection of a price level which it is considered possible to maintain, and, secondly, a financial and banking policy really capable of giving stability to this price level. The currency's parity with gold will be determined by the price level thus fixed.

On the other hand, a stabilisation of the world's exchange conditions cannot, as apparently people sometimes try to imagine, be attained by the separate countries now at once attempting to stabilise their exchange rates. The stabilisation of the internal values of the currencies must come first. In that sphere each country can have any aim in view it likes. But it will be unable to control the exchange rate as against another country so long as that other country has not stabilised the internal value of its own currency. If the re-establishment of a certain definite exchange rate is deemed desirable, this can only be effected by some sort of international co-operation.

Further, it is essential that people learn to realise that stabilising the price level precludes all further efforts at reducing it. Curiously enough, we are still far from realising this truth. We often see mentioned in conjunction with one another a stabilisation and a gradual fall in the price level as being the object of monetary policy. When a country is determined upon stabilising its price level, it must positively give up regarding a fall in prices as in itself an object to be aimed at and must absolutely exterminate the idea that the 1914 price level could in any way serve as the normal price level of the future. This means complete dissociation from the argument which finds its expression in the proposal of the Cunliffe Committee that for the circulation of uncovered notes the preceding year's average should be taken as the maximum for the following year. I am not so much concerned with this particular recommendation as with that widespread idea as to what should be aimed at in regard to the future development of the price level which lies behind the proposal just quoted. When once a country has decided to regard as normal a certain definite price level, this decision must not be altered the very first time the price level happens to fall below the normal level, nor must any attempt be made to set up the new lower level of prices as a normal level. It is, therefore, a condition of the policy of stabilisation that a fall below the normal level must also be counteracted. Now, changes in conditions, with their accompanying fluctuations in the price level, can never be wholly avoided. There will always be times, therefore, when prices fall below the normal, and when consequently the banking policy must aim at raising the price level. The sooner such an aim is achieved the better. The most serious faults in banking policy in all countries during the past year seem to have been due to the necessary steps having been taken too late. When prices already show a decided tendency to rise, then time is ripe for a restrictive banking policy. I may add that such endeavours to raise the price level can only be a function of the banking administration. It would be exceedingly dangerous if the State authorities were to take the opportunity once more to launch a scheme for financing State expenditure by means of inflation.

My pointing out that banking policy must therefore adapt itself now to raising, now to lowering, the price level, seems in certain quarters to have caused some surprise. Nevertheless, there is nothing new in this idea. Even under normal conditions a sound banking policy must be pursued along those lines. The only difference is that the fluctuations of the price level are now so much

18

more violent, and that now each individual country has
to consider independently what is to be the level on
which it desires to have its prices stabilised, whereas
under normal conditions this question would be determined by the international purchasing power of gold.

In discussions that have taken place over my second
Memorandum the question has been brought up as to
whether it is at all possible to stop inflation without at
the same time bringing about a deflation. This question
is perfectly justified. The measures that have to be
adopted in order to put an end to a serious inflation are
bound to be of so powerful a nature that they are very
apt to cause the reaction to be followed by a more or less
violent deflation. It is just one of the reasons why it is
at present so difficult at once to attain a stable price level.
Stabilisation can only be won gradually. But in order to
win it at all the administration, while combating any
upward tendency in the prices, must hold itself prepared
to insist upon modifying the downward tendency it strives
to produce.

Finally, emphasis must be laid on the fact that the
policy of stabilisation cannot be merely concerned with
a particular group of prices, such as wholesale prices.
Stabilisation must rather be extended to all prices, and
consequently even to wages. Under normal conditions
the natural formation of prices always tends to form a
certain economic equilibrium between different groups
of prices. A fundamental condition for this equilibrium
is that produce-prices correspond to the costs of production—that is to say, the sum total of prices that have
to be paid for producing the article. This condition seems
at present to be far short of fulfilment in most countries.
During 1921 wholesale prices dropped in a number of
cases so excessively that they reached a level far below
the costs of production. In such cases an adjustment

is essential either by raising the price of the produced article or by reducing wages or other costs of production. If a severe reduction in nominal wages might be attended with very serious difficulties, due consideration must be taken of such a contingency when choosing the price level which it is desired in future to establish as normal. This inevitable connection of ideas politicians usually seek to expel from their minds. It is inopportune to talk of a reduction of wages, and the subject is studiously avoided. And people are all the same quite prepared to hold out prospects of an improvement in the country's currency. This is a futile game of hide-and-seek. It is now a primary necessity for all nations and all classes to learn to look reality in the face. There are no grounds whatever to justify the idea that it will be possible to maintain wages at a relatively higher level than the prices of commodities. Indeed, this would mean that the productivity of labour had been increased through the disturbances we have suffered since 1914. Still, there can be no one who would ever seriously champion such a theory.

There remain to be added some remarks upon the actual transition to a gold standard. The restoration and maintenance of a gold standard depend on certain conditions whose relative order and importance we must have clearly defined. The fundamental condition is that the purchasing power of the currency is kept on a level with that of gold. In the second place comes the redemption of notes with gold. Only the third in order of importance, as a guarantee that this redemption will be practicable, comes the demand for certain gold reserves in cover for the notes. There is a very peculiar disposition, especially on the part of the central banks, to reverse this order of priority and to make the maintenance of a certain amount of gold reserves the principal point. The fact has been borne out everywhere that the central banks have refused to redeem their notes, not because they had no gold with which to redeem them, but because if they did so their gold reserve position would fall below the prescribed or the desired quotient. According to this irrational view it is believed that one can best pave the way for a return to a gold standard by accumulating as large stocks of gold as possible in the vaults of the central banks, and while interest is being entirely absorbed by secondary considerations of this sort, the essential point—*i.e.*, the stabilisation of the internal purchasing power of the currency in a certain fixed relation to that of gold—is completely lost sight of; in fact, people go so far as to declare that the solving of this problem lies outside the scope of the central banks' duties, and that they lack the means for dealing with it.

The restoration of an international system of gold currency at the present juncture, as is clear from what has been said in the foregoing, involves the additional difficulty that to a certain extent the value of gold itself must first of all be stabilised. For this purpose some restriction of the demand for gold is necessary. But if the central banks compete with one another in their efforts to accumulate as large stocks of gold as possible in order to prepare the way for the restoration of the gold standard, the result can only be that the value of gold is forced up in a manner quite incompatible with the fundamental need for a fixed gold value. Any attempt to reintroduce a gold circulation would have the same effect, and a warning must therefore be constantly uttered against all efforts in that direction. As an argument against what I have said regarding the danger involved in an excessive demand for gold, it has been pointed out that most countries would nowadays be too poor to be able to acquire gold, and that therefore there is no danger of the demand becoming too great. However, in face of the enormous rise in the value of gold that took place from the spring of 1920 to the spring of 1921, there is hardly any occasion to regard the matter any longer in that light. One of the principal factors underlying this increase in the value of gold has been the vast accumulation of gold in the banks of the Federal Reserve system of the United States, and this accumulation has taken place concurrently with a serious economic depression in that country.

It is obviously important for the restoration of the gold standard that the value of gold is not now unnecessarily enhanced. And it is equally obvious that, to attain this end, a restriction of the demand for money on the part of the countries belonging to Western civilisation is necessary. It is simply a question of whether it is likely to be possible in the long run to maintain, as against the demand for gold in the East, the present value of gold, which, nevertheless, in spite of the latest rise, is considerably lower than the value ruling before the War. During the past year Asia has not been able to afford to purchase much gold. But a change in this situation is not unthinkable, in which case the countries of Western civilisation will be faced with the problem whether they are in a position to meet the demand for gold from the East by reducing their own monetary gold requirements, or whether they can find any way of reducing the demand from the East. As far as that is concerned, one has in the first place, as I have previously pointed out, to think of making vigorous efforts so to develop the Oriental people's requirements of real commodities that these nations will no longer find themselves able to afford the acquisition of so much gold.

In each individual country it is important to observe the order given here in which the conditions for restoring the gold standard must be taken. It is first of all, therefore, a question of conforming the price level to the gold standard that is to be introduced. It has sometimes been urged, particularly in Sweden, that, irrespective of this primary condition, the redemption of notes with gold should at once be resumed. But this is absurd. If the price level really is considerably higher than the maintenance of the gold parity warrants, then no amount of gold reserves can be sufficient to meet the demands for gold which an immediate resumption of the practice of converting notes into gold would call forth. If this conversion into gold were really made fully effective, the result would only be that some few persons would possess themselves of the entire gold reserves of the country, and would make a considerable profit out of it. The country would thereby have come no nearer attaining its object of restoring the gold standard. Those who recommend a policy of this kind naturally imagine that the disappearance of gold would prove the most effective means of compelling the central banks to reduce the note circulation and bring down the price level. Resorting to such forcible measures can scarcely be regarded as reasonable. At any rate a more direct way would be to see first if it would not be possible to provide the central bank with a more rational management.

As I explained at length in my second Memorandum, it is hardly possible for a small European country by itself to resume the practice of redeeming notes with gold. With the present enormous fluctuations of the exchanges the effort might easily prove too much for it. The redemption of notes with gold, therefore, will probably have to be resumed in a number of countries simultaneously, and it seems practically inevitable that England will have to lead the way. In order to enable a country to meet the demand for gold which might possibly assert itself in the event of the gold standard being restored, a considerable reserve of economic strength would be required.   Only if London is a free gold market, prepared at first hand to meet such demands, is it likely that small countries will be able to undertake an unconditional conversion of their currencies into gold.   As against this it may be objected that a country can always convert its notes into gold so long as its gold reserves hold out, and that the loss of the gold reserves does not represent any economic loss to the country.   The only possible answer is that no security could thereby be given for the maintenance of the gold standard.   The idea of now resuming the redemption of notes with gold, only to be compelled later on to suspend it, would scarcely represent a method of procedure calculated to restore that confidence which at the present juncture is what is most urgently required.   On the other hand, it stands to reason that those countries who want a gold standard must to some extent hold themselves jointly responsible for demands for gold being duly met.   If any of them close their gold reserves against such demands, the only result will be that the demands will fall so much the more heavily upon the remainder.

The effective maintenance of a gold standard in a country further demands not only that gold be surrendered against that country's currency, but also that the country be prepared without restriction to accept gold at a fixed price.   Only if gold is thus constantly accepted in a number of countries can adequate security be obtained against a violent fall in the value of gold.   Thus, all countries possessing a gold standard are jointly responsible for the value of gold being maintained by always ensuring a free market to gold.   Those who declare their intention of returning to a gold standard must not start by shirking this duty.   But this was exactly what Sveriges Riksbank attempted to do when, in February, 1922, under pressure

of a temporary decline in the dollar rate, the bank claimed
continued exemption from its liability to buy gold at a
fixed price. From the point of view just discussed this
policy was to be condemned, but it was also unwise in
other respects. If in the case of any European country
the market situation should chance to develop in such a
way that gold is attracted to that country, it can only be
considered an advantage under present circumstances to
have its gold reserves thus reinforced. There may very
easily come a time when this additional reserve—and
more still—may be badly needed to enable that country
without hesitation to redeem its notes with gold. For
the next few years a country possessing a gold standard
will doubtless have to be prepared for far more violent
fluctuations in its gold reserve than ever used to take
place in pre-War days, and it must be realised that
an anxious insistence on keeping to the old rules for
the regulation of gold reserves will no longer prove to
be compatible with a rational monetary policy. The
required stability in the value of gold can only be attained
if the central banks in countries which have returned to
a gold standard are prepared without reserve both to
accept gold and to part with gold in strict accordance
with what the market situation demands. Such a policy
will in the long run bring about the stabilisation of the
gold market, and thereby a limitation of the gold reserves
to more normal proportions, whereas any attempt to
obstruct the free movements of gold must react on the
steadiness of the market.

Lately the idea of a " gold exchange standard " has
frequently been mentioned in discussion. If it has been
intended by this to mean that the European countries
should go over to a gold standard without introducing,
for the purpose, a gold coinage into the circulation, then
that idea is fully in accord with the opinion expressed by

me when I uttered a warning against reverting at the present time to an actual gold circulation which would lay far too severe demands on the world's gold stocks. As I have frequently pointed out, the one essential element in a gold standard is that the gold has a fixed price in the country's currency—that is to say, is purchasable and saleable at rates deviating only very slightly from the established parity. In order to maintain such a gold standard, it may perhaps be expedient to possess a gold reserve. But sight balances in effective gold currencies— such as the dollar—may in most cases serve the same purpose. The idea, therefore, that the introduction of the gold exchange standard would in itself necessitate a fresh distribution of the world's gold stocks, in which case the United States in particular would have to part with a considerable portion of their unnecessarily large gold reserve, can hardly be justified. It can scarcely be said to be necessary for the countries of Europe, with their weak finances, to contract additional debts abroad by laying in stocks of non-interest-bearing gold with the purpose of founding thereon a well-regulated economic life. The main point is that the purchasing power of a currency be kept in a fixed relation to that of the dollar. No amount of gold reserves can render this primary condition superfluous; if, on the other hand, this condition is carefully fulfilled, it is likely that in a majority of cases quite a moderate gold reserve is all that will be required. Thus, even in the treatment of this question we see clearly how necessary it is to fight against the old superstition about the importance of gold reserves. A wise policy of stabilisation is conditional upon the world's getting rid of the superstitious idea that a gold reserve is capable of giving a currency a value which it does not possess by virtue of there being a definite scarcity in the country's provision of means of payment.

There are a number of people who, against all—even the most rationally conceived—schemes for restoring normal exchange conditions, raise the objection that it is no use introducing artificial remedies, that developments must be allowed to take their course, and that time alone can repair the damage that has been done. It is a rather cheap kind of wisdom that finds expression in utterances of this sort. Anyone who closely studies the exchange problem will soon discover that it is practically impossible for either the State authorities or the central banks to avoid exercising an influence on the monetary system of the world. In some way or other policy will always affect its development. Is there really any reason for calling this influence a natural one when it is poorly thought out or else dictated by harmful political motives, while describing it as artificial when it is a link in a chain of systematic endeavour to provide a rational solution of the monetary problem ? All civilisation represents one mighty effort of man to overcome difficulties instead of passively allowing himself to be carried away by them. At the present moment the future of civilisation rests in no small degree upon this central will to conquer being able to assert itself in the sphere of money.

INDEX

AGIO: 63, 77, 88, 98

Allies, the: 5, 159, 165, 191, 199, 201

Alsace-Lorraine: 41

America: 66, 68, 141, 199, 201, 238, 239

American embargo: 75

Amsterdam: 43

Argentine: 75, 111

Armistice: 65, 154, 187, 256, 261

Artificial purchasing power, creation of: 9-19, 25-29, 97, 104, 112, 119, 129, 203

Asia: 277

Balance of payment: See Trade balance

Bank of Austria: 31, 65

Bank of England: 64, 109, 189, 194, 203, 205

Bank of France: 31, 32, 65, 66

Bank of Norway: 195

Bank laws: 4

Bank policy: 97, 225, 226, 238, 247, 249-250, 273; Federal Reserve Board's: 220-226, 235-237

discount policy: 101-136, 189, 194, 258; Federal Reserve Board's: 196-199

Bank rate: See Discount rate

Barclay's Bank *Monthly Review:* 206, 257

Belgium: 40, 43

Blockade, the: 165, 168

Bolsheviks, the: 66

Bond market: 127

Bonds: 15, 43, 121, 198

Liberty Bonds: 197

Long term bonds: 117

State Bonds: 10, 11

Brest-Litovsk, Peace of: 65

British Empire: 68

Brussels, International Financial Conference at: 124, 212, 213, 214, 216, 228

Bureau of Labour: 70, 188, 225, 244, 259

Capital market: 109, 112-114, 119

Capital, real: 115, 121, 122, 126

abnormal dearth in: 126

" floating capital," surplus of: 113-115; reduction of: 109

scarcity of capital: 109, 112

Central Bureau v. d. Stat: 234

Central Europe: 161

Central Powers: 165

Cheque payments, encouraging of: 32

China: 69

Christiania: 88, 98

Circulation, increase in: 31-41, 57-59, 61, 62, 72, 124; contraction of: 42; decrease in: 244; pre-war: 243

gold circulation: 33, 71

note circulation: 35, 40, 41, 42, 65, 71, 77, 98, 125, 126; Swedish: 36-38, 42, 272, 89, 91-94, 130-134, 242; English: 204, 212, 243 ; United States: 234, 243

silver circulation: 34, 35

Civil War, the: 216

Congress, session of 8th August, 1919: 219

Copenhagen: 88, 89

Cost of living: 46, 125, 132, 208, 210, 220, 221

Credit expansion: 131, 194, 197, 203, 221-224

Credit policy: See Bank policy

Credit rationing: 213

Credit, speculative: 220; legitimate: 220 ; measures for limiting: 101

Cuba: 239

Cunliffe Committee: 203-207, 272

Currency, export of: 42, 45. See further German Mark, function of: 115

Currency problem: 174, 176, 211, 213

Eastern European currencies: 44

D'Abernon, Lord: 208-210
Danish National Bank: 3, 124, 127, 195
Deflation: 213, 215-217, 232, 236, 237, 240, 242, 245-250, 256-258, 271, 274; in the United States: 228, 237, 238
Deflation policy: 217, 224, 230, 231, 236, 240, 271; Federal Reserve Board's: 225, 226, 227, 235
Deflation programme: 213, 217, 258; in England: 206, 207, 211, 212; in the United States: 218-224
Denmark: 41, 42, 83, 85-88, 90, 92, 95, 96, 125, 126, 133, 134
Depression period 1873-75: 216
Disagio: 87
Discount policy: See Bank policy.
Dollar: 65, 75, 76, 94, 147, 148, 160, 161, 196-201, 218, 220, 221, 231, 232, 235, 236, 237, 258-261, 263, 265, 269, 281
Dollar circulation index: 244
Dollar exchange: 98, 99, 147, 217

East, the: 68, 69, 75, 277
Eastern Europe: 40
"Economic Declaration" (Supreme Council, 8th March, 1920): 211
Economic Journal: 122, 182, 208, 214
Economist, the: 188, 191, 205, 233, 236, 243
Egypt: 24, 69
Ekonomisk Tidskrift : 131
England: 33, 34, 67, 70, 75, 76, 108, 111, 154, 157, 162, 170, 171, 173, 182, 189, 190, 201, 203, 207, 210, 233, 243, 262, 263, 271, 278
English, the: 207
Europe: 75, 126, 146, 190, 192-194, 199-201, 202, 211, 240, 267, 281
Exchange market: 80, 184
Exchange policy: 230, 231, 254, 270
Exchange problem: 165, 167, 212, 218, 269, 282
Exchange rate: 44, 86, 98, 107, 135, 137-146, 147, 151, 154, 156, 157-168, 171-173, 175, 176, 178-185, 203, 204, 208, 209, 211, 212, 239, 240, 256, 261, 262, 265, 270, 271, 278; theoretical: 182

Exchange, theory of: 163, 170-186
Exchanges, equilibrium of: 155-158, 161; illicit trade in: 167; "pegging the exchanges": 261

"Fair Price Committees" (U.S.A): 219
Far East, the: 75, 193, 194, 200
Federal Reserve Bank of New York: 196, 223
Federal Reserve Banks: 196, 197, 222-227, 239, 263
Federal Reserve Board: 198, 221, 223-226, 235
Federal Reserve System: 219, 221, 222, 227, 228, 243, 259
Finanstidende: 234
Finland: 190
Floating debt: 10, 239
Franc, French: 41, 160
France: 33, 65-67, 111, 188, 234
Frankfurter Zeitung: 153, 234
Free coinage, free mintage, suspension of: 79, 83, 85
French, the: 30, 39
"Frozen credits": 38, 248

German mark: 15, 41, 158-160; export of: 42-44, 150-154; export prohibition of: 199, 200
    mark rate: 60, 61, 65
German Reichsbank: 32, 65, 109, 114, 115
Germany: 5, 14, 33, 39, 41, 43, 65, 67, 114, 116, 150-154, 159, 161, 165, 168, 190, 191, 234, 253
Gold coins: 33, 34, 63, 85-90, 92, 93, 104, 280
"Gold exchange standard": 280, 281
Gold-exclusion policy: 79-100
Gold market: 70-71, 264
Gold, movement of: 63, 64, 68, 70; export of: 64-69, 72, 75; licences for export of: 88; depreciation of: 92, 99, 100, 202, 211; forced import of: 23, 92, 99; rise in the value of: 97, 215, 236, 258, 277; scarcity of: 215; industrial consumption of: 69; premium on: 177; purchasing power of: 97
"Gold points": 176
Gold production: 67-70
"Gold Question," the : 217

Gold standard: 63, 65, 77, 81, 82, 84, 96-107, 116, 142, 174, 180, 181, 186, 203, 205, 206, 211, 213-215, 217, 230, 231, 259-265, 269-272, 275-278; restoration of: 185, 207, 257
Gold stocks, the world's: 281
Goschen: 177, 178
Great Britain: 66

Hitchin: 68
Hoarding of notes: 38-40, 61, 245, 246
Holland: 43, 72, 76, 96, 113, 116, 122, 123, 264
House of Lords: 208, 210
Hungary: 190

Index numbers, calculation of: 45-51
India: 67
Indian mints: 84
Inflation: 11, 20, 21, 25, 26, 27, 29, 33, 37, 40, 56, 61, 63-78, 101, 111, 112, 120, 145, 146, 147, 149, 162, 167, 168, 173, 182, 184, 187-202, 214-216, 221, 232, 235, 247, 250, 254, 260, 266, 268, 273; in Sweden: 90-95, 133-135; in neutral countries: 96-100; in the United States: 223, 228; in England: 205; responsibility for: 100, 101
Interest rates: 97, 103, 104, 109, 110, 112, 115, 116, 118, 120, 121, 123, 128, 129, 131, 133, 151, 178, 217
International Chamber of Commerce, Congress held by (London, 1921): 265
International Institute of Statistics at The Hague: 51
Italy: 67, 188

Japan: 64, 68, 70, 233
Japanese Central Bank: 233

Keynes: 184; "The Revision of the Treaty," 183

League of Nations: 141, 212; Financial Committee of: 214

Loans, long term: 112, 117, 118, 123
    short term: 112-114, 117, 211
    war loans: 39
London: 196, 202, 265, 279
London Joint City and Midland Bank: 64

Maximum price: 23, 24, 47, 48
McCullogh: 170
Memoranda to the League of Nations (Cassel): 141
    first Memorandum: 216, 217
    second Memorandum: 269, 279
Mexico: 200
Mint Laws: 2
Moll: 131-133, 135; "The Riksbank and the High Cost of Living," 132
Moratorium: 30, 38, 239

Napoleonic Wars: 174
Netherlands, the: 84, 99, 123, 234
Netherlands Bank, the: 96, 110, 123, 124, 128, 129, 195
New York: 160
Norway: 42, 83, 85-88, 80, 92, 95, 96, 126, 133, 234

Ökonomisk Revue: 234
Oriental peoples, the: 277

Parmer: 217
Peel, Viscount: 210
Poland: 170, 171
Policy of Labour: 144
Pound sterling: 98, 138, 155, 157, 160, 173, 204, 237, 260-265, 269
Prices, social economic function of: 113; natural formation of: 23
    fall in prices: 161, 188, 189, 205, 215-222, 225, 226, 231-234, 238, 240, 242, 243, 246-252, 272
    peace prices: 219
    price statistics: 155
    retail prices: 46, 70, 233
    rise in prices: 19-25, 33, 40, 46, 50, 56, 61, 62, 70, 82, 93, 101, 103, 104, 120, 134, 141, 145, 150, 154, 155, 163, 167, 169, 187, 188, 189, 194, 195, 198, 199, 209, 232, 247; in the United States: 160, 188, 192

Prices, rise in—*continued*
 193, 220, 244, 259, 260; in
 England: 183, 188, 205, 208:
 in the neutral countries: 58,
 59, 98, 99, 122-125, 129, 131,
 133
 wholesale prices: 46, 47, 70, 71,
 93, 123, 187, 244-247; index
 for: 242; index of: 76
Profiteering: 22, 23, 163
Protective tariffs: 162
Purchasing power parity: 140-144,
 147-162, 168, 172, 182, 183, 185,
 237, 262
Purchasing strike: 226

Quantity theory: 26-29

Reparation claims: 34, 150, 153,
 159, 160
Reparation Commission: 151
Reparation payments: 151, 153
Ricardo, the (Sweden): 14, 79-95,
Ricardo: 170-174, 176; "Principles
 of Political Economy": 170
Riksbank, the (Sweden): 14, 79-95,
 110, 118, 129-136, 189, 195,
 279
Roumanian Central Bank: 66, 68
Roumanian War: 66, 68
Russia: 35, 66, 182
Russian Central Bank (Russian
 Imperial Bank): 66, 68

Safeguarding of Industries Bill:
 157
Scandinavian Central Banks: 134
Scandinavian countries, the: 35, 88
Scandinavian Monetary Conven-
 tion: 87-89
Scarcity of Commodities: 60, 120,
 132, 169, 191
Share issues: 126
Silver coins: 34, 35
Silver, exclusion of: 83, 84
Skandinaviska Kreditaktiebolaget,
 Second Quarterly Report: 245
South Africa: 200
South America: 75, 193, 200, 239
Social Board (Sweden): 58, 94;
 price index for food: 242
Spain: 72

Speculation: 127, 128, 131, 194, 232,
 234; period of: 120; speculation
 in shares: 39; in exchange: 150,
 151, 163, 164, 253; speculative
 mania: 125
Statistique Générale: 234
Stock Exchange: 123, 126
Stockholm: 89, 98, 99, 155
 Commercial College: 192
 Conference in: 89
Stuart Mill: 176, 177
Svensk Handelstidning (Swedish
 Trade Journal): 58, 93, 234,
 242
Svenska Kronkreditaktiebolaget: 13,
Sweden: 7, 17, 19, 34, 35, 50, 54, 57
 61, 76, 79, 81, 83-89, 94-96, 98,
 111, 118, 126, 129, 131, 147, 182,
 187, 192, 193, 216, 234, 237, 242,
 243, 245, 264, 278
Swedish Central Bank: See Riks-
 bank
Swedish economists: 95
Swedish krona: 79, 82, 88, 94, 130,
 133, 138, 147, 237
Swiss notes: 42, 98, 253
Switzerland: 7, 32, 35, 72, 113, 264

Tables and Diagrams:
 Circulation in Sweden: 36, 37,
 38, 58, 59, 60; in the United
 States: 244
 Exchange rates: 86
 Gold production: 68, 69
 Gold reserves: 67; in Sweden:
 90
 Prices in Sweden: 58, 59
 Swedish Riksbank's losses on
 foreign currencies: 135
 Wholesale prices: 76
 "Theoretische Sozialökonomie"
 (Cassel): 105, 179, 181
 Trade balance: 141, 165, 166, 171,
 179, 193, 194, 209, 211, 239
 Trade statistics: 200

Unemployment: 17, 251, 256, 257
United States, the: 11, 33, 64, 68,
 70, 74, 76, 147, 160, 162, 174,
 188, 192-194, 196, 199-201, 206,
 216-218, 220, 224, 227, 228, 230,
 232, 234, 235, 237, 239, 240,
 243, 251, 258, 259, 261, 263, 264,
 269-271, 281

United States Customs Commission, the, " Depreciated Exchange and International Trade" : 160

United States Senate, the: 223

Upper Silesia: 151

Vissering, head of the Netherlands Bank: 122-124

Wages: 16, 17, 47-50, 70, 144, 172, 226, 243, 244, 274, 275

Washington: 160

Western Europe, countries of Western civilisation: 54, 63, 70, 277

Wilson, President: 219

Zweite Denkschrift (Reichsbank): 114

PRINTED IN GREAT BRITAIN BY
BILLING AND SONS, LTD., GUILDFORD AND ESHER

WORLD AFFAIRS: National and International Viewpoints
An Arno Press Collection

Angell, Norman. **The Great Illusion, 1933.** 1933.

Benes, Eduard. **Memoirs:** From Munich to New War and New Victory. 1954.

[Carrington, Charles Edmund] (Edmonds, Charles, pseud.) **A Subaltern's War.** 1930. New preface by Charles Edmund Carrington.

Cassel, Gustav. **Money and Foreign Exchange After 1914.** 1922.

Chambers, Frank P. **The War Behind the War, 1914-1918.** 1939.

Dedijer, Vladimir. **Tito.** 1953.

Dickinson, Edwin DeWitt. **The Equality of States in International Law.** 1920.

Douhet, Giulio. **The Command of the Air.** 1942.

Edib, Halidé. **Memoirs.** 1926.

Ferrero, Guglielmo. **The Principles of Power.** 1942.

Grew, Joseph C. **Ten Years in Japan.** 1944.

Hayden, Joseph Ralston. **The Philippines.** 1942.

Hudson, Manley O. **The Permanent Court of International Justice, 1920-1942.** 1943.

Huntington, Ellsworth. **Mainsprings of Civilization.** 1945.

Jacks, G. V. and R. O. Whyte. **Vanishing Lands:** A World Survey of Soil Erosion. 1939.

Mason, Edward S. **Controlling World Trade.** 1946.

Menon, V. P. **The Story of the Integration of the Indian States.** 1956.

Moore, Wilbert E. **Economic Demography of Eastern and Southern Europe.** 1945.

[Ohlin, Bertil]. **The Course and Phases of the World Economic Depression.** 1931.

Oliveira, A. Ramos. **Politics, Economics and Men of Modern Spain, 1808-1946.** 1946.

O'Sullivan, Donal. **The Irish Free State and Its Senate.** 1940.

Peffer, Nathaniel. **The White Man's Dilemma.** 1927.

Philby, H. St. John. **Sa'udi Arabia.** 1955.

Rappard, William E. **International Relations as Viewed From Geneva.** 1925.

Rauschning, Hermann. **The Revolution of Nihilism.** 1939.

Reshetar, John S., Jr. **The Ukrainian Revolution, 1917-1920.** 1952.

Richmond, Admiral Sir Herbert. **Sea Power in the Modern World.** 1934.

Robbins, Lionel. **Economic Planning and International Order.** 1937. New preface by Lionel Robbins.

Russell, Bertrand. **Bolshevism:** Practice and Theory. 1920.

Russell, Frank M. **Theories of International Relations.** 1936.

Schwarz, Solomon M. **The Jews in the Soviet Union.** 1951.

Siegfried, André. **Canada:** An International Power. [1947].

Souvarine, Boris. **Stalin.** 1939.

Spaulding, Oliver Lyman, Jr., Hoffman Nickerson, and John Womack Wright. **Warfare.** 1925.

Storrs, Sir Ronald. **Memoirs.** 1937.

Strausz-Hupé, Robert. **Geopolitics:** The Struggle for Space and Power. 1942.

Swinton, Sir Ernest D. **Eyewitness.** 1933.

Timasheff, Nicholas S. **The Great Retreat.** 1946.

Welles, Sumner. **Naboth's Vineyard:** The Dominican Republic, 1844-1924. 1928. Two volumes in one.

Whittlesey, Derwent. **The Earth and the State.** 1939.

Wilcox, Clair. **A Charter for World Trade.** 1949.